OFF THE RECORD

One woman's global search for the world's greatest music producers

MEL BAMPTON

Copyright © 2021 by Mel Bampton

All rights reserved.

ISBN: 978-1-922486-11-0

Cover art: *Gracelands* by Kelly Sullivan

No part of this book may be reproduced in any form or by any electronic or mechanical means, including information storage and retrieval systems, without written permission from the author, except for the use of brief quotations in a book review.

Acknowledgement of Country

I acknowledge the unbroken and continuous belonging to this land, sea and sky of the Minjungbal people of the Bundjalung nation, upon which I live and work. A deep bow to the intricate knowledge systems of all Aboriginal and Torres Strait Islander peoples who have looked after this land with deep knowing and connection, since the dawn of human consciousness. I pay my respects to Elders past, present and emerging and hope for a future where your knowledge will be heard by all who reside here, so we all may learn how to live with the land and with each other.

OFF THE RECORD

ONE WOMAN'S GLOBAL SEARCH FOR THE
WORLD'S GREATEST MUSIC PRODUCERS

MEL BAMPTON

1

The Seed

It was in the triple j lunchroom – which wasn't as much of a room as it was the table nearest the kitchen. The table was a place of unity, it functioned much like the UN in that around it, all were equal. It didn't matter if you were a music presenter, a news reporter or from middle management; the only thing that mattered here was the story of your lunch.

Sometimes meetings were held here – which weren't as much meetings as they were chats over a cuppa about stuff you'd talk about outside of work anyway, like radio and music, but we'd call them 'Editorial Meetings'. This was one of those.

I'll hazard a guess at it being sometime in March 2005 when my then producer, Jordie Kilby – music obsessive and all–round snappy dresser – proposed I start interviewing music producers for my morning radio program on national broad-caster triple j.

'Why?' I immediately thought, slurping my spicy chai. 'Do we really need to further intellectualise the emotions coming from the speakers? Or demystify the end result by examining the process any more than we already do as music presenters?' I wondered if anyone other than Jordie, who had grown up in a household of radio broadcasters and record collectors, would have the inclination to care. But thankfully, what came from my mouth was a compliant, 'OK'.

Besides, what kind of beast could say no to a man in a baby blue suit? Not long after, planning began on what would become the first of The Producer Series: the stories behind ten of the finest sonic craftspeople in the world, taking the nation inside some of the biggest albums ever made, defining what it really meant to be a producer. It was a decision that would kick off a journey through studios, bars, desert seas, homes, golf buggies, band rooms, cobbled streets, hotel foyers, underground clubs and cocktail glasses all over the globe. Needless to say, it's been an eye–opening experience.

Until that first series – when I spent hours talking on the phone with producers who, despite their busy schedules were in no rush to end any of our chats in a hurry – I had not even spared thought for the difference between producer and engineer. I actually felt like the role of producer was somewhat superfluous; made up, like so many jobs in the industry, by folk who either desperately wanted to be in it but couldn't succeed as musicians, or simply wanted a piece of the fiscal pie. But those kinds of thoughts proved to be terribly erroneous. Turns out that many of the great idiosyncratic moments that have ended up defining some of the most famous songs in the world, have come directly from the producer's touch. Although most would be hesitant to admit it.

In the case of musicians, it's fair to assume that for most, the right-side of their brains – the creative side – is the dominant, but producers have to be equally as artistic as they do logical, technical and administrative. This access to an entire brain that's firing in all areas delivered the most fascinating, unpredictable interviews I would ever do in ten years as a music broadcaster. Steve Albini, a great example; a man who is as much famous for the bands he's produced (Nirvana, The Pixies, The Breeders) as he is for his raw, warts–and–all, style of production. When I asked Steve if he had to like an album in order to produce it he gave the startlingly, deadly serious reply: 'I don't think a gynaecologist should be getting turned on by all the vaginas he has to work with each day, he should have a more professional relationship with the vagina and I feel like I need to have a professional relationship with the music I'm working on.' Articulate, creative and just a little bit inappropriate – an interviewer's dream.

It wasn't until I had left triple j after eight years on air, that The Producer Series became the travelling circus it did. After the calibre of stories within the first series, it was felt that each episode for the second series should be more extensive. In order for this to happen the audio quality had to be vastly improved – listening to someone speak down a phone line for half an hour when you're in your car or surrounded by general life–noise is a type of torture that one should only ever employ on someone most annoying. I had to get these interviews face to face, there were no two ways about it.

There were other factors at play too. One; it's impossible to get someone to open up in the same way on the phone as they do when you've travelled halfway around the world to stare directly at them and two; for some of those producers who were extraordinarily busy, it was only my seriously real presence in their city and the threat that I may never go away, that suddenly made a couple of hours free up in their chock–a–block schedules. On a whole though, all the producers I've chased (bar Rick Rubin who could potentially claim the title of world's most well–known producer and who still remains my bearded abominable snowman to this very day) have been so graciously giving of their very valuable time. And not one of them has proved to be anything less than fascinating. My one despair has been the disproportionate representation of the sexes. When we set out to create this series, we thought we could potentially – if we dug really deep – have a 1:4 ratio of women to men, it turns out we were extremely lucky to get one in ten. Of the two women producers we did manage to find, there was a common thread both with them and myself – we were all lovers of music on the heavier side and used to the full brunt of a male–heavy existence. An essential comfort zone in a music world that still very much swayed in favour, at that time, to the masculine. In 2018, the USC Annenberg

School of Communication and Journalism looked at 600 songs that made the Billboard Hot 100 from 2012 to 2017 and found that only 2 percent of producers on the list were women. Whilst those figures seem dire, the wheels are definitely turning – with many more young women coming up in the last 5 years as part of a new wave of ladies behind the console bringing their finesse to the tunes of others. It will be fascinating in another decade to observe much more music produced through a female filter and how the producer role will look with the needs of women at the helm, highlighted in the awesome tale of Trina Shoemaker who refused to stay in the role as it's been constructed by generations of men, instead moulding it to her needs and the needs of her womb.

Producers are like limestone, they wear the imprints of an age; standing consistent whilst each new trend washes through them and over them one decade after the next. If we were to cut a producer open down the centre from head to foot into two halves we could see entire eras of music fossilised into their hearts, their minds, their muscle mass and definitely into their livers. Producers are the carbon daters of music history.

Take a portion of Australian rock producers over the age of fifty; surrounding the intense focus of their sonic brilliance, there's a certain similar soft fuzziness around the neural edges of some. This struck me as a mystery for some time but over several interviews, over several years a theory became apparent. All had lived hard and worked harder through the octane–

fuelled heyday of 1970s Australian rock n roll. This was a period, in Australian history famous for the alcohol excess of the working class followed not long after by the heroin heyday of the mid–to–late eighties. The music as always was reflective of its surrounds; bands like The Birthday Party, The Beasts of Bourbon, AC/DC, The Scientists and The Angels were ruling the music scene with wild abandon; the whole industry was gritty and reckless – expected to be so, and at the heart of it all: the producers. Those times had left a lasting impression.

Take Tony Cohen for example, who worked with half of the above plus Powderfinger, The Go–Betweens and more. Our wonderful interview was preluded first by determining, of the albums that he produced, which ones did he remember producing.

The many stories, that Tony did recall though amongst the mayhem, particularly those that contained the words Tex Perkins and Young Talent Time in the same sentence, were hilarious and also remarkable for the fact alone that they were not already part of Australian music folklore.

Like Tony Cohen, not all of The Producers made the cut for this penned version. This time round at least. Within the conversation of each producer was enough to write a single book alone. Producers are in many ways like the Nanna who doesn't get a lot of visits. She rightfully should. She knows things. She has stories to tell and wisdom to share yet instead, people go visit the young 'uns who may be more dynamic than old Nan but less likely to give out the juice. It's the same with producers, we tend to go to the musos, but if you want the dirt you go to the person with lesser fame to protect, a lot less ego and approximately twenty fewer people telling them at any given time how to think and act. Courtney Love might not tell you that she was showing up to the studio nine hours late, then getting yelled at which made her cry and run away. But Michael Beinhorn will.

The other similarity that producer folk share with Nannas, is that a lot of their stories are in their nick–knacks, one small item of bric–a–brac can be the unveiling of a musician's mental state/creative genius. Who would ever think to ask Luke Steele of Sleepy Jackson/Empire of the Sun fame, if he'd ever thought of putting a colander over a light bulb to make sparkly patterns on the ceiling whilst recording his vocal takes? No–one. But when you're there in the inner sanctum of Big Jesus Burger Studios in the heart of Sydney staring up at them, it's the next natural tangent of conversation.

In this DIY digital world, there are more bands self–producing than ever before, but just as it is with life in general, when the right person is by your side, the chances for greatness multiply exponentially. Whether you're in a band or you're just fascinated by humans and the human condition, I hope by the end of these pages you'll have laughed and wept your way through this crazy hunt for characters that are all, in varying degrees, psychologists, tech–heads, chameleons, spiritualists, magicians, alchemists, pragmatists, referees, encouragers, sex–symbols and ball–breakers. I hope that the role they play in taking talent and turning it into a soundtrack for the lives of the masses is more greatly understood and that fingers–crossed, you find me to be a good travelling companion on such an adventure.

    Shall we go?

2

Michael Beinhorn: Master of Charm

Blinking grittily, I feel the slowest of cogs begin to turn achingly in my mind. I can almost hear the small screams of their resistance as tiny, blunt thoughts try to surface and tell me that I'm in a house in Santa Monica. I think it might be Saturday, perhaps Sunday? I'm fairly certain in that strange space between passing out and being given another chance at life that the year is 2006, but in this dusty moment I wouldn't throw all my chips at that either. My buddy, Kate, is beside me sleeping blissfully; her earplugs in, eye mask on, covers unmoved. Oh yes, it is resentment I feel as I look woozily in her direction knowing she has slept dreamily whilst I've done the usual traveler's toss and turn. 'Probably doesn't even have a hangover,' I think dourly from the disheveled side of the bed, pieces of the night before slowly returning in unpleasant fragments … along with bits of garlic … in my teeth. Oh god, a kebab had been consumed. There was a party

… in Venice Beach … a beautiful lady in a Mexican wedding dress, a lounge room lit in red and … errgh … keg stands; the ungodly act of doing a handstand on a beer keg whilst its contents are propelled at force into the mouth of the inverted idiot.

I get out of bed, I hate everything. Even the floor, failing to pass on any of its steadiness to my feet, offends me. Heading to the shower, I massage my head, trying the squeeze–really–hard–and–release technique that alleviates the pain and nausea in one–second bursts. Towelling off, I make it ten metres before curling up in the warmth of an insultingly cheerful Santa Monica sunbeam roller skating its way through the curtains onto the lounge room floor. I lie like a cat that's eaten a mouse that's eaten Ratsak, chastising myself for being in such a state on such an important day.

Only by the sheer motivation of dire consequence do I manage to make the 3pm appointment I've travelled twelve thousand kilometres for and have been thinking about since a conversation I'd had with my old friend, James Tweedy, several years earlier.

James was the original bass player for LA punk band The Bronx and whenever the band would come to Australia we would catch up, have an amazing time filled with live music, beers and nonsense, then as they veered off to the next city I would generally veer toward the hospital or pass out close to one, unable to make it the final few metres.

One night in 2007 at the famous Annandale Hotel in Sydney's inner west, where the band were headlining, James and I were chatting about the recording of The Bronx's second album. Apart from sharing the same name (self-titled), the sophomore album was vastly different from the first. Still very much full of Bronx grit and power straight from the kerbs of Long Beach and West Hollywood, the second record had indulged in a few debauched weekends in the penthouse and bought itself a top-of-the-range surround-sound home entertainment system. The songs were just as anthemic, but there was definition where there had previously been sheer force. The jugular-bulging vocal work of frontman Matt Caughthran was just as powerful but the skills of that voice as a singer were crystal clear.

As I looked further into Beinhorn's work after that conversation, I could see a pattern: a trail of artists – the Red Hot Chili Peppers, Hole, Soundgarden, Marilyn Manson and more – that all possessed a certain force of nature. Loose, wild, incredibly talented but not, by any stretch of imagination, well-behaved, trend following, manufactured pop-stars. They were instead fringe folk who found themselves at the heart of the industry machine but with unwieldy sounds, personalities or both. They had major label deals with capacity to make millions but possessed anarchic 'artistic' unpredictable dispositions. What was a major label to do when so much money was dependent on artists with famous drug habits, ego-problems, emotional issues and more? Sending them to Michael Beinhorn seemed a consistent response; a man with enough confidence, bossiness and charm, he could harness the undiluted force that made these artists incredible; he could win them over, antagonise them, piss them off, gently cajole them and along the way package up all this wild talent into a sonic envelope that would be welcomingly played by commercial radio worldwide.

All of this I ponder, sprawled out on the grassy verge of Maxella St in Marina Del Rey across from Ballona Restaurant, like a roadkill starfish, happy just to be alive and looking up at the big, blue Californian sky. I desperately try to employ some yoga techniques I'd learned along the ways in a last–ditch attempt to rescue some dignity. With the in–breath I imagine my professionalism swimming up from the soiled depths of my liver and settling into its rightful place at the front of my skull. It's at approximately the heart region when I notice an athletically–built Caucasian New Yorker coming down the road with two Asian kids. I recall Beinhorn's last text, 'I'll be the white guy with the two Asian kids,' and leap up to greet them in as business–like a manner as is possible when one has grass in hair and professionalism left behind in a porcelain s–bend.

Oh, and while I'm already regaling you with horrific tales of personal flaws, I'll confess right now to having at this point a soft crush on Michael Beinhorn. No, we'd never met, it was an email/discography crush – enough to bring butterflies to a place in my belly where there was already an unruly protest and only further destabilising any opportunity to gain ground in a situation akin to climbing a mountain during a landslide. So, with grass in hair and heart on sleeve (or possibly sweet chili sauce) we settle into a booth at Ballona's and get the interrogation underway. James Tweedy had described Beinhorn to me that night at the Annandale as a *Times/Life* kind of producer: big albums and presumably, big money. To the man accused of earning a gourmet three mill on Hole's first album, I hear myself saying, 'So, you go into a bakery and you buy a sausage roll and a white bread roll, then put the roll in the roll … apparently.' My brain hasn't even had time to think about closing the gateway of shame located just below my nose before gagging on the next pill of professional suicide. 'Or you buy a loaf of bread, some hot chips, well 'fries' in your case, hollow out the loaf and put the fries in it. Awesome.'

Why I am using the Australian surfers diet as an ice-breaker, I cannot say, there's not a lot of neuron connection happening at this stage, but strangely, it seems to be working, Beinhorn adding to the food hall of shame the revelation that he microwaves leftover fries. Disgusting, I think. What kind of human being would *do* such a thing?

This culinarily laid–back and easy–going man certainly seems a contrast to the controlling, meticulous, arrogant–yet–charming man I was for some reason expecting: a revelation that I clearly feel comfortable in sharing.

'Meticulous doesn't necessarily mean focusing on every sonic detail or browbeating people into adopting a different way of thinking,' Michael says in gentle defence of the reputation he had gained over his years on the job. 'It just means getting in there and tackling the philosophical aspects of what the album is going to mean; what the artist themselves are trying to say. That really is something that requires a bit of thought.'

By default, Michael does however accept the title of 'boss' stating that as the producer people are going to be looking at you as the person they've hired in that capacity. 'I don't necessarily want my ego to infiltrate a situation like that so I don't characterise myself as boss per se, but to sort of steer the boat? Then ok.' The big albums that have defined Beinhorn's career, and his reputation, have been Hole's *Celebrity Skin* and *Nobody's Daughter*, Soundgarden's *Superunknown*, Red Hot Chili Pepper's *Mother's Milk* and the one that got it off the ground in jetpack fashion – Herbie Hancock's *Future Shock*.

'It was like a shockwave,' he says between mouthfuls of sushi. 'I was twenty–three when we did that record, I had no idea what I was doing; I had no idea about studio etiquette, I had no idea how to place a mic, I didn't know what I was doing on any level at all. It helped refine me as a creative person … I mean it was just a stunner of a record to be working on at that time.'

The big song from that record was *Rockit*, the video of which was one of the very first to feature African Americans and still make its way on to MTV. For a young whippersnapper like Beinhorn, that success came with some lessons. 'The success of that song was as much to do with the film clip as it was anything else. I had a very clear mental picture of what that song was; this extension of black music, of R&B, where Herbie was as a jazz artist combined with electronics all from the hip hop school. So, when I saw this video that had been directed by this pair of really clever white English guys, I hit the ceiling. I was furious! I was like this is like a joke! This song is not a joke!'

His voice suddenly goes up an octave as the re–enactment of fury becomes somewhat a reality. 'This is a piece of serious... *what the?* I wanted to kill these guys! Then all of a sudden it starts getting played all over MTV and slowly I just shut up. I was like, 'Oh, ah, maybe it's not all that bad.'

In the later eighties, Beinhorn started working with the Red Hot Chili Peppers. He worked on two albums; the first being *The Uplift Mofo Party Plan*, followed two years later by *Mother's Milk*; the making of the latter providing all the right elements to create one of the most defining signposts on the tough road of Beinhorn's formidable reputation.

I'd heard the difficult–to–believe rumour that he'd fired the lead singer but I needed to hear it direct from source.

'Um yeah. At one point, I did throw him out of the band, literally, kicked him out.'

'Wow', is all I can manage for a moment, soaking in this idea of the omnipotent producer who can fire a band's *frontman*. So, what was Michael planning to do without a singer?

'I had no idea. It was a really spontaneous move, I don't know where it came from but I mean the guy was doing an incredibly large amount of heroin *daily* and it just turned into a situation where it was bringing everybody down. Those guys didn't know what to do, the manager didn't know what to do, someone had to do su'm. But it worked. I think Anthony realised that this band was his only means of survival and he had to pull it together, and he did. He really came back as a champ.'

Within the Red Hot Chili Peppers during that time, there were a stack of problems, generally relating to drugs, as was well documented in singer Anthony Keidis' autobiography *Scar Tissue*. Keidis also suggests that Beinhorn and lead guitarist John Frusciante, didn't get along so smashingly. 'John and I actually got along pretty well,' Michael disagrees. 'I'd done *The Uplift Mofo Party Plan* with them and that was a kind of defining moment cos it not just took them to a slightly higher level but it also addressed a lot of problems within the band – namely the drug use – and there were a lot of residuals from that, put it that way.'

Those residuals made their way deep into the sticky carpet of creation underfoot during the recording of the next album, *Mother's Milk*. So, was it the drug use Michael couldn't tolerate?

'I didn't back then, and they weren't in much of a position to do anything about that. At that point, they were the red–headed step children of EMI and no–one cared if they existed or didn't. In fact, there were people on their label who I think were actively trying to see the band go under, because they simply didn't like them as personalities. They just went against the grain of everything that was supposed to be successful back then and I think it offended a lot of people at the company. So, no, I didn't tolerate it and I think that's where any issue that Anthony had with me may have come from.'

Whilst Michael's kids Mia and Tae, who are sitting across from me in the booth, show as much interest in Daddy's stunning career as any child of any parent (bless their truly egalitarian perspectives) our talk moves onto the next big spike in Beinhorn's career; the making of an album that contains one of the most unique studio tales of all time.

As the grommets gnaw indifferently on their burgers and fries I ask their impactful pop if there were difficult things about making Soundgarden's *Superunknown*? Michael suddenly starts laughing. *Really* laughing. The laughter soon turns into a giggle, then into the best happy place of all – the *silent* giggle. He gasps for composure then almost inaudibly, between breaths, he expels, 'Is pig mostly pork?'

Once back in full control, Michael begins to give an intimate insider's account of an album that has won two Grammy awards and sold five times platinum. 'It was kind of nightmarish – to begin with at least,' he explains. 'These guys did not get along and there was really one principle guy who was writing the music, one guy who really wanted to be more of the songwriter and one other guy who felt like he should be the guitarist and the songwriter and didn't write anything and just sat around a lot and another guy who was just surly all the time and probably needed to be locked up.'

'Woah, woah, woah, let's back this pony up', I suggest, a bit stunned by these revelations of chaos behind one of the greatest rock records of the nineties. Let's just talk for a moment about where the *music* for that album was at when it first came to Beinhorn's ears.

'Ok, so, I got a tape when they were first thinking about working with me, which were basic demos for their record and it was just *RAMBLING*. There was no cohesion to it whatsoever, only one maybe two of those songs made it onto the record and one…'

Michael suddenly pauses, noticing the ever–increasing flaccidness of my arm that has been outstretched with a microphone in it, in the general region of his face for near on twenty minutes. 'Am I leaning too far back?' he asks politely of his distance from the microphone. 'Alright let's rearrange', he suggests, 'cause I know what that can do to a person's arm over time and you can't have it getting all stiff – you need two arms for the road in this city!' We individually shift some body parts and continue.

'I heard this tape and I was like, 'We can't do this, this record is not ready.' From that alone they were like, 'This guy's an *asshole*.' 'Maybe I am,' I said, 'but I'm *your* asshole now."' he says, bursting into another round of infectious giggling. 'After that, I had conversations with Chris (Cornell – lead singer/songwriter) over like, a two–month period. I'd come out and visit them, and they'd rehearse, and no–one wanted to hear me. A couple of people in the band pretended I wasn't even there, so I realised pretty quick that they didn't want to feel like they were being dictated to.

'I had a conversation with Chris, I'll never forget this … they were writing songs that were kind of jammish which were similar to their previous record and I knew as a listener that I didn't want to listen to Soundgarden songs with these long drawn out guitar solos (*proceeds to sing long–drawn–out example in drop D*), I heard that on Black Sabbath records. Be Soundgarden, for God's sake! I was like, 'Chris, what's your favourite music, what do you like to listen to?' 'Well, Beatles and Cream,' he says. And I'm like, 'Ok Chris, those guys wrote *songs* didn't they? They're real proper songs. You just sit down and dedicate yourself to writing a great song.' 'He was like, 'But what if it doesn't sound like Soundgarden?"

'Who gives a fuck if it doesn't sound like Soundgarden or not, you guys *ARE* Soundgarden; when you orchestrate it and your band plays it, it will sound like Soundgarden.' He came back to me with a tape that had on it *Fell On Black Days*, *Tighter and Tighter*, *Anxious* and *Black Hole Sun* – I heard that tape and man, I still get goosebumps thinking about when I was sitting there listening to it.'

And what about '*Spoonman*'? I ask feverishly, about the album's biggest hit and possibly the only song containing a spoon solo *ever* to reach number three on the US charts.

'It's funny, it was one of my least favourite songs. I'm still not that crazy about it, but I think the best thing about that song was watching that guy Artis come in and do that spoon performance. He said to us, 'Get a video camera out cos you're gonna wanna tape this.' He had all this stuff, it looked like he was setting up for a torture session and it was kinda like that too. We did about four passes and this guy was beating the *shit* out of himself! I've never seen anything like it! He was hitting himself with pieces of metal that were big – things that I'd never seen before and don't ever wanna see again cos they look like they're for taking limbs off, bloodletting equipment ... but I'll tell you something, by the end of the second take there was blood all over the place it was flying everywhere ... we were all sitting in the control room like this ... (*Pulls look of stunned, secretly amused horror – the kind that might be seen on the expression of a teen who's just seen their principal fall down an embankment, then get hit by a golf buggy*) aghast! I've never seen anything like it.

'Oh man, he came into the studio after that and everyone just couldn't wait for him to leave cos it got so tense, I mean he's a street guy, this guy, and he's like talking all this crazy stuff then he wants money for like a meal and I was like wait a sec ... surely these guys worked out some kind of financial arrangement, but he had to get a burger or something like that ... you take a boy outta the country so to speak. God knows what's happened to this guy.'

Michael chuckles in recollection of that crazy day and downs a piece of salmon sashimi, which has been flirting with him like a two–bit hook, line and sinker since it arrived at the table quarter of an hour ago. As he swallows I reflect that by this point in his career he had dealt with some pretty confused characters and a fair share of relationship fireworks. So how much did all that come in handy for work with Marilyn Manson?

'Brian (*the name Marilyn's Mum gave him*) was actually one of the most professional people I'd worked with. Apart from some of the hijinks he pulled, which was easily some of the most childish crap I have ever seen in studio. One thing he really enjoyed doing was that he really liked to dig at people to see if he could find a weak spot, you know a place where he knows he can always work on to break someone down psychologically.'

I can't help but wonder how this prepared him for Courtney Love and her cracking 1997 album *Celebrity Skin*; an album that saw the grunge and fuzz of previous Hole offerings honed to power–pop perfection, introducing them, with heads held high, to the mainstream. The Beinhorn signature move, and one of the most wonderful moments in Courtney Love's career. One that as a powerful woman and a musician, she thoroughly deserved.

'I have no point of reference with which to compare,' Beinhorn says of Courtney's headspace during the recording of that record, 'But from everything that I'd heard, I would say that she was probably in the best creative space of her life at that point. She was very lucid. She didn't show up all the time however,' he laughs. 'I remember one time, I mean you wanna talk about excess – OOHH – she kept having these healers and these yogis and these chiropractors and so on coming to the studio. And we'd taken over the main office – it was our lounge, as the lounge areas in the studios just weren't gonna do so I said to the guy who owned the studio, 'We're gonna have to take over your office, it's just the way that it is,' and he was cool. But she was spending so much time and money having all these people come in selling her tea that was like a thousand dollars a bag or something, I don't know, then she'd be off meeting with people about movies and I just remember a couple of days where she just didn't show up for hours – one day she was nine hours late – and I really lost my temper (*his voice goes up into the high key of fury again*). I was on the phone to her publicist and I was like, 'You better get her down here or I'm gonna fucking kill somebody, this is really gonna be bad!',' he laughs. 'Then eventually she showed up and it was crazy, I went right up in her face and I was like, 'Where the fuck... don't you fucking dare do this kind of shit.' She was like, 'I don't want to hear about it!' and just ran away. The confrontation was too much for her.'

As stories continue about Hole, they lead to another firing. This time it was the drummer who got the Beinhorn boot. Rumour has it that he and Patty Schemel just didn't get along.

'Didn't get along, huh?' Again, that jolly sounding but loaded–with–evil laughter. 'That's funny. No, Patty Schemel didn't play on the record because one, she couldn't remember anything we worked on for a month and a half on pre–production and two, because she was taking heroin. I didn't fire her from the record, that's always a decision for the band, but I did bring it to their attention however.'

I'm on the edge of my seat.

'We were about three weeks in and we were still working on drums and it was a train wreck. I said to the band – obviously Patty was *not* present – and I said the tracks weren't coming out that well. Courtney was like, 'No, no we're a band, I told you in the beginning we're a band we're going down like a band, that's our ethic, she's on the record to stay and that's it.' She said, 'I don't care what you got to do, do it.' I was like, 'Ok, I'll do the best I can with what I got."' He's chuckling now, the build up becoming palpable. 'About a week later Courtney walks into the studio and we're playing back a drum take and she's like, 'What the hell is that?' And I say, 'That's one of Patty's takes.' And she's like: *'FIRE HER!'*"

While Dad is having yet another sinister chuckle, ten-year-old son, Tae seizes the somewhat jovial moment to ask for a coffee – a request that is shut down quicker than a drumming circle in the Oval Office. 'Keep dreaming, eat your hamburger.'

'You guys are being so awesome,' I say apologetically for the hour that has already passed.

'Yeah, you'll definitely get a little surprise when we're finished,' promises Papa Beinhorn. Back to Courtney, and I make mention that she was once quoted as saying, 'I don't know what he did with our three point two million but I still like the guy.'

'If that were the case, that I got paid three point two million,' Michael says convincingly, 'we'd definitely be meeting up the coast ten or twenty miles in my palatial estate overlooking the magnificent Pacific Ocean ... so um no I've never seen that kinda money. As a matter of fact, I recall going to the head of the record company saying, 'Do you have any idea how much money this fucking record is costing?' And he just looked at me and said, 'So? Just get in there and make a great record for us, that's what you're getting paid for'.'

Ok. So. He's fired Anthony Kiedis, fired Patty Schemel, made Courtney Love run away and recorded a homeless man maiming himself, how did The Bronx – a down-to-earth bunch of rowdy gents from Los Angeles, go recording their second album with this mercenary of musical professionalism? Band intact? Body parts…?

'Oh man,' he says in that, have–I–got–a–tale–for–you kinda way. 'Matt (Caughthtran – the band's lead singer) worked so hard on his vocals and between him, Joby and myself, we really didn't want to leave the studio without the right vocals and it took a really long time. I have a letter that Matt wrote me,' he says as he starts giggling again … this time in the octave of maniacal joy. 'He left me a note, cos at one point I wasn't coming into the studio – I think it's the only time I've ever done that – cos it started to feel like he was getting frustrated because he felt like I just wanted him to rise to this level, that he didn't even know what I meant. I kept saying, 'Just be true to your emotions, you'll feel it when it's there.' But for so long it was rough going for him, yeah so at one point he left me this note that said 'Dear Michael I'm going to the beach now and jump in the ocean and drown myself.' Something like, 'I want to cut my own penis off and eat it, I hate you, I hate everybody, I wish you'd all die.' It was one of the funniest things I ever saw and the best part is that he meant every word of it. He was *so* frustrated. I'm sure that if someone had handed him a paring knife he would've become a monk.' *Giggle giggle giggle.*

Suddenly, over Michael's shoulder, someone's presses themselves up against the tinted glass, looking in. I squint but they are gone too fast for me to notice that it's actually my very fresh and well–rested friend Kate. Tae jumps up and runs away. It's a motion which seems simply like a common case of ten–year–old ants–in–your–pants until he returns, with a crinkled–up note. He holds said note at my eye level whilst making perfectly polite clearing throat noises. The scrawl reads: 'Our hangovers have now also kicked in, we wish to go home. Get your ass out here now or your share of the Berocca gets it.'

'Sorry Michael,' I say equally amused and appalled by the hilarity of my 'support' team. 'One last question then freedom is yours.' I say to Michael, and in the direction of Mia and Tae, I say, 'and yours and yours.'

'What leaps out at first thought as the all–time studio experience, and does that make it also your favourite album?'

'Actually, just being in a recording studio and working on something is the best, I just feel so buoyed by it, it just kind of takes me and carries me along, probably the best feeling in the world. It's incredible. And for that reason, I love 'em all.'

With that, I pay the bill, give Michael a squeeze, congratulate the kids on their wheelie–popping awesomeness and hit the road back to Santa Monica. For near on twelve hours I lay still, the last of the hangover waning in the exhilaration of the conversation had and in anticipation of the trip I was soon to take.

3

Dave Catching: Beneath the Mojave Moon

From Santa Monica we head south to Long Beach to make contact (and to collect) another old buddy from OZ who will play an important role in the next story's unfolding.

Leslie and I had become best of pals about six years earlier, when she was living in Australia on a student visa. Under bad guidance from Immigration she'd rather unfortunately gotten her arse, and her dreams, kicked out of the country. The situation for us as friends was made all the worse by my deportation from America the year after, meaning that neither of us were allowed into each other's country of origin. Thankfully though, after nearly three years and much fiery–hoop–jumping, the Department of Homeland Security finally decided that the 1.5 grams of marijuana that had mysteriously made its way into my wallet at the age of eighteen didn't necessarily make me a threat to national safety, and I was allowed to enter the country of her birth. As an aside though, every single time I want to go to the States – even now – I have to apply for this same clearance visa and upon arrival have my passport retained, am then taken to the Department of Immigration at the airport where everything is rechecked, and once they have suitably added another ten premature grey hairs, I am free to go. When it comes to communicating with American Immigration, their disproportionately extreme actions do not necessarily promote honesty as the best policy when filling out that little green card. Something to bear in mind.

The drive to Leslie's place, like so much of California, is constructed with contradictions: four lane highways where everybody speeds but no–one seems to get anywhere, glimpses of pure blue sea lidded by massive oil refineries and where there exists the constant dichotomy of wealth and poverty that litters most of America. Here in Long Beach, where the working class rubs shoulders with those of the Coastal View, it is amplified. It is where the ghetto meets the sea, where I'll soon be tattooed on a boat that never sails and where punk, ska band Sublime, cut their teeth, putting Long Beach forever on my musical map.

As we drive in over the sweeping highway, over the massive oil plant that stretches for blocks, I finally understand how Elvis fans must feel pulling into Graceland. This gritty hamlet bred those Sublime tunes that had soundtracked so many amazing moments in my life. Being here now, seeing the streets and the struggles and the beauty, I *really* get it. 'The Sublime style is straight from Long Beach.'

Leslie's place turns out to be a small granny flat tucked in behind a home owned by a pair of mosaic artists. Across the Mexicali–inspired footpath that the couple are in the midst of compiling, we tip toe in on broken shards of tiles, the adhesive not yet dry. Leslie is at the door and before I can say, 'Who is Long Beach's sexiest lesbian?' she embraces me with part hug, part wrestle and then immediately has me throwing supplies into the back of the jeep: sunscreen, hats, cowboy boots, bottles of water, tinned corn, cameras, recording gear, dress–up frocks and white rum – everything we'll need to meet up with Producer Dave Catching of the famous Rancho De La Luna. This adventure is my most anticipated. No matter how it pans out, out there in the desert I predict that only death, a serious drug habit or degenerative brain disease will steal the memories of having been to Joshua Tree: birthplace of the Desert Sessions, haunt of Josh Homme, home of the Rancho, inspiration for U2's finest album and birthplace of a thousand road tripping movie clichés.

As we cruise the wide–open highway and LA finally loses its quest for domination to the ever–lengthening spaces between, we become the epitome of those clichés. Windows open with feet dangling out, marvelling as the buildings give way to palm trees that eventually give way to nothingness. The heat in the breeze rising as the lengthening distance from one In–N–Out Burger to the next signals our ever–increasing distance from Hollywood. Spat out in the open expanse of the

Mojave, I suddenly remember the startling fact that California is a desert, that LA doesn't even have its own natural water supply; the whole place is a constructed set.

If the sudden sparseness isn't weird enough, sparseness suddenly invaded by a thousand triffid–like windmills is as odd as it gets. With the weighty *voosh–voosh* of their slow lazy turns, the windmills cluster surreally along the outer rim of the clifftops, standing high on the hills and low on the flats, the massive wind farm appears to the unfamiliar eye alien, robotic, omnipotent. As Highway 10 winds through the desert, the beginnings of the bizarre California that I will see over the next few days stands proud: welcoming us around the bend rears up the Indian–owned Casino Morongo – a capitalist oasis in an otherwise economical and botanical wasteland. It stands so tall amongst the flatness of the red earth, it would appear arrogant if owned by white fellas: instead I cannot help but think of the silent sobs of a decimated culture drowned out by the *ch–ching* of a thousand unflinching poker machines.

After another thirty miles or so, we roll on in to Palm Desert. It's a strange vibe here; half outlaw–ish, half retirement village. We're there to intercept a man who'll play a starring role in the retelling of this adventure for years to come: a rockstar, a renegade, a moustachioed romancer, bandmate to the man of our mission, outspoken supporter of the right to bear arms: Mr J Devil Huge, otherwise known as the frontman of hip–shakin', whisky swillin' outfit Eagles of Death Metal, of which Dave Catching, our producer of prey, is lead guitarist. As we pull the jeep up to the address given, it is with a bit of shock. It appears that it's within the closed confines of a large gated community in which The Devil resides; now cycling toward us in a leather hat, aviators, buttoned down black shirt, black jeans and all the right tattoos on a layback, black bicycle.

'Hello baby girl,' he says in the smooth, dapper ruffian style for which he is famous, as the gate slides silently open.

'Hey Jesse', I say in return with a friendly cuddle and the kind of kiss that's as equally flirtatious on my behalf as it is frigid. Jesse's high–octane energy is slightly daunting to this currently–sober version of my otherwise shamelessly adventurous self.

'Come on up,' says Jesse. 'Let me show you 'round.'

As The Devil leads the way on two–wheels, I take the time to reflect on the space between point A to my current location of Point B. My friendship with Jesse began in 2004, off the back of the band's debut album. I was all set to do my first interview with the charismatic frontman after the release of Eagles of Death Metal's very first cheeky, hand clapping sonnet of a somewhat sleazy persuasion, *Speaking in Tongues.* The track tapped right into my primal love for tunes perfect to get drunk to, and I was excited to meet the fella behind such a ditty of good times. There I was those years ago in the j studio – questions, phone number and DAT tape ready – I always waited for the precise scheduled time before calling an artist in case they too were living their life right up to the minute. The clock struck two exactly and I began dialling. The phone rang….and rang....and rang. I tried again with the same unsatisfactory result. J Devil Hughes was MIA.

Not long after toddling back to my desk, I received an apologetic email from Eagles of Death Metal's Aussie record label Inertia, saying they weren't sure what had happened but they'd arrange another interview for the same time the following day and this time things could not have gone any better. Take two was an expectation–exceeding success; Jesse delivering one of the most dynamic and hysterical interviews I'd ever done.

Turns out that two days beforehand, Jesse had been passed out on the couch having a lovely, old–man nap when a knock at the door caused him to leap up in a dazed and confused state (of the kind that one awakens to when one has been awake in a heightened state for too many days and finally passes out, only to be awoken far too soon). Caught between the waking world and the dead, Jesse ran down the stairs, jumping the last few and simultaneously slamming his head into the ceiling. He then slid toward the front door, turned the handle and pulled it open all in one dazed fluid motion. At the precise moment the door swung open a fifteen–centimetre geyser of blood started shooting out of his cranium in the general horrific direction of his guests – Josh Homme, the indisputable title–holder of stoner rock, and his terrifyingly breathtaking wife, Brody Dalle.

Needless to say, the day after the morbidly comedic pantomime, Jesse was at the mercy – and pleasure perhaps – of some pharmaceuticals to soothe the pain and ensure that he would sleep right through his allotted interview time with me.

It was only on this trip to the Mojave that I would find out that that chat was the first ever international interview for Jesse and the Eagles of Death Metal and it meant quite a lot. So much so that our first face-to-face meeting in the triple j corridor, some two years after that initial phone chat, was actually a little awkward – the over-the-top Don Juan transforming into the shy, uncertain guy of his past for just a flash of a moment.

Back to this gated community in the heart of Palm Desert, I tail the man that Josh Homme had assisted in making into a megastar. I'm baffled at this contained, very structured way of living – orderly and repetitive. You'd certainly never know that a world-traveling, trouble-loving, music-making Giovanni resided here. The interior of his modest townhouse has the same quiet air of normality – a few souvenirs of tours gone by – posters and pics – but at first glance it resembled the home of probably most of our mums; the reason for that becoming soon apparent: that Jesse lives with his Mum. There are proud pictures of her son taken during a different life – ones pre the tatts, handlebar mo and pocket comb – the furniture is that of the post-middle aged and it's very tidy. We go out on the balcony so Jesse can have himself one of many cigarettes he'll smoke across this adventure and out there shows us his nine-year-old son's toy collection, and as has been the case many times already that day, I'm startled by what I see. The wooden box is filled with nothing but toy guns, of all shapes and sizes – plastic pistols, mini–glocks, massive water blasters, metal guns, fluorescent guns – it's Play School meets Terminator.

'Errr…What's with all the flouro firearms Jesse?' I ask, a tad conservatively.

Turns out that J Devil Hughes, international man of rock n roll mystery, purveyor of free love and preacher of non–stop bootee shakin', was once a former speech–writer for the Republicans and is in full support of the right to bear arms. *(Whilst that's a globally well–known secret now, at that time it was a bit like finding out all of a sudden that your aunty is actually your cousin or that your best mate's first name is actually their middle name, or your best friend voted for Pauline Hanson. It was to be a verbal conflict of opposing views between Jesse and I that would last all the way out to Joshua Tree and sporadically in various locations around LA for the entire duration of the trip.)*

Soon after Jesse's revelations, Mamma Devil walks in. She makes us cups of tea, whilst we go hang out in Jesse's bedroom. In here the atmosphere dramatically changes, there is awesome stuff everywhere! Recording gear, rock n roll figurines, block mounted music posters, a pink lacy g–string hanging on the wall and lots of guitars – it's the kind of room you dream about as a teenager but don't have the design nous or the funds to pull together. Jesse wants us to listen to some new tunes that he and buddy Josh Homme are working on, as well as some stuff he's just started working on with Money Mark. The décor sets the perfect tone for the music; the basis of what will become the Eagles of Death Metal's third album *Heart On*.

After jumping up and down on Jesse's bed and taking photos wearing an array of different hats, we bid Mamma Devil goodbye and jump in two separate cars – Kate leaps back in the jeep with Leslie and I roll out with Jesse. Before long as the asphalt of 29 Palms Highway winds out in the soft glow of dusty headlights, Jesse's wickedly hilarious and unstoppable mind has me in tears of laughter. I am strangely at ease in the unknowingness ahead; as much at peace with the uncertain length of the journey out to the Rancho De La Luna as I am with the excitement of soon arriving at the hub of the Californian desert rock scene.

It's well past dusk by the time we pull into the wide, open drive of The Rancho, birthplace of so many sonnets and home to the man who didn't create a recording studio as much as he did a Dali–esque destination where minds melt in the most wonderful of ways and melodies make their way into the net of his own, almost accidental, making. Seeing the sun set over the great expanse has to wait until tomorrow – this night is all about meeting new folk and sipping mojitos under the Mojave moon. There are a handful of people at The Rancho already; a strangely social place considering its isolation. It draws people out of LA like embedded splinters, once free of the hand that feeds, they find space and spirituality out here amongst the spinifex. They might only roam here for a few days, taking in the peyote and the heat, howling at the massive sky in a cry of liberation before heading back to the concrete and steel, but they go back refreshed, re–earthed, rebirthed. It's the same with the musicians who find their way here. There is no advertising for this place, your cards have to have scattered a certain way to show you the path to The Rancho. There are rarely strangers, only friends and friends of friends – it's a system that not only allows the artists a unique sense of privilege and freedom but also provides The Rancho's sole resident – Dave Catching – the peace to throw open his heart and his home with trust and generosity.

Stepping feet out onto the dusty desert driveway, I feel the sense of wonderment and perspective of being a tiny human *bean* in the vastness. In the driveway Dave's ice blue Chevrolet pick–up truck sets a tone of perfection only to be matched the following morning by the 10 gallon hat he will don for our trip out into the expanse. The glorious scene enhanced as I stand on the porch by the foldout bed set up for Josh Homme and Brody Dalle, whenever they're out here having sleepovers under the stars. I hear the clinking and chatting inside of a community connected by their place out here. It's amazing to think that where I'm standing right now, in the middle of a desert in the middle of the Americas, so much music has been created that has made its way so far out into the world; Ween, Josh Homme, PJ Harvey, James Lavelle, Mark Lanegan, The Arctic Monkeys and Snow Patrol have found inspiration on this very porch. As Dave will tell me later, 'It's the house – it gives music to people.' And I believe it too.

As the spring-loaded screen door swings firmly shut behind us, ensuring that the many things in this desert capable of scurrying, could not scurry in, we find ourselves standing in a micro–universe of art. This main living area is dimly, yet warmly lit. As we adjust to the soft lighting, we see every surface covered, *COVERED,* in creativity. Porcelain ducks, dogs and horses line every horizontal space, there are wooden carvings, instruments and lanterns; the place's sense of care-free anarchy is represented on the walls and on the shelves. There are paintings of all subject matter, in all styles, side by side; the absolute commitment to the themeless–ness of it all is the very theme that brings it all together. This place is designed to spawn creativity and in every corner, there is something to look at, with the potential to spark a thousand imaginings.

Dave is by the kitchen chatting with his neighbour who lives in one of the other two dwellings on the same property and who is also the girlfriend of Hutch from Queens of the Stoneage. Dave stops mid–sentence as he hears the door close, 'Hey!' he says with deep southern warmth and an even warmer embrace. The first time Dave and I met was when Eagles of Death Metal toured Australia off the back of their *Peace Love Death Metal* album only some six months before. Dave's hospitality is that of a friend who I may well have known for years. He introduces me to his friend Kristy – a stunning translucently–skinned, platinum blonde, silver–screen looking thing who turns out to be a designer studying to become a taxidermist – and to his very old buddy Barry Conley. Barry has been the in–house engineer at Paramount

Studios in Hollywood for years, he's engineered everyone from Cypress Hill to Zakk Wylde and tonight he has with him an invention he's been working on. But first, Dave decrees it's time for dinner. Like the family time of rock'n'roll dreams, everyone gathers round the table outback by the barbecue pit underneath the stars. 'It's my favourite place to cook,' says Dave, who was a chef down in New Orleans, in a former life. On this night he's cooked up a pile of Creole–style chicken, covered in spices, peppers, celery, onion and splashes of his favourite hot sauce – Black Widow – which he puts in near everything he cooks (even the soyrizo omelette we have for breakfast the following morning). As soon as the meal is down, Dave and Barry hover over the strange metal case that Barry has carried outside with the nervous excitement of a hymen on prom night. At first, talk is at a whisper, it soon becomes louder, more excitable, there's a flashlight involved, then a sudden strange warbling sound akin to a cat being sodomised by a moog. 'The Outtacontrolatron!' Barry declares with triumphant pride as he turns to look at his audience of three. The device, covered in knobs and dials, transforms light into bent unpredictable sound – it's an experimentalist's masterpiece, 10 years in the making and perfect for Dave's other band, the psychedelic rock experience, The Earthlings.

After several eye–crossing goes on the Outtacontrolatron, the party drifts out front. Jesse and I engage in a passionate debate about gun–control as we sip our mojitos – as promised - under the big Mojave moon. It's during this discussion that my suspicions about Jesse are reinforced – he is razor sharp and quicker than lightning. Beneath the tattoos and his Moustache of Rock n Roll Grandeur, sits a man of almost savant-like intellect. Fuelled by the speed and confidence of certain lifestyle choices, he is an unbeatable opponent in a volley of words. And whilst offensive to boot, Boots Electric offends so equally across all factions that discrimination neutralises into equality. Accepting that I am well out-matched, we drift inside to set up camp in Dave's back room, which is also the recording space and for the next few days, home to our pyjama party. In it sits a drum kit, a piano, one entire wall lined with guitars and the other a Tetris of amplifiers from floor to ceiling. In fact, on closer inspection, there are amps *everywhere*. It's like when you sit on the grass and only when you've been there for about ten minutes do you notice that there are hundreds of ants moving all around you going about their business on every strand of grass. I walk by the dryer on my way to the toilet at one point to find that yep, there is a little baby amp in there too. Kate, Leslie and I get snuggled into bed and Jesse comes into say goodnight whilst managing to make a crack about Jews and lesbians for Leslie's sake – who is of course a Jewish lesbian.

'Is there anyone safe from your humour, Jesse?' I ask.

'Absolutely,' says Jesse without twitching, 'The Japanese. How can you insult a race that can be blindfolded with dental floss?' And with that he's off, into the night and onto another crazy mission from which he will not be seen again for another five or so days.

Dave and I get up nice and early, eat the aforementioned Soyrizo (vegetarian chorizo) omelette and head outdoors for our 'official' radio chat. The heat pushes into me like a shirtless bodybuilder at a music festival, offending my senses and throwing me momentarily off balance. It's only 9 am.

'We're looking at lots of Joshua Trees, mountains, a few cars and a very huge expansive sky – which is my favourite part of living out here – but not too many animals today, it's a bit warm,' Dave describes the landscape we see before us as we lean up against the stone outer wall of The Rancho. As well as huge blue sky the view also takes in the little township of Joshua Tree in the valley below and the national park beyond. 'On a cooler day we'd be seeing lots of rabbits, chuckwalla lizards, rattlesnakes if you're really unlucky, scorpions…and lots of solpugids I've been seeing lately…oh and little ground squirrels.'

In 1990 Dave's friend, Fred Drake, moved here searching for something other than Hollywood. 'He'd been coming out here for a while and one day he came out with some friends and found a sign that said three houses for rent. Straight away he fell in love with the place – it was $500 a month and he was paying probably double that in Hollywood even in 1990, so he decided to move out here even though he didn't have a fridge or a truck or anything. Somehow, he just made it happen. He went from wanting a studio to having three in one month and I don't know how that happens other than as Leonard (Cohen) would say, 'You just let it'.' Dave chuckles happily, remembering the good fortune and the good decision of a good friend who passed away in 2002.

'The first time I came here was in 1982 on my first trip to Los Angeles, my friends and I drove through the park and we loved it. Once I settled in LA, I didn't really come back here until the late eighties, just for day trips and when I say day *trips,*' he laughs, 'that's kinda exactly what I was doing! I would come out to the park, have lunch and climb around waiting for the moon to come up – I'd generally come out on the full moon because it was beautiful. So, when Fred told me he moved out here I decided I wanted to come visit him and we started hanging out. I was actually living in New Orleans at the time. I got the call from Fred telling me a friend of ours was selling his studio and asked me if wanted to go partners with him, which I thought was kinda funny because I was 1800 miles away in a different city with a business of my own, but it was so cheap and cool and fun that I just went for it. We bought the whole studio for $6000 and all we had to do was make $100 a month repayments until it was paid off. Then in the same month, his friend Hugh Harris brought his 1 inch 24–track machine, then about 2 weeks later Mark Howard who was Daniel Lanois' engineer, came out and asked if Daniel could leave his gear out here because he wanted to record some stuff out here. So, being Fred's favourite producer, he of course said yes and they left their gear here for about a year. That's when Fred recorded Kyuss and Wool and The Earthlings stuff. That was the beginning of everything.'

'Space often breeds craziness,' I say to Dave as we wander

in to the shade of what looks like a Poinciana Tree, thinking about the years I'd lived up in Far North Queensland where there seemed to be a direct equation of madness to the distance you were from a metropolitan centre. 'Do you find that about Joshua Tree?'

'Yes. Not so much for me because I get to leave a lot, but for the people who live here all the time, definitely.' This statement is undermined a little as we approach what looks to be a cross between a sunken dining table and a large vat for broiling things of human–size 'And what is this exactly?' I ask curiously.

'That used to be a great wood–burning hot tub that some kids who came to record from Canada said they'd fix.' Dave explains with a hint of lingering annoyance. 'Their way of fixing a red wood hot tub was to paint it with roofing tar, which ruined it and the deck. I can't remember the name of the band, but I do want to kill them. Anyway, the solution was to use the bottom of the hot tub and build it into a dinner table for a New Year's Eve party. It's worked out well, we actually used it a lot during the Duke Spirit sessions for dinner parties. Sometimes damage happens but I generally don't have people out here that I don't know or don't at least love their music. It's not really a professional studio you know, I don't have ads, I don't have a phone number, if people really want to come here they have to get through someone else before they come here.'

'They have to make their way into your heart before they get into the home?'

'Exactly.'

We enter the house through the side door. There's a little outdoor alcove at the entrance, which, like every other part of the house, is filled with organs, ornaments, omnichords and other such things. You could insert a crazy cat lady into this house with little shift to the atmosphere. 'Between Fred and I, we always liked collecting crazy stuff and so our friends give us crazy stuff,' he says, taking me inside and pointing to a large oil painting just inside the door near the kitchen. Dave explains it's a gift painted by his friend and singer-songwriter, Victoria Williams. Victoria became known to a whole new generation when Pearl Jam covered her song 'Crazy Mary' to help raise dollars to aid Victoria in her battle against Multiple Sclerosis.

'This is Fred's horse', he explains, 'and it's painted over a seascape but that's The Rancho and that's the chorale and that's Fred and Victoria there.'

With a slow, sweeping, theatrical twirl of wonder, I ponder what Dave's favourite pieces are in this artistically–laden room.

'I gotta couple at the moment.' He says, answering my musings. 'I kinda like the guy playing the guitar here – Fred found him at a swap meet and I like this cowboy thing, it's kinda like a cowboy ghost that we also got at the swap meet, oh and this one, a picture a friend of mine painted of a house in New Orleans that's kinda famous. Hey,' Dave says, suddenly taking a diversionary thought, 'you should speak to another friend of mine from New Orleans, Trina Shoemaker, she's a producer and an engineer.'

'I will do that on your recommendation, Sir. Do people see

all the kooky stuff and decide to then leave you such things in thanks?'

'Yeah possibly, or they buy it and realise it's way too goofy for their house and dump it on me!' Laughs Dave mostly good–naturedly. At the back of the room sits the tell–tale sign of The Rancho's purpose. A bit like Captain Kirk's chair on the starship enterprise or the deep fryer at the local fish and chip shop – this is where the magic happens. It's the mixing desk of The Rancho – a giant retro thing, a 1978/9 Neotech Elan board that Dave describes as 'pretty good but not the best ever.' Thankfully he doesn't sell cars for his supper…

'People come here for the vibe,' he says to flesh out the previous comment regarding the sub–par equipment. 'It's very giving in musicality, this place. It sounds really weird but it is. The amount of things that have been recorded here have not been because I have the best gear, but because of the sky and the heat and the house, it's definitely built for giving songs to people.'

Possibly the definitive project that put Rancho De La Luna on the map internationally is The Desert Sessions: a series of currently ten albums featuring a conglomerate of artists including Twiggy Ramirez, Dean Wean, Josh Freese, Mark Lanegan and PJ Harvey instigated by Josh Homme.

'At the time of the Desert Sessions, Kyuss was a very focused group,' says Dave speaking of Josh Homme's pre–

Queens of the Stoneage band, heralded as possibly the greatest stoner rock outfit of all time, largely responsible for the 'desert rock sound'.

'They didn't really jam with other people as far as I know and I think the Desert Sessions were born because Josh really loved Fred's drumming. So he'd come out here and I think he really saw the freedom that we had, you know with everybody getting involved and playing whatever they wanted on any instrument, and he really took it to the next step, inviting more amazing musicians, and because he's such a great musician himself he could pull other people in that he'd never even met, and we'd just plop here for five or six days. It was never like, 'Oh, bring songs' it was like, 'Come here, Dave'll cook, Fred will play drums and engineer.

'There was no set rules, it didn't matter what happened, if it was something that we didn't think was cool, it didn't get released. We didn't expect it was going to be something that people would really latch onto, especially that first Desert Sessions, it was pretty out there and it was just such a core group of people who really grew up together. It's still very true now though, to those original sessions, but the last few have definitely been really incredible, you know, having PJ Harvey calling out from the kitchen, while I'm engineering (*bungs on terrible pommie accent*) 'Dave would you like a spot of tea' and looking over and thinking 'oh look there's PJ Harvey making tea in my kitchen, that's pretty weird'. But at the same time having Mickey from Ween and Allen Johannes sitting on my front porch writing a song, while Twiggy Ramirez (Nine Inch Nails/Perfect Circle/Marilyn Manson) is on the back porch singing Shepherd's Pie* making us piss our pants.

There were days where we would do five songs in a row which felt like they took no more than fifteen minutes.'

As we move round the back of the mixing board toward the room where I had slept, Dave plops himself down in front of an organ big enough to lift the lid off a Louisiana parish.

'I love this Lowrey organ!' he suddenly exclaims. 'It has a synthesiser built into it by Bob Moog so you can never get it to do the same thing twice, you have to capture it right there and then.'

Without any form of disclaimer Dave begins belting out a mass of noise. It's the sound of a Mamma howling out in distress to her tiny offspring which may very well be the Outtacontrolatron.

Soon, there are beats as well. Even after Dave stops, the sound continues to bounce around the walls and then the hills.

'That's the other thing about this house…' Dave says, 'half the stuff doesn't work right and that's when you get all these interesting noises, half the stuff that we've recorded are sounds that no–one else is ever going to get, not even us if we tried to do it again.'

*(The closing track on Desert Session's Volume 9 & 10: a bit of a 'you–had–to–be–there' moment with the lyrics Shepherd's Pie being sung over and over again. A very candid insight into the desert madness of The Rancho and those who find a bond there)

Together we stroll into the room where my mattress lies and I (a terribly messy traveller) do a quick and desperate scan to make sure there are no pairs of underwear hanging over the necks of any guitars. 'I've got about fifteen now I think,' says Dave misinterpreting my gaze in the direction of his fifty plus strong *guitarsenal* as one of awe and calculation, instead of a frantic search for undergarments. 'Any faves?' I say, satisfied that all smalls have been tucked away satisfactorily. 'Yeah, I've got a '58 Stratocaster that I really like and a really old, old customised Les Paul from the early seventies that I really like. I've had both of those for a long time – about thirty years.'

'So, with so many choices how do you decide which one you're going to play?' I ask as I walk past the line–up, imagining all of the collective stories contained in these strings and the mystical attraction in choosing which one would get strummed on any given occasion.

'I think you just go for the one that's closest to being in tune....' Says Dave bursting out laughing, deflating my spiritual rock imaginings.

'So, genius is attained through laziness?' I ask, astonished by the sheer lack of poetry in the process.

'Of course! You don't want to be halfway through the flow of writing a song and have to stop and mess around tuning for an hour. You just want to pick one up and go, yep close enough!'

At the end of the guitar runway sits a delightfully demure looking drumkit; it has an air of confidence about it that suggests its sweet appearance may pack a little more punch than it's giving away. I wonder if it's instrument or sculptural art?

'Not many people have opted to use a different kit.' Dave says in its direction. 'It's an old Gretsch from the seventies and it has a very unique sound. It's not a huge, big, eighties–rock–sounding kit, but it is a very natural sound. It's been used on pretty much every Desert Sessions song, Kyuss, Victoria Williams, Daniel Lanois stuff, in fact the only people I can think of that didn't use it the whole way through were The Duke Spirit, they only used it on one song – I think they were looking for a bigger sound on the Neptune album.'

With the mercury climbing faster than Pemba Dorje Sherpa, (I'll let you google that one) we make a spontaneous, unanimous decision to hit the road and see some of the sights. For some bizarre reason, maybe due to the five of us all suffering Mojave mojito hangovers, we stupidly decide it would be a great idea to drive three hours sou–east into the desert toward all that is lawless and liberated, in Leslie's un–airconditioned, beat–up jeep. Dave wants to show us some of the things that make this place so utterly defined, the real California he says, the one filled by those with a desire to be different from the superficial Californian stereotypes.

Our first destination is the Salton Sea. Yep, the place put on the map (well, the 24–inch map of the straight–to–video screen that is) by Val Kilmer, in the movie of the same name. The flick does nothing to change the idea that the desert attracts insanity. With this in mind, it's with comical levels of trepidation that us non–Americans pull into the tiny 'sea'–side township of Bombay Beach. Driving in is desolate. It's impossible to tell if locals are hanging indoors to hide from the heat or the stench. All along the Salton's edge, which laps up onto the shores of this little hamlet, lay the bodies of dead tilapia. 'It's heavily polluted from underground seepage and fertiliser run–off,' Dave reckons. It's also extraordinarily salty; too much for any fish less hardy than the tilapia, which only survive when the lake is full, not half evaporated into the salty concentrate it is right now. What a perverse cruelty; this enormous sea of coolness is too dirty even to dip a sweltering toe into.

'You think this is bizarre come look at this.' I follow Dave along the water's edge, up over a gravelly embankment. There are no trees here at all, just a haze of grey sand underfoot leading into a haze of silver water. As we reach the top of the small rise, I have a sudden epiphany – in life there are things stranger than imagination: art imitates life and all we do is merge its masterpieces to come out with a brand new picture. Before me there is a desolate plain of destruction – half submerged trailers, clinging in utter fruitlessness to the air above, their half–sunken windows taking in those last glimpses of blue sky as the soft depths of the salty bog pulls them achingly slowly and suffocatingly below ground. There are skeletons of homes so ravaged by their environment that even the memories have been picked clean. There is furniture left exactly where it beached some 30 years ago. There is the carcass of a small dog or a large cat, it's impossible to tell. And for the final flourish, there is a plastic child's doll – a girl with blonde hair and one plastic eyeball missing – sitting on an oddly grand but filthy Tudor–style armchair. Tarantino himself could not have detailed this place better.

With the heat now pounding down on our pounding heads, thirst overrides fear and we head into the one commercial building we can see. It looks locked tight, there are no windows, only taunting signs of cold beers and refreshing, sugary drinks. We presume it's a bar, the kind where inside sits a small group of 5th generation locals, hunched over their ales talking about rattlesnakes and Ol' Drunken McFuck–Fuck's latest indiscretion. Their banter only stalls when interrupted by the heat and sunlight that streams in when us pasty city slickers swing open the door. All heads turn when it does, and they notice we're not from around here. They glance at each other with a subtle and well–practiced glint and a nod. They'll pull out their knives, rape us then dismember us…and not necessarily in that order.

By the time I reach the building I've completely freaked myself out, it takes more mental strength for me to pull that door open then it did to dive off a bungee tower some years earlier. I yoik it and peer inside, the dark imagery of my mind shattered like the retinas of a stoner that's waltzed into a 7/11 without sunglasses…in fact this is a 7/11! There are flouro lights and small aisles of grocery items, there's a man and a woman behind the counter looking about as murderous as a floral apron. My dehydrated, adrenalised mind takes a few moments to put down the imagined schooner glass that I'd picked up in my mind's eye to defend myself from non–consensual carnal sin.

'Hi there!' The couple say chirpily….in an *IRISH* accent!

They proceed to tell me that there was a sea surge back in the seventies when the Government decided to divert water into the Salton sink. They gave the residents two weeks' notice and then flooded their little village. Apparently, this couple came to visit Bombay Beach sometime before that and fell in love with the place, moving from Ireland not long after. They claim also to swim in the Salton, but only at night – no doubt to avoid the gazes of a thousand dead fish. We thank the couple for their cool beverages and the story of their mind–bending life choices and jump back in the jeep heading toward and beyond a little town called Niland – population 1200. As we motor through the barren terrain the ever–increasingly translucent Kristy – sitting in the middle, in the back – starts to feel very ill. It makes me think of the pasty little Brit–folk from The Duke Spirit who've recently been at The Rancho, wandering around in the spinifex in a million-degree heat for six weeks.

'They loved it out here they really enjoyed it,' says Dave when I ask about their experience. 'We had another band out here from Britain called the Eighties Matchbox B–line Disaster, another Chris Goss project, and they are amazing, they're a great band and they have a really great look; the guitar player wears, like, Edwardian jackets and has giant green hair, and just seeing those guys wandering around the desert was priceless. You know like the Duke Spirit guys look like they could be from around here but the Eighties Matchbox guys they look like they could be from Mars, so it was just awesome to see them wandering around aimlessly.'

I can't help but wonder what the folk of Joshua Tree think

of these odd meanderings and of the host that draws them here. What is Mr Catching's social standing within this very vast environment but very small community?

'I don't think anyone really knows about it. The few musicians that live in the area love it, but I don't really venture out much when I'm home. I'm on tour so much that when I get back here, I buy a bunch of groceries and cook – I don't wanna go anywhere.'

Except of course, in moments like this, when he is entertaining his Australian lady friends and his good mate Kristy (who's now gone from porcelain white to milk–mould green), when he is willing to risk life and lung to venture out into the middle of territory so remote that even the American government won't claim it. We hang a left at Niland, pass a few power stations when suddenly looming in the distance, is a brightly coloured mound of biblical proportions – Salvation Mountain: a message from God, using half a million litres of paint. The tale goes that the man behind the mount, Leonard Knight wandered into the desert sometime during the eighties dragging his damaged hot air balloon behind him. He was looking for a space big enough to lay the silk out and repair it; space that Los Angeles could not offer. For some reason he started painting the earth instead, and just never stopped.*

---

* *Leonard lived out there with no water, no electricity, no home; just a mountain of joy and a message of love until he was placed into care for dementia in December 2011. Leonard passed away on February 10, 2014, in El Cajon.*

When we roll in, he rushes out to greet us. With no idea if we're serial killers or saints, he asks us if we'd like to stay the night. We um and ahh until Kristy says, 'I don't feel so good,' and promptly vanishes before our eyes, suddenly becoming nothing more than a green crumpled frock on the ground, so devoid of nourishment in that moment, her tiny mass may well have blown out of a car window somewhere along this desert road. Dave scoops her teensy body up effortlessly as we exchange smiles and thumbs–ups with Leonard, gratefully decline his offer to stay, and drive away, Salvation Mountain fading slowly in the rearview mirror along with one of the most pure–hearted and free human beings I'd ever met. Leonard doesn't stop waving until we are no more than a speck on his horizon.

After Kristy is revived – a victim of heat, whiskey and a fragile constitution – talk returns to guests of The Rancho. One of the more recent being James Lavelle of Unkle fame, who came out looking for somewhere to finish off his *War Stories* album.

'How did James end up all the way out here?' I ask Dave who has resumed his place behind the wheel.

'He was recording in LA with Chris Goss and Chris brought James and Rich out here, just to record one song – to maybe be out here for two or three days.' As he speaks he hangs a right back out onto the main(ish) road at Niland. 'I saw them get outta the car and they were just going 'holy shit' looking around the place. James came up to me and said, 'Can we stay here for five weeks?' I thought that was funny because he hadn't even been *inside* yet! I was like, 'Yeah sure but you might want check the place out first.' I told him I'd have to be here though, too, and he was like, 'Yeah we want you to be here to write some songs with us.' I love Unkle so it was an honour, especially hanging out with Chris, who is one of my best friends. It was a blast.'

The Rancho proved exceptionally generous to James. It seemed he understood the place and The Rancho De La Luna repaid in kind.

'They wrote more songs here than anyone ever has. We had a little pro–tools set–up in the tracking room and they would record something, and then when they were editing in that room, Rich or James would come back and write a song in the other room, or if something was happening in that room they'd be writing something out on the porch. I think they wrote something like 40 songs in the five weeks they were here, it was crazy and they were all great songs. I think the album has about 13 songs on it and about six of those were recorded out here – at some stage he's going to have to release a triple album of just Rancho stuff.'

So creatively abundant was James's time here, he ended up singing on this particular album: the first time he had ever done so. He sang on two of the album's songs – *Hold My Hand* and *Morning Rage* – both penned in part by Dave.

'Yeah they were both riffs that I'd come up with and he'd never done that before – sang – so he was pretty excited about the whole experience.'

Whilst Dave himself doesn't embrace the Producer title, he's been involved in the making of around 50 albums – either in the main role directly, or alongside Chris Goss and Josh Homme, whom Dave describes as both amazing producers and two of the funniest people he knows. He's become a producer almost incidentally; as a musician and by osmosis – James Lavelle was part of that process as another incredible producer, cementing Dave in the rightness of his direction.

'When someone's here and they are getting more inspired than they've ever been, I feel great, like I'm doing something right. I don't own The Rancho, I rent here and I don't have just anyone out here. There are a million studios in this part of the world all with way better gear than mine, so when people come out here and get it, I just feel like I'm doing something really right.'

As we return to The Rancho I settle myself in to spend many hours gazing at the Mojave moon on its immense black canvas, for the last time, knowing the next morning we'll head back to LA where the night sky loses its sharpness to the manufactured glow of humans below. There is one last catch up to be had there with Michael Beinhorn; for dinner in a beautiful restaurant in Venice Beach and onto a club where bizarrely I run into desert–dweller and Outtacontrolatron inventor Barry Conley once again. Michael and Barry, remembering their connection in Zakk Wylde – former Ozzy

Osbourne guitarist and creator of the *Black Label Society* – with whom they had both worked with at different times.

As I drift off to sleep, thinking of my babies far away on the opposite curve of this enormous sky, I realize that only for something of this magnitude – to meet with these people, to feel these parts of the world – could I be this distance from them. As I fall deeper and the poetry of being both content and wistful simultaneously begins to blur into unconsciousness, I make one last note to self…call Trina Shoemaker.

4

Trina Shoemaker: A Tough Cookie

Trina Shoemaker was not difficult to locate. Being, incredulously, one of very few female producers in the year 2008 and incredibly, one of few who actually has a website. I sent her an email a week ago detailing my time out in the desert with Dave. She promptly sent me her phone number in return and today I sit here in the triple j studios, dialling those digits. I'm not sure what this ensuing chat will have in store, but certainly the lead in has been the most effortless and organic to date. Listening to the ring that's reaching out to her on the other side of the globe, I ponder again just why there are so few women working in this role? Other than Trina, the only other woman that I've spoken to in this capacity, who has worked with enough bands of a high enough profile for the Series is Sylvia Massey – a ballsy, switched–on producer, most renowned for her work with Tool.

Snapping me back to current location is the sudden sound

of the infamously capable Trina, holding phone in one hand and pressing play on a Baby Einstein DVD with the other. She's slightly breathless as she chases her diaper–less son around the house, before plonking the little fella in front of the tele in the hope of buying herself some talk time. In this moment she represents the epitome of the highly skilled but overstretched modern woman; reinforcing perhaps why she is just one of a teensy handful of female producers in the world and possibly one of the only to have achieved both career and family.

'There were probably three main things that saw me go down this path,' Trina explains of her decision to follow this road in the first place, whilst attempting to rectify the no–diaper situation on her young son. 'One was a devotion to music, but two was knowing that I didn't want to be a musician. I'd look inside albums starting with my Dad's record collection, then moving onto my own as I got a little older, and I'd see the studio shots and I was attracted to all that equipment in the control room. The third thing was underlying, and didn't really occur to me until I was grown and I was already doing this – I was raised mostly by my Dad who worked for a natural gas company and they had a control room which was underground, it was dark; a very controlled environment filled with all this equipment. I used to go with my Dad when he worked nights and I think there was something about the safety of those control rooms at Midwestern Gas that later maybe made me seek that same kind of environment; a place where I could be all cut–off, in this little world all unto itself. It must all have played a part, because I knew I wanted to be an engineer from when I was a teenager.'

Trina's Dad was also a major factor in her unflinching ability to enter a world bobbing with testicles. 'Both of my sisters are the same, my younger sister has a PhD in solid–states physics, and my older sister works in high–end business banking, writing corporate software. So, we all entered very male–dominated fields. My dad, you know, he was just one of those guys that said you can do anything you want to do, but you better figure out how because I'm not getting it for you. He would help of course but he wasn't an enabler, we had to figure it out – when we were eighteen if we weren't in college, then we were moving out. I remember once going through some kind of pubescent depression moment – my boobs didn't grow and I was bummed or whatever my problem was – my Mum was like, 'She needs therapy,' and I remember my Dad going, 'She doesn't need a goddam thing, she's fine.' I was listening and I was like, 'You know, he's right, I am fine.' He was just very much, 'Figure it out, pull yourself together, make yourself a cup of tea and go and make your life happen.'

'In my career I've never met with a single ounce of sexism,' Trina says, taking a moment to think it through. 'And if I did, well then, I was completely unaware that it was happening, cause if I came up against someone like that I would probably just plough right through them. I'm tall, thin, rather muscular – I'm not a little petal – so most men who might have treated me with a little disrespect were probably a little scared of me and stopped right away. It wasn't until I got pregnant and had my little baby that I could see the difficulties in being a woman and a producer. It wasn't sexism I was coming up against, it was my maternal desires – I want to be my baby's Mummy, I want to be home for him at night.'

Trina's voice drifts away from the phone for a moment and goes up an octave 'You want a banana? You want to watch more Baby Einstein? Ok sorry, where were we? Oh yeah, the aim for me now is to be working on records I get points on,' her voice suddenly becomes much deeper with its conviction. 'If I don't secure my future in that way, I don't know how my kids gonna go to college – I am not gonna be in the studio when I'm sixty, tracking.'

Trina was thirty–nine years old when she decided life needed to change. She'd spent more than two decades in the studio–scape and simply refused to enter the next decade of her life in the same space. An amazing strength of will prompted a massive leap of faith and resulted in a fairy tale; all of which began far from home – on the shores of New South Wales, Australia.

'I LOVE it around there,' Trina says enthusiastically of the place far from home that gave her the platform for a life–changing decision. 'I mean a lot of the time was of course me behind an SSL Board, which is how my life always looks, but then you'd look out the window and have this incredible tape bay that was all glass on the back and…I took this picture with the Steuter 827 mixing board in the foreground and in the background, the moon. I used that picture as my computer screensaver, it was a very special moment.'

Mangrove Studios on the Central Coast just north of Sydney is where Trina found herself staring at the sky, beginning to quietly build an unshakeable resolve for a different future. She came out twice to exactly the same location, both times to work with Australia's Something For Kate.

'They sent me some demos for *Echolalia* and I have no idea how they came up with me, but I was sent these demos and it was just at an odd time in my life. My Mum's name was Kate, so that immediately drew me to the band and I just really liked what I heard. There was something very unique about Paul's voice and writing that prompted me to call them. I just went with my gut… and they were very funny on the phone, all three of them, at one point, we were just laughing and it didn't become about the record anymore it just became about the ridiculous. I made a comment that in Australian terms actually means to give someone a blow job, and I had no idea that that's what I was actually saying, and I could hear them all snickering and it was Steph who told me about the lingo… so yeah, right away we felt comfortable. I took a huge leap of faith and so did they and I jumped on the plane and flew over there.

'Right away Steph and I connected,' she says. 'She was still finding her feet in the band at that point and I think she could see that I wasn't going to dismiss her for the genius of Paul – because Paul is a genius, not just a musical genius but an all–round genius, he's also seven foot tall... he's possibly the most intelligent person I've ever met, he comes out with this shit, and you're like, 'Are you talking about nuclear physics right now? Are you talking about sub–atomic particles? You are!' But Steph could see right away that I wasn't going to dismiss her and go 'Oh, here's just Paul's girlfriend who happens to play the bass.' I respected them all, Clint too, and I think they could see that. For example, I spent a lot of time working with Steph on her bass parts, she was new to bass then, and rather than just go, 'OK Paul (who is an excellent bass player) you play this part,' I worked with Steph. She wrote all those bass parts and she deserved a chance to play them up to album quality. She was also great at seeing the big picture, she'd walk in when Paul and I were agonising over the board during mixing, and pick whatever it needed straight away. Her lucid ideas would fill in the big picture whilst Paul and I would get lost in the minutia.'

After the massive success of *Echolalia* (it was voted by triple j radio listeners as the best album of 2001) Trina returned to work on the follow–up, *Official Fiction*. It was during the making of this album that Trina's previously quiet resolve turned into a loud, self–enforced personal contract. With a decree of 'buggerit' to the world, Trina announced she was throwing in the towel.

'It was bizarre to me... it was what, three years later? We

were in the same studio and they were the exact same band, only better players. It was history repeating; the only difference was that we were in different bedrooms and Paul had a new Volvo. But it was during that record that I cancelled all records after that, because I decided, then declared on live Public Radio during a phone interview I was doing with them while I was there in Oz, that I was quitting until I found someone I could share my life with and start a family. I was not going to turn forty alone in a recording studio.' With the same determination that drove her to all of her destinations Trina threw herself whole–bodied, whole–heartedly in. She enrolled with the University of New Orleans to study, signed up to go on archaeological digs as a volunteer in Israel and France and had her flights booked, she was very, *very* serious. 'I flew back to LA with Paul to master the Something for Kate record,' Trina says, beginning to explain the precise moment that would make her life whole. 'I was standing out front the Beverly Loyal Hotel on Beverly Ave, waiting for a cab to take me back to the airport to head back to New Orleans. I hadn't been home in three months, I was real burned out, real tired. Then this weird guy with a turban on came up to me while I was waiting outside and said in very broken English, 'I want to tell you something' and I just scowled at him and said WHAT? And he said, 'The best thing in your life is about to happen to you but you can't see it yet and you're gonna live till more than 90' then he walked off. I was like, 'Ahhh ok… that was weird.' Then I got in the cab and flew back to New Orleans where I went to meet a friend at this little club at about 6pm – who didn't show up. I was still so tired, I'd hardly slept and I was jetlagged, but I stayed, and up on the stage that night was Grayson. That's when we met, and we've been together ever since and have a baby together.

'Steph called me a few days later, because they knew how lonely I was and how tired I was of being in hotel rooms year after year after year, alone, alone, alone, alone and I was like, 'Um, you're not gonna believe this – I'm in bed with a guy right now.'

'You're bloody not!' She said. I left Something For Kate and walked straight into the arms of my husband and fell pregnant 8 months later. I was alone for my whole adult life until Grayson, I sacrificed that part of my life to become great at what I do and it became a vicious cycle – I could never meet anyone because I was always in the studio and because I was never meeting anyone I turned myself even more into my work. That's why I needed to make the grand gesture and actually quit to allow anything else in. About four months after we'd been together I was like, 'ok I guess I can book a few records in now, I've done it'. I don't have to go to college, yay!'

The strength in Trina emanates from her voice like a thick, desert breeze, she's a take–no–shit kinda lady who might stare at some and make them scamper into hiding or invoke in others more cheeky a desire to push her buttons and see what happens. Nick Oliveri, original bass player for Queens of the Stoneage, decided to take the latter path.

'It was hilarious.' Trina says of tracking and mixing Queens of the Stone Age's second record *Rated R*. 'They had a floor bong right as you walked into the control room and at one point whenever I looked at Nick, the former bass player, all he would do was act like he was blowin' somethin' and do these lewd hand movements and I was just like, 'Whatever dude, not only am I old enough to be your mother, and two not only does that *not* gross me out or offend me, it does nothing, I don't care, you could pull one off in the corner over there, not impressed, don't care.' I think they learnt pretty quick that I'm pretty rock n roll with all that stuff. You wanna watch porn whatever all that stuff goes right by me, I couldn't care less. But yeah, doing the Rated R record… that was a crazy, crazy amazing record to work on.

'It was all analogue!' She suddenly exclaims. 'ProTools was only wheeled in once, for one thing, we tracked it on two 16–track analogue machines that were locked together which equals lo–fi and hi–fi, that's the warm fuzzy sound but hi–fidelity. Following Josh and Chris Goss's bizarre, creative ideas all around the damn place, there was really no special recipe there, just the strength of the music itself. Oh, we did over–dub the drums, Josh wanted no cymbal bleed whatsoever and he wanted the kick and the snare very compressed and punchy but not the cymbals going crazy, so the only choice was to use the old heavy–metal trick to overdub the cymbals which is extremely difficult but it worked on this record.

'Josh had a very clear vision; he is an incredible musician and an incredible producer, he had it all pretty much laid out, all I had to do was turn EQs until he said, 'Yep, that's it right there'. At one point I said to him, 'Josh what am I doing here, I've never done a kind of metal, heavy record like this, why am I doing this?' And he said, 'Because you've never done a record like this. I don't want somebody here who thinks they know something telling me how to get my guitar sounds. I want to tell you how I want my guitar to sound and then I want you to do it.' And I was like, 'Cool. How do you want your guitar to sound?"

Trina had the underlying connection also to the Mojave, her friendship with Dave was cultivated through The Rancho and all those that had deeply felt its call.

'It was back when Josh was in Kyuss, out in the Mojave. A lot of my friends used to hang out there, Fred Drake, Dave Catching, Victoria Williams all those people….and when I lived in LA and even when I moved to New Orleans I used to still go and hang out in the desert. And then Dave started showing up in New Orleans and then I think both he and Fred mentioned me to Josh, and made him aware of me, and if those guys think I'm cool then I've already passed Josh's integrity test through people he definitely trusts.'

Five years later, in 2005, Josh would again call upon the exceptional technical skills of Trina to mix the band's live album *Over the Years and Through the Woods*. It couldn't have come at a better time, Trina receiving the phone call at one of the most intense moments of her life.

'I hadn't seen the house yet. I knew it was flooded but

they wouldn't let us in for another four weeks, then Queens called and said, 'Look come out here for two weeks and mix the live record.' So, it was great because there wasn't much I could do in Alabama at Grayson's mum's house, apart from sit there and stare at the computer and wonder how bad my house was in New Orleans. It was actually while I was out there in LA during that mixing that I found out the flood lines were 6 feet on my house, so I knew that that was it, it was done.'

Hurricane Katrina not only took Trina's material possessions but, as was the case for millions of others, it also forced her and her brand new little family to completely rethink and then reshape their lives from scratch.

'I pretty much lost everything, my house, everything in it, my studio, all my equipment, my record collection all of it was under about 6 ft of water for three weeks. Unfortunately, none of the studio gear was insured for flood because I couldn't get commercial flood insurance in New Orleans that I could afford. It was insured for fire and theft and meteors and every other calamity but not flood. I lost my Grammies, my beautiful Neve (*a brand of much–loved, high–quality recording consoles that began their life courtesy of Rupert Neve back in the 1960s*) and my DATs! All the old mixes I'd done – Sheryl Crowe, Pearl Jam, hundreds of tapes. Luckily, I took with me the tapes I was working on at the time, because I just couldn't risk losing the masters of those. I decided not to go back and rebuild, it was just too devastating, so my partner Grayson and I decided to move up here to Tennessee, at least for the next few years.'

The choice of locale was based on more than just a desperate throw of the dart but not by much.

'I used to go through Nashville for work once or twice a year anyway and I came up right up after the flood to mix a record for this woman Joanna Cotton and her Producer Peter Collins, a good old friend of mine and he said, 'Where are you gonna go?' And he said, 'Why don't you move up here?'

'So, just for a lark we went out with a real estate friend of his to look at some rural properties, because I said, 'Well, if I'm going to live up here I want to live out in the beautiful Tennessee country,' and sure enough she showed me a place that was 11 acres with a converted barn and absolutely beautiful.'

With a creek out the back, a mountain and a cave for their boy to explore, the place proved to be their silver lining.

'All afternoon today, I sat with my feet in the creek and I was like, 'Wow I live here!' I'm in debt up to my eyeballs, but this land is getting more and more valuable every minute, we bought in a very sought–after area in Williamson county, so even if my career dried up tomorrow I could sell this place for twice what I paid for it two years ago.'

Whilst Trina's roots ran deep in New Orleans, a lack of fully functioning studios already meant that much of her life was spent constantly on the move, all over the globe. To New York, Nashville to LA, Japan, UK, Australia and Germany, Trina took her packed bags and made records in locations determined by the artists with whom she worked. She knew even before motherhood, that when her baby came she was going to have her first big Producer–Who–Parents conundrum to solve. 'When I got pregnant before the flood, I didn't know what I was going to do. I knew I didn't want my son, Waylon, to grow up in hotel rooms, and so I was already faced with the fact that I may have to move somewhere with a thriving recording scene. New Orleans has a thriving music scene, but not a recording scene, then the flood came and well, that took care of that. I love it here but there's a lot of days where I still just want to pack up my shit and move back there.'*

Back in the studio in Sydney where I've now sat for the past hour and a half, mesmerised by Trina's tales, other triple j announcers start increasing the hand gestures universally symbolic in radio stations around the globe of 'get the fuck out of the studio, we need to go to air dickhead.'

I shuffle my papers in a, 'Ye–ep just packing u–up,' fashion, asking Trina one final question. 'You've now won three Grammies – Best Pop/Contemporary Gospel Album in 2004 for Steven Curtis Chapman's *All Things New* and two in 1998 for Sheryl Crowe's record *The Globe Sessions* – one for Best Rock Album and the other for Best Engineered album – making you the only woman to have won a Grammy for engineering, ever. Are there parts of your time with Sheryl that you can put your finger on, that pinpoint the magic?'

'I don't know, I don't do anything different with Sheryl

than I do with anybody else so it's just Sheryl I suppose – she wins prestigious awards. There was definitely a chemistry there though, in the way we heard music, and something about the way we two crabby, skinny, single women were in the studio together. We were both willing to be in the studio 18 hours a day and focus all our life on this one purpose for a year and a half. Every ounce of me went into those records, I travelled everywhere with her, sometimes for months at a time, and I can never make that commitment to anyone else ever again.'

Whilst those Grammy's did bring the cred and respect that such shiny things tend to do, not just for her, but for women in the industry in general, they didn't change the type of albums that Trina continues to work on to this day.

'I'm still very much a middle class engineer, if I ever get points on an album that sells a million copies I'd quit and from then on I'd just do labours of love – work on records for people that I adore, like Grayson and Something For Kate – I would put working with Something for Kate in my top five greatest times I've had in the studio in my entire twenty years. If they had another record happening when Waylon was older and they'd have me, I'd be on a plane in a second. I love 'em. I only want to be in that space now, I don't want to be around people who are in a bad mood and it's like, 'You get to make records for a living, how can you be in a bad mood?' I want to be around funny, positive people and help support brilliance and ignore mediocrity... although it's often mediocrity that pays the bills! So, I won't complain too much!'

On cue little Waylon suddenly starts squealing delightedly

in the background in an I'm–*very*–chuffed–with–myself way and Trina's voice immediately goes up in volume and in octave with that special enthusiasm for bodily fluid that only a Mother can employ. 'Good job!' she proclaims. 'Good pee in the potty! But you don't always have to bring it out to show Mummy. Be very careful you don't spill it… but really good work!'

'But as far as the Grammy goes, in terms of pride,' Trina says without skipping a beat between Diligent Mother and Internationally–Acclaimed Producer and Engineer, 'I was suddenly like, 'Holy shit I'm the prom queen, I got the crown, I'm head cheerleader, every failed dream that I had starting with not winning that Office–friendly colouring–in competition to not being asked to the prom, all of those were suddenly gone because I just won a Grammy for Engineer of the Year and I'm the only woman who ever has, still to this day.'

Fast forward two years and 17 941 kms (11 148 miles) away to a couch on which QOTSA frontman Joshua Homme sits in a dimly lit portable donga, backstage at Soundwave 2011 in Perth and says, 'Trina worked at Kingsway which was Daniel Lanois' place in New Orleans and Daniel had actually brought a desk to the Rancho in the very early days. I also knew Trina's work from all the stuff she'd done previously and I really felt like what we were about to do with *Rated R* needed a woman's touch. I don't care what colour, if you're gay or a woman or a man none of that has ever mattered to me – it seems so stupid – but there are real benefits in the differences between people and she also has such an acoustic raw sensibility and I knew that we were going to do strange brash things and I needed them to be encased in a natural and delicate delivery. I also knew that we were wild and I wanted the responsibility of having to be quasi–gentleman holding me back a little, to actually feel the pressure. I love creating a little bit of positive anxiety in the studio. You also can't offend Trina and you shouldn't try. She's a tough cookie.'

5

Wesley Pentz aka Diplo: Man of Many Colours

Worldwide curiosity (including my own) began about Diplo, when a Sri-Lankan dynamo with a riveting lineage and an unconventional approach to music, suddenly exploded out of the pages of the UK music press. M.I.A. was all bright colours and dark skin, grew up in London, had family ties with the Tamil Tigers and could make a song work with fewer words then galang-a-lang-a-lang-lang. He was a white boy from Florida, obsessed with Brazilian funk, her DJ, producer and on further investigation, her boyfriend too, way back then.

M.I.A.'s eclectic mash of sounds, that borrowed styles from all over the world, overlaid with her distinct offbeat, syncopated way of rapping about salt and peppering her mangoes, piqued the interest of numb music journalists around the globe, scooping Diplo up into the atmospheric slipstream with her. I wondered about Diplo's tale from that day on. How did a lad from deep-fried America find himself entwined in the life of a soon-to-be famous Sri-Lankan/British ragga-style rapper with such a backstory? Why was it that just five years on from producing M.I.A.'s debut, *Arular,* folk of Janet Jackson/Christina Aguilera notoriety would come snooping around for some of his anarchic, hipster cred? Was he a brat, was he blessed, was he too cool for school or was he just a really lovely guy who worked really hard and coincidentally happened to move one-step in front of the dance-music zeitgeist?

The theory that I'd formed in my mind based around his free-wheeling production sound and hip hop attitude, was that Wes Pentz (aka Thomas Wesley Pentz aka Diplo) was a bit rough around the edges with little care for what the hell he *should* be doing, he was just doing and doing it well. So now, four years on from the release of MIA's striking debut album, and 21 hours of flight time, I'm soon to hear how that theory sits with the reality of Diplo.

Despite being an Australian-born British citizen, this is my first trip to the UK. I never had any connection, any pull, to come here. I'm not sure if it's to do with the astonishing similarities between Australia and this here country that colonised it or simply my genetic imprint but I feel as disappointingly comfortable here as I would stepping off a train in Sydney. I have been shocked by just how little unique identity Australia has on its own, thanks to the dominance of that first and ongoing European assault, just how extensive the eradication of culture really was when the British invaded the shores of the country I call home some 250 years before, and how little we've moved forward to embrace our individuality of a land that still hosts the oldest living culture in the world. To come so far and see so many similarities; to discover that my homeland is still a carbon copy of Britain has been confronting. To momentarily placate my white shame, I go look for the most British food I can find, in the hope of discovering something culturally more here that I've missed.

Just across the way from the Hoxton Hotel where I'm to meet Diplo is The Rivington Grill, it turns out to be more of a restaurant than a bar, but there's a stout to be had and a thing called a Welsh Rarebit. Bingo! As I order it, knowing nothing except that it's vegetarian, I congratulate myself on my daringness, my sense of adventure in a land so pale! It's a moment of back-patting that ends quickly when I discover that my exotic delicacy is little more than embellished cheese on toast. After the initial disappointment, I do feel a strange small sense of affection for a country that's willing to put the cholesterol count aside for such an unpretentious national dish.

With stout down and a couple of cheese toasties devoured, I walk the two blocks to the Hoxton Hotel. Upon entering I discover something I never knew - that few things scream 'doing alright' more than a hotel foyer containing a life-size, flouro orange Lamborghini made out of pipe cleaners. I'm intercepting Diplo during his European tour and by the looks of his artsy digs, life outside the box is plush indeed, at least in a very boutique way. Diplo is here in London to do a couple of

DJ gigs and to catch up with his colleague Switch - the two having collaborated on M.I.A.'s debut album, *Arular* and the follow-up, *Kala,* as well as their own gangbusters project Major Lazer. It's been nothing short of a miracle intercepting him here - his two days off on the whole European tour falling right on my arrival into England and just two days before I leave for Paris to chase down Philippe Zdar, the big bass god of the French music scene.

With the rarebit and the pint of stout sitting like lead weights in my feet, my head feels like a hot air balloon; a combination of jet lag from the flight and a few pre-interview butterflies that are now a little tipsy. Staring at the Lamborghini helps, it's right inside the entrance of the hotel and up on a platform about one foot off the ground with a cosy brick wall backdrop. It's hypnotic and indeed it is made of pipe cleaners. Really, really bright ones. Its silly awesomeness makes me happy.

It's about 5.20pm and Diplo was due to meet me at five. Considering how far we've both travelled to be here, a couple of minutes elasticity spread across some twenty thousand kilometres is almost punctuality in lieu. A black cab soon pulls up out the front. A young fella steps out whom, I presume instantly by his tired, focused expression is Colin - Diplo's tour manager. Diplo steps out into the grey street behind him. He's wearing a black shiny bomber jacket. It's more subdued than some of the shiny jackets of a similar style I've seen him donning, but it's still absorbing all of my attention; I can't decide what to make of it. Artists always wear things that no normal human would wear, things that make them instantly recognisable as musos even if you have no idea who they are. This look states, 'I am creative from the depths of my soul to the tips of my sculpted hair.' Having spent my entire radio career with many a famous creative, I can say that sometimes it takes a moment to figure out if the look is working in real human terms. In this case I would say that only Diplo, and possibly John Travolta during the final scene of Grease, could get away this ensemble. It's working perfectly.

Mr Pentz has got the boyish looks of a young Hollywood brat-pack actor circa 1988, but with an air of Oliver Twist about him. His short, blonde military-style hair cut is made prison-like by the tiny bit of 'I-might-steal-your-car' stubble on his top lip. The rest of his face is so devoid of any facial hair, it looks like the only time it might ever see a razor is in the backstreets of one of the gritty cities in which he dwells. He looks a tad tour-tired already…another country, another hotel, another interview.

Colin spots me in the corner - I've not made myself known but there's something about the radio gear in my lap and the headphones around my neck, that give me up as I attempt to spy on them for as long as possible.

'Hi' he says. 'Mel?'

'Colin?' I say in return. We shake hands as Colin explains that they'll just check in and get organised, they'll be about five minutes. Colin arranges to use one of the hotels smaller conference rooms and conveniently, they designate us the one with the air conditioner that sounds like we're chugging along on board the P&O Pacific. The table that Diplo is leaning on creaks too, whenever he shifts the weight of his elbows, reinforcing the sensation that we're out at sea, full-steam ahead. He has to sit very still in order to avoid the table-noise carrying through the microphone, he's not very good at playing statues so he resigns to keeping his body off the table completely.

Diplo is fidgety, he's buzzing with energy and it becomes clear pretty quickly that hyperactivity plays a large part in his creative output. He opens his mouth and speaks with a more measured Southern drawl than I'm expecting, making me question if the Diplo family are in fact from further into the swamp than Florida.

'I was born in Mississippi,' he admits, 'but I grew up in Florida, which is where I spent my teen years.' During his pre-pubescent years (which he barely looks like he's out of) Diplo says the Pentz family moved around about ten times from Mississippi, to South Carolina, then onto Florida, Tennessee then to Georgia, Virginia, back to Tennessee then to Florida. As Diplo morphed (somewhat) from boy to man he spent time bouncing around different cities before settling in Philadelphia about eight years ago. 'My family moved around a lot,' he says slowly, when quizzed about the transience, 'we were just constantly on the run from the law…always having to stay one step ahead of the police.' He stays deadpan for a couple of seconds, I stay deadpan with him, not knowing yet what I'm dealing with, but he soon breaks out into the sort of smile that belongs on the face of a fifteen-year-old boy chatting up one of his mum's friends.

He says he comes from a line of big country families - his mumma being one of ten brothers and sisters, his grandma popping babies out since she was the ripe old age of thirteen.

'Some of 'em live out in the woods still,' he reckons, 'and use airboats to get around.' I can't honestly tell you if he's taking the piss or not, but the Cheshire grin doesn't appear, so I take it as truth.

His beginnings as a border-hopping producer began on the blurred county lines of Florida, where the radio was filled with the sounds of Cuban-American rapper Laz and famous Floridian DJ, Magic Mike, who would mix Merengue and bass music, pop and dance hall. And just to round it out, during his middle school years, Diplo would discover heavy metal too. 'It's kinda what all the white kids did in Florida - played in metal bands or make Miami bass, so I was into both those things. When I was a bit older I'd travel around and go and see punk and hardcore bands, things like Hot Water Music, even Marilyn Manson before he got big, when I was like eleven or twelve... oh,' he suddenly adds drifting off into a fond music memory and laughing. 'There was also a metal band I really liked called Ass Suck.'

Not feeling the need to elaborate on Ass Suck, I ask how all those sounds came together into the Diplo soundstream that we're hearing now.

'I'm still waiting to see where my streams at!' He says laughing excitedly. 'I'm still in the rapids! In a giant river of music that I can't even yet see the sides of!'

Diplo describes Florida as the place that had the biggest impact on him musically and as 'a real messy place'. 'It's really disjointed,' he reckons. 'It has that east coast feel but that really Latin and Caribbean feel also cause you know South Florida is mostly Haitian and Cuban but it has that real southern feel to it too.'

When he was fifteen or sixteen, Diplo started to become somewhat of a 'treasure hunter' finding used toys, antiques and other such bounty to sell on eBay and make himself more coin to buy old records. His absolute fascination for all styles of music led his mind in behind the music and onto thoughts of production where chopping and splicing genres together became his new passion. 'I never really got good at DJ-ing,' he confesses, 'until I was about nineteen when I moved to Philly and started to try and make money from DJ-ing. It's only been in the last five or six years that I've been able to quit everything else and be a DJ and producer full time.'

Like everything that makes Diplo Diplo, his production life began in makeshift fashion. Picking up samplers and mixers and other ye olde worlde gear from the flea markets, (getting busted shoplifting a mixer once too) Diplo would glue beats and loops together with little more than the substance of his entire success - unwavering enthusiasm.

'No one else was really into what I was into, so I had to be self-taught,' he says of the way he went about things. 'You know, when I'm here in London, every kid knows how to use a computer - they all know how to sample and produce records really well. When I was that age, I couldn't even figure out how to use the computer. But around 2004, when I was already in my twenties, I sent some tunes that I'd been making, here to Ninja Tune Records and they signed my first album called *Florida* - which was basically me being stoned a lot and making weird music.'

Diplo put that first record together with a cheap program called Cool Edit. Without any multi-tracking, Diplo had to simply loop things over and over, using a calculator to keep track of how many bars he was using. Being arsey as well as gifted has proven a powerful combination, and one that's left Diplo free from the rules of the industry to a large degree, yet in strange demand from the major players he's innocently sidestepped along the way.

As we sit in this sterile little room, air conditioner rumbling away behind us, I realise just how fast Diplo has found himself here; touring the world, being interviewed by an Australian for an international series to feature alongside some of the world's best and most longstanding producers. He's risen to production fame at a rate of knots, sailing right by all the structures and ladders people believe they are supposed to climb, instead just making that one bangin' record that threw his name into the stars. I wonder too, if his place in my own hunt has come too soon.

'Yeah, it really only jumped off in 2005,' he admits with no hesitation, 'when I started producing for M.I.A. When I met her, I was still doing more mixtape type stuff, but they were the first proper records I'd ever done. Learning to record vocals and produce and do the whole thing myself.'

It's an amazing bit of trivia considering that album's impact around the globe and even more so when he goes on to reveal a little later just how crudely and cheaply MIA's *Arular* album was made. But maybe that's why it cut through so successfully: it was gritty; no bright lights, no make-up, no hype, just a coupla passionate folk making music without giving a fuck what anybody else thought.

'Nowadays I have to go into big studios and make everybody comfortable and act accordingly,' he says without complaint but a touch of nostalgia for times past. 'Back then with her, it was still like working in my backyard. She wasn't even signed yet to XL when she reached out to me, it was still local to London. I was doing my first gig in London at Fabric when I met her and that's a really big deal, even today, it's like the head club that has the tastemakers, and she'd come because she'd heard a song I'd done called 'Newsflash' from my first album - this raga thing with weird beats - and she just really liked the whole vibe about it, so she tracked me down and we hit it off; we traded some music and then she came to Philly to work with me to finish off her first album.'

Diplo already knew of MIA by then from her first 12" *Galang*. 'I thought it was really cool, it had all little influences in it, which I was really into and she came to Philly and we worked for like a week and we didn't even do anything.' He laughs a naughty chuckle. 'We just went to eat fried chicken everyday and went and saw movies and the label were like,

'Okaaay, you gotta leave tomorrow to come back, did you guys get that song I needed?' And we were like, 'Oh yeah, things are really good, things are almost done, can we get like one more week…?' So she ended up staying for like, two and a half weeks and we ended up making the whole mixtape *Piracy Funds Terrorism* because I didn't even know how to make a song back then. So we made that mixed tape just full of sketches and ideas, but two of those songs did end up making the album - *Bucky Done Gun* and *You're a Cutie*. That mixtape opened doors for both of us.'

'I can't believe I haven't been sued,' he suddenly comes out with, before cracking up laughing. 'Two of my mixtape records made New York Times top 10 lists, and they weren't even real records!'

As Diplo continues to speak in more depth about MIA, the amount of respect he has for her becomes more and more obvious (despite her saying in a 2016 Pitchfork interview in reference to Diplo 'I know that I should stab you, and you probably still want to stab me, but if we get on, that's actually quite a cool thing'). When he starts reminiscing, he goes all soft and sweet and cute. 'It was strange you know, she's this Sri Lankan girl who grew up in London, but we had a lot in common - we both went to film school, both really interested in the music that was coming out of Florida and shared a lot of the same ideas about music. We actually dated for a while - for about two and a half years, up until working on *Kala* and finishing that record.' And when he starts talking about the music they made together, his sparkly reminisce turns to excitement. 'It's really weird, because her first album didn't really pick up, it wasn't a huge seller, but it was really interesting and had a big impact because it was so interesting. The fanbase for that record was like a new kind of kid, they weren't hip hop kids, they weren't rock kids, they weren't like indie kids - they were a bit of everything, like the record was. So, after that we really got to take off and do weird things for the second record.'

As the attention on MIA's music grew, so did the interest in her personal and (apparent) political life. The media latched onto her father's alleged connections with the Tamil Tigers and it became quite the beat-up when she was denied entry into the US in 2006.

'MIA had this politicised aspect to her life that they really liked to exploit at Interscope Records,' reckons Diplo of the whole kerfuffle. 'It gave her a lot of press, but apart from one lyric about the PLO* on the song *Sunshowers*, she's not really political at all. It was all politicised more when she wasn't allowed into America, because when she was like eighteen she went to jail in LA, so she had a criminal record. Even when I picked her up the first time in Philly, I had to wait like ten hours at the freaking customs. It was for like, shoplifting or something, when she was seventeen!

'A lot of people were picketing her at Coachella though, Singhalese Sri-Lankans that didn't like that kids were into the Tamil side, even though the kids didn't even know anything about what was going on. Yeah, there were negatives and positives.'

At this point Wes drifts out of interview mode and off into the land where fluffy memories live. 'Her father was a really important intellectual,' he says with admiration, 'who wrote books about sustainability. I even read one…she gave it to me for my birthday. I really get it you know, she's like a post-modern creation, she's past rap and past everything - the daughter of an immigrant but an art student, she lives in both worlds all the time, she's not some girl from the hood, she's not some girl from West London, but she is a bit of both. What she is, is even more dynamic than what people think, straddling so many worlds. It may not be as sexy as being a gun-toting terrorist,' he says cynically, 'but I think it's still cool.'

Talk soon turns to the actual making of MIA's albums - this is what I've been curious about for several years. I've read interviews with MIA where she almost seems angry, feeling like people are saying that without Diplo her first two records would not have been what they were. I'm on the edge of my seat to hear Diplo's version of events when suddenly he starts chuckling, he begins speaking and his voice takes on a new tone as it moves right into the back of his throat, delivering his words on a healthy gust of laughter.

'Everything we ever worked on always seemed to be a work in progress. Even the whole second record was like…I don't even know, like half the hooks…were like the same hook 'nan-nana' used like three times! I'd be like, we're gonna fix that later, right? And then suddenly the song was out and it was too late! My whole life as a producer…*everything*…

seems to be a work in progress.' He bursts out laughing again. 'And then ...the time runs out ...so yeah, that's kinda how it goes.'

Things didn't really change for MIA's second album either, in fact, they may have gotten even looser, courtesy of the confidence gained by the success of the first.

'None of that record was making any sense,' Diplo says of *Kala*. 'None of the whole idea of it, the label just trusted us at this point.' He says that last statement with the cheek of a kid who's just gotten away with stealing twenty cents out of mum's purse and downed a bag of mixed lollies. 'We were like 'Um, we're in Trinidad, we're going to make this Aboriginal hip hop song...' and the guy cutting the cheques was like, 'Ooookkaaay.' But eventually, it all came together.'

The biggest track from that album was *Paper Planes*, its defining moment existing in the chorus in the form of four gunshot sounds followed by the ker-ching of a cash register. In typical Diplo style it was an accidental stroke of genius. 'It was hard, because I'd already forgotten about this record,' he says, going off on a bit of tangent from the question posed about the ideas' beginnings. 'And, like, a year later, after we'd released it the labels like, 'Can you do another version of this with no guns?' And I was like, 'What?! that doesn't make any sense.' So, I was putting like these snares in and gave them this like 'clean' version and it was really whack and then radio started playing this 'clean' version and all the other radio stations were like, 'Well, we're gonna out-do those other stations,' and started playing the 'gunshot' version anyway. But um…yeah…' he says, relocating the cerebral path he was supposed to be on. 'Oh yeah, the reason we put the gunshot on there was because we didn't have a good take of her voice doing the 'boom boom booms' so we tried to get away without having to clear Wreckx N Effect cos it was kind of a take on that old *Rumpshaker* track. The vocals were the very first take, we tried to record a coupla times more and just couldn't get 'em right. I think we recorded those vocals on a porch with a pillow as a wind guard…' he says with a little chuckle. 'She was just relaxed and having fun. Our writing and producing sessions are always like that, really loose, not really serious you know?'

Of the actual origins of the effects, Diplo confesses to the gunshots being, 'The standard ones, like when you type it into iTunes.'

At this, he starts giggling in a, 'Yep, I am fully getting away this,' kinda way before continuing on. 'And the cash register is off, like, a Sesame Street CD or something…yeah they were the only ones I got. I got more gunshots now though,' he says proudly, 'I got like, plenty!'

I see in Diplo's eyes that precious spark, that if he actually were ten years old, would have him prescribed to Ritalin, his creative process labelled ADHD and his anarchist approach marched straight to the principal's office. He's one of those great adults, that has somehow managed to come out the other side of childhood and into adulting with a bit of that spark still burning, hopefully the more success he gets because of that very thing, the brighter it seems to burn. But just how well does that spark dance with other full-grown adults?

Here's a recipe, if you'd like to get involved:
Welsh Rarebit
Serves 2 as a main course, or 4 as a starter
- 4 large thick slices of white sandwich bread
- 1 heaped tablespoon of finely chopped sage leaves
- 2 spring onions, finely chopped
- 6 ounces mature cheddar cheese, grated
- 1 rounded teaspoon of mustard powder
- 4 TBS brown ale
- 1 large egg, beaten
- few drops Tabasco sauce
- pinch cayenne pepper

Pre-heat your grill to high. Place the bread onto a grill pan and toast under the heated grill on both sides, until crisp and golden brown.

Mix the cheese, sage, onion, mustard powder, ale, beaten egg and Tabasco sauce together in a bowl, until very well mixed.

Divide equally amongst the 4 slices of toast, spreading the mixture completely to the edges of each slice.

Sprinkle each with a light dusting of cayenne pepper.

Place under the heated grill again, grilling until the cheese is melted, golden brown and bubbling.

Serve immediately along with some salad on the side.

6

Diplo Does Brazil/Santigold Calls Him An Asshole

The most intriguing element to the Diplo sound up to this point in his work, has been his utilisation of Brazilian music, known as Baile Funk. By seeking out the sounds of life and uprising within the massive illegal housing estates known as the favelas, Diplo plugged into the Brazilian version of dancehall. It was gritty, honest and a perfect condiment for smoother hip–hop and electronic production. This was another piece of the Diplo puzzle that had me wondering. Was he truly tapped into this scene or was he just a preppy white–boy pirating the sounds of a culture that couldn't afford its own way into the international spotlight?

Diplo first went to Rio in 2004 to research this mish–mash of samples and screaming that was slowly creeping out of the favelas, across borders and into Diplo's sphere. Musing as to why his imagination got caught up in the tangled power of Bailie Funk, Diplo says it simply came down to an insatiable appetite, 'Growing up as a music fan devouring everything I could get access to – old soul records, psychedelic rock records, jazz, new wave, eighties and the rest, the fascination of music just carried on, so once I got my fill of all that, it was like 'what next, what else is happening?' The funk stuff was the first stuff I wanted to access because I hadn't heard anything about it outside of Brazil. It was quite connected to what I'd grown up on because it was kind of a bastardised version of Miami Bass, but with kids screaming, like, it's heavy metal on top! That kind of homegrown music exists because Brazil had a complete breakdown in its music industry, so people are now doing whatever they want, dictated by nothing.

'I was writing for a mag back then called *Fader* and I brought this story to them where I said, 'Hey, you should send me to Brazil.' The head editor was like, 'OK, I'll bring you there but you *can't* write the story *and* you can give me the contacts.' Which was cool, cos I got a free trip and that would've been a lot of money for me back then. Instantly in Rio we hooked up with one of the biggest DJs, DJ Marlborough and he's on one of the radio stations there which is an all Baile Funk station. He brought us on the air and interviewed us that day, and then that night took us to all the parties and gave us connection with everybody. So, I kept going for another year after that, making mixing tapes and doing production for kids and researching, eventually I turned it into a documentary called *Favela on Blast*.'

As Diplo goes on excitedly, it's clear that this is a topic he could talk about for days. 'The kids that I meet in Rio who *aren't* from the favelas are amazed that we go in there, they're more scared of entering the favelas than we were.' Diplo glazes over a little as he thinks about the country that's given him so much, 'It's such a weird place, Rio, you have such division between the classes, people don't even look at each other as the same identity – as fellow Brazilians. But you'd be surprised how *normal* the favelas are, like there's a big one in the South Zone that's right next to a big country club and it's 200,000 people living in this favela, on this illegal unclaimed land, but they have their own McDonald's! They have banks, they have a whole Chinatown even, because a bunch of Chinese moved there! So even though the development of the place and the homes, is unorthodox – there are big giant balls of power chords running everywhere – people live normal lives. There's of course a lack of education and a lot of poverty and each favela is somewhat run by the drug lords in each area, but at the same time they also help to develop their community – if someone needs, say antibiotics for your kid, you go to the drug lord there and he'll help you out.

'It's such a strange scene you know because you have this downtown scene in South Zone – the country clubs and the playboys – and those kids like to use drugs and these guys in the favelas are selling the drugs so the whole system runs on itself.'

This connection he feels with the nothing–to–lose freedom of Baile Funk, makes sense in the context of Diplo's own disposition; a ferociously hungry music–head, burning with passion to consume everything out there and throw it all back up again, completely unimpeded; no–boundaries, no set course, no rules and no authority except his own. 'I'm living like Mad Max,' he says in response. 'Driving round the music industry in my busted–up jeep, shooting people and blowing up stuff.'

I still remain unsure as to what's in his heart. He's cute and clever, loves the scenes and the sounds, but does the community move him? Is he stirred by the social or political issues of these places he feels drawn to? Is he putting anything back into the neighbourhoods he's gained so much from? This contemplation fires him up with excitement, breaking out of his more serious demeanour as he talks about some studio type set–ups he's kicked off around the favelas, teaching the kids how to advance their music making skills. Turns out that this charitable project in Brazil got its life all the way around the other side of the globe in the deserts of Australia.

'On my first DJ tour there,' he explains, 'these kids were giving me this really cool Aboriginal hip hop – the *Down River Record* by the Wilcannia Mob – it was even being played on the radio there, and I was fascinated by that record, how cool it sounded, how organic and cheap it was, in a really cool way. I met Australian hip–hop producer Morganics, who hooked that project up and eventually we put that song on M.I.A.'s second album, she did a little verse on it and gave those kids a bit more exposure. At the same time, I was on this big club tour DJ–ing and all the white kids were in the club going crazy and I just felt a bit weird you know, that I was fascinated with this real homegrown hip–hop meanwhile playing in all the clubs where the kids had to pay a fee to see me play.'

It was at this point that Diplo decided to go back to Australia a second time and do his own workshops with the kids. With former triple j host and all-round producer bombshell Nina Las Vegas, along with their buddy Levins, they formed Heaps Decent, an organisation to support young people develop technical, creative and social skills through engagement programs. Together they packed up their toys and headed to the little community of Maningrida in the Northern Territory.

'We took some computers and other gear up there for the kids to use and it became this really cool workshop. We then went down to Wagga Wagga in central New South Wales to a juvenile detention centre, 'cause Nina's mother was actually the principal there at the time, and it was cool to have that contrast between these rougher city kids and those who play football and walk around barefoot. At the end of those workshops in Maningrida, we had this big party and a dance off where I was DJ-ing and dropping that song, *Land Down Under* and all the Aboriginal kids were singing it a cappella… it was crazy bizarre! Like, I was at the end of the world or something!'

At this point Diplo suddenly reveals that pre-global-adventuring, he was a school teacher. As I look at his shiny bomber jacket and first-day of middle school crew cut, struggling to see that there would be much gap between the teacher and the students, he continues, in response to the bemused look on my face.

'Yeah, I was a teacher before I was a DJ! I was an after-school–care teacher for students in North Philadelphia, and then I moved onto being a full time teacher and a social worker there but the job was like *grinding!* You might think it's hard to go and DJ at 2am until 4am, then wake up and do the things that need to be done, but working with kids in the daytime was like…man, I just wanted to die, it was the hardest work ever! I'd rather DJ for twenty hours straight than work with kids for three!'

There's always this point in an interview, like there is any relationship I suppose, which is a lot like that moment when you're lying in bed on a cold night – you get in and the sheets are freezing, you lay there not making a move, trying not to think about the cold and all of a sudden you realise you've gotten warm and cosy. The interview just hit that point. More comfortable, less professional more conversational. This is where things always get great.

Right then there's a knock on the door. It's Diplo's tour manager Colin, I look down at my recorder. We're 40 minutes in. I hope he hasn't come to wrap things up. 'Just checking into see how it's going?' He says, looking to Diplo for signs of needing rescue. This moment happens a bit with artists – particularly those who are also producers, as their time is bulging with commitments and they are also more subject to being punished on the promo trail than producers are.

Diplo simply replies to Colin with, 'Did you drop off the clothes?'

'I'm aah, washing them by hand at the moment,' Colin says, somewhat embarrassed, knowing I guess that he's conjuring images in my mind of him with sleeves pushed up scrubbing Diplo's tighty whiteys.

Diplo laughs, 'Do you need a washboard?'

Colin retreats with a half sarcastic, half playful, 'HA!' before returning to just one of a million duties that make up the glamorous life of the Tour Manager.

Aware now that there's a bit of time pressure with the first appearance from the TM ticked off, I move things along to Philadelphia new wave/hip hop artist Santigold. Much like M.I.A., Santigold is a fascinating creation of the modern world. She traverses many territories sonically, having foundations in punk, dub and rap. Socially she is a fiercely focused and driven woman. During a catch–up I had with Santi over the phone whilst she was gigging Paris, she began out our chat by describing Diplo as 'a charming asshole'. Then clarifying with, 'I call him an asshole all the time but I love Wes, I really do, he's a really good friend of mine.'

When Diplo starts talking about Santi, his face becomes more serious, describing her as one of the strongest artists he's worked with. 'She needs no coaching, she knows exactly what it is she wants to do. I definitely wouldn't tell her what to do, she'd be like, yelling at me, so I'd never try to.'

He says that he's known her for about eight years through the Philly music scene. 'She used to be in a band back then called Stiffed, which I really didn't like that much and she was always like, 'Wes, you've got to mix my band, you gotta remix this thing.' I was always like, 'Ahhh I dunno man, I'm aahh kinda busy but check out this dude Switch, he's British he's got like a lot free time, he's about to move to America'.'

Diplo has a little chuckle at the memory of his silliness at the opportunity he almost missed. 'About a month later, Switch was playing me *Creator*, a track from her *Santigold* album, and I was like, 'What the hell is this?' Cos I remember back in *Stiffed* she was singing and now she was rapping on this track and it was like the most amazing thing I'd ever heard. Still to this day, I love that record, the lyrics on it are crazy! I was just super–jealous then, I was in the studio like, a week later trying to work on her album. Later on, I made a mix tape with her called *Top Ranking,* which was kinda the bizarre version of her record, as Switch and I kinda envisaged it.'

One of the other tracks that Diplo worked on was called *Superman*. A slow, down–tempo, dark sounding thing, with a whole lot of dominant swagger. For me, it really encapsulates the strength that Santigold emanates, so I ask where that track got its life.

'It came from this track called *Redlight* by Siouxie and The Banshees, and I changed it so much…' He turns all naughty–vibe again, '…so I wouldn't have to pay! I even changed the melody, but Santi just ended up telling the label and I was like, 'No! Don't do that!' But yeah, that's how it began and for me as a hip-hop producer, that's probably the most out–there thing that I've done…it's like a straight–up gothic record…something like Bauhaus would produce or something…I don't even know what Bauhaus sound like, that just what I think they'd sound like!'

According to Santi, when her and Diplo met she was already friends with all of his friends – people like Amanda Blank and MC Spank Rock; those who represented the new crew of underground Philadelphian hip hop at the time. When the pair first met properly, it was on a couch at a party, where they sat awkwardly beside each other for a good ten minutes before even acknowledging the other's existence. 'I obviously knew who he was, and he knew who I was, but we'd never been properly introduced,' she would tell me. 'So we both just sat there for like ten minutes not saying anything,'

Santigold burst out laughing at that memory. 'Finally, he asked me if he could borrow my lip gloss or something, and I said, 'Ah okay,' and then he's like, 'Come here, I want to introduce you to someone.' That was, like, the first real thing he said to me! And then he took me over and introduced me to Switch and said that we should work together.'

As Santi talks about Diplo she has genuine affection in her voice, there's also an underlying tone of eye–rolling that comes with thinking about him – like the love one has for their adorable but annoying little brother. 'He acted that night like we'd known each other forever with his, 'Oh you guys *so* need to work together!' But it worked out great because Switch was only in town for a couple of days and in that time we made

Creator. And that was a real testament to what Wes does best – he is an amazing connector of people.'

Nina Las Vegas from triple j radio in Australia had also said something along those lines to me before I left for the UK, suggesting that this was definitely one of the skills, way up there, in his bag of tricks as a producer.

I ask Diplo what *he* sees as the most important traits for a producer to have. He ponders this for a moment; he's not a huge way into his journey so it's clear he's still not sure himself. Ironically, it's the knack for seeing things through that he puts at the top of the list. 'I guess it's because it's something that I'm not that good at!' He chuckles. 'I start so many projects, so being able to keep a vision all the way through and having perseverance, basically, is so important. Good ideas are really important too, for me being able to have ideas is bigger than being able to play music – I can't play music for shit, but I would never trade my ideas about music and the weird creativity that I have, to be a piano prodigy or something like that.'

As the clock ticks over the hour and a half mark and we both grow restless, I ask him one final question. 'Is there anything that is not cool with you in the studio? Anything that gets under your skin?'

'One thing you can't do in the studio when I work with you,' he spits out with the vigour of recent experience, 'is Google yourself! But don't put that in there!'

On that note we indulge in an awkward selfie and an even more awkward high five and go our separate ways. Diplo heads back to his room to do whatever it is he needs to do before DJ–ing at three in the morning, and I head down to a little pub I spotted down the road called, cleverly, *The Bricklayers Arms*. As I stand on the corner beneath the street sign, downing a celebratory schooner, happy to have the first European interview in the bag, a familiar face appears walking along the road. It's Colin, with a white sack in hand. 'Laundry.' Is all he says, as he nods and waltzes back to the glitz of life on the road.

7

Philippe Zdar: French Connection

If there is a deity up there, eyes-glued to the antics of humanity, they must be looking down on me proud, if not a little shocked, as I walk purposefully through the streets of sweet Pareee. Unbelievably, I stand seventeen thousand kilometres from home, piggy in the middle of the Arc de Triomphe and ye olde Eiffel Tower with a quiche aux épinards et au fromage in one hand and a croissant in the other, knowing precisely where I'm going. It's afternoon time in Paris, and thanks to the omniscience of modern technology, I've made my way over to famous hipster club *Le Regine*. The place is virtually invisible; there's nothing to be seen from the street but an open doorway and a blackness that suggests steep stairs and a literal definition of the term 'underground club'. Down below there are levels of lowlight seeping from various furnishings. Sun squiggles soon turn into neon squiggles. I blink, slowly the squiggles form a phrase, *le monde est a toi* -

the world is yours. Brilliant! It will go well with my spinach quiche. In front of the phrase are two dance floors. Lit-up coloured squares cover both - one has a panther painted on it, there's a red Perspex bar top - which is also a light box - and plenty of Victorian-style red velvet lounges that don't so much say 'sit down' as 'drape yourself upon me'. Possibly the most spectacular accessory in the room, though, is the low ceiling, embracing the philosophies of both Vogue Living circa 1974 and Tutankhamun's tomb, if he'd had the opportunity to be preferential to modernism. The roof is wall-to-wall mirrored glass, covered in small inverted pyramids. It's such a spectacular display of kitsch that it's been heritage protected by the Parisian council. Seriously.

Le Regine was first opened back in the 70's by world famous socialite and professional extrovert, Regine Zylberberg. A holocaust survivor, jet-setting titilator of the playboy set and self-proclaimed Queen of the Night, Regine was the lady responsible for opening the world's first discotheque back in 1958, *Chez Regine*. *Le Regine* is owned these days by *La Clique*, a group of France's most-cool in the club scene.

I'm here to chat with Chris and Branco from Phoenix about working with the man behind the mixing of their debut album

United and co-production on *Wolfgang Amadeus Phoenix,* Mr Philippe Zdar.

'Careful, he is very unpredictable,' says Branco when I tell them I'll be interviewing Philippe two days from now. Unfortunately, he doesn't mean in a might-snap-and-beat-you-with-a-French stick kind of way, more in that he tends to turn up when he feels. 'He's like Fonzie, he's very cool. Sometime he turns up seven hours late. He's not like an American professional producer.' A small restriction grips my chest as I remember I'm due to fly out of Paris just four hours after my interview with the time-defiant Mr Zdar is scheduled.

'We met him because he was friends with Guy-Manuel and Thomas from *Daft Punk*. Which were my friends too,' explains Branco in the thickest, handsomest of accents, of the beginning of the love affair. 'We met him in a shop and we didn't like him because he ah… looked so perfect.' He chuckles recalling the memory. 'He was just so good musically, his technique, that's why we wanted to use him, but we didn't think he was very nice. We found out very quickly that he is the nicest guy on earth. We got him in to mix our first record, *United,* and within 5 minutes it was like a blood brotherhood.'

'And actually, it was funny,' says Chris. 'Because, when we became friends later, we learnt that he felt the same way about us.' It was a friendship that began with misunderstanding that blossomed with Moët and the intense emotional expression that is the poetry of Paris.

'He's a crazy French guy. Every day, he comes with a bottle of champagne and he's always very intense about the music. On the new album, he would come for five minutes and hear what we were working on, and be nearly crying, either out of joy or out of sadness that we had ruined a song. He would call us at five in the morning and say, 'I've been listening to your song and I like it. My girlfriend likes it too!''

'This is true,' confirms Chris. 'He's passionate about everything - like a kid.' Chris and Branco describe Philippe's producer persona as 'spiritual; more like a guru', constantly filling spaces of despair with enthusiasm, inspiration and that French passion that could only exist in a culture that can eat a three-course meal made from naught but chocolate…for breakfast. 'He could do one-hour inspirational speeches, for real. I would say that his major input was to save us from sinking in the quicksands of creation. And it's just what we want, we don't want it to be just a series of technical processes when we're recording, we want a human adventure. With him, it is very much like that.' Although so very philosophical, Philippe is still very much technologically meticulous. His ability to make things enormous, no matter how flimsy the sound to begin with, has been a big bass monolith rumbling on the one-dimensional French landscape for two decades. 'It's just like in photography when you work with very good lenses,' reckons Branco. 'They don't capture reality, they add a thickness, a light. With Philippe he does this with sound, I don't know how he does it but he makes it thicker, enormous and magic somehow.'

'If you have been chosen by Philippe,' adds Chris, 'it's going to be good. He doesn't just work with anyone. He's like an animal, he feels people out. If he's chosen you it's going to be good… but intense… but good intense.'

Phoenix songs with that special Philippe touch

Fences *'This track, we did not even want on the album. Philippe fought for it for days, weeks. He took a demo of the track with him to Ibiza with his girlfriend and he said 'you cannot do this, it is our song, it* must *be on the album.' Philippe believes in girls. He believes one girl is worth 10 000 guys and he believes in their judgement of music. I think in this he is right. So we ended up putting it on the album and we love it.'* Branco **Lisztomania** *'Sometimes with a track you can have it 99% for months and you just cannot figure out that last 1%. It was this way with this track. Then Philippe walked past and said 'you must double the chorus'. It was just a small trick but without it the song did not work.'* Branco **1901** *'I recorded the keys on this track very low and then put lots of compression on it, that way you get the hiss again, the hiss that I love from all my favourite records from the seventies and eighties. I put three different equalisers on those keyboards - one very old valve, a neve and one that is very clinical but it is enormous. Then the hiss becomes enormous! If your grandmother put this song in her player she would say oh no you are going to blow my speakers! But no, we control everything.'*

Two days, three Nutella pancakes, four croissants, seven different types of cheese and a trip to the Louvre later, I jump aboard the Metro to Montmartre. I've been excited about this interview for months, and being here in Paris now to do it, feels absurd. The train pulls into Chateau Rouge station. It's not where I should be, but I figure it's close enough and one thing I love to do when traveling, is walk. Plus a bathroom-stop is calling, so I make my way out of the station amongst the masses and begin search for a public and legal place to *uriner*. There's a KFC up ahead, and with the comfort of franchise familiarity, I figure it a good, easy option. The queues for the toilets are lengthy but I've got plenty of time, so I jump in and wait. Five or so minutes pass. There's a small boy staring, he's been staring for a while. It's a stare of mistrust. I smile. It doesn't land the desired effect. Instead, he starts saying something to me I think is in French. He turns up the volume. 'Whiii-tee … whiii-tee… Whitey?' With my embarrassingly blonde hair and stereotypical Dutch blue eyes, I look around and suddenly notice that every single other soul in this fast-food outlet - employee and customer - is black. Not brown. Not burnt umber. Amazingly, beautifully black. I feel like Richard Pryor in *See No Evil, Hear No Evil*, in reverse - discovering just how disappointingly lacking in melanin I am. 'Bagu-e-ette…bagu-e-ette.' *Baguette?* Is this cute-as-a-button chocolate muffin calling me a baguette? As far as skin-based slurs go, that's pretty good – especially for this piece of white bread who grew up in Brisbane's low-socioeconomic western suburbs - a baguette a vast cultural elevation from the dirty back streets of a downtown Goodna bakery.

I head out of Chateau Rouge and wander up hill. Soon I am in the heart of beautiful Montmartre. This part of Paris is simply ridiculous. Both stoic and sexy, its fingertips stretch out to fondle the Basilica of the Sacred Heart whilst its legs wrap firmly around the Moulin Rouge. It's a gorgeous sunny day, I've travelled seventeen thousand kilometres, through three different countries and I'm fifteen minutes early. Bloody hell. Philippe's studios are in an apartment block. There is an intercom with no names or numbers, beside two oversized blue wooden doors with no door handle. They swing open as if by the power of my confusion. 'Bon jour, I'm Julienne, Philippe's assistant,' says Julienne, before adding the four words I was dreading. 'He is running late.'

Inside, the studio is as classy as the district it nestles in, but instead of ancient history this is French couture. Big open spaces, shiny pale wooden floors, clean lines, carefully placed instruments - a Wurlitzer over there, clear-skin toms over here - a room for nothing but vinyl, a loft-style relaxation area and the control room, containing two French lads and the unmistakable aroma of quality. Julienne is taking photos of all the compressors. 'This is to make sure we can mimic exactly the sounds that we achieved yesterday during mixing,' he explains. Time ticks away, Philippe is already an hour late. My plane leaves in three, the interview will take almost two. 'I saw him in here at 1pm once.' Says Julienne. It is only 11 o'clock. Suddenly Mr Zdar appears in the doorway. His presence takes me aback and not just because he is (relatively) on time. I hope my facial expression is deadpan but I'm fearing it's a bit like when you see someone with a thalidomide arm - your mind is saying, 'Don't look at the arm, don't look at the arm,' and consequently mid-sentence completely out of context you say the word - arm. I'm sure he registers the expression on my face for what it means which is 'dammit man, pash me now!'

'I'm so sorry for running late,' he says.

Pash me now and all will be forgiven I say mentally as my mouth says, 'It's fine.'

'Do you mind if I smoke?' he asks.

Oh, you are *already* smoking, exquisite creature. The man is stunning! Despite my wide-eyed awkwardness, Philippe bravely pulls up a chair and winds the conversation back to the little lad days when he was still known as Master Cerboneschi.

'My early introduction to music was very bad,' he explains in a voice even more impossibly handsome then Branco's. 'It was when I was eight. I hated music because my sister, who was four years older than me, was spending all our money on records. When I was eleven, I said to her, 'I will never buy a record in all my life.' Now it has been thirty years and it's still the only thing that I do. Every day, I buy records. She was listening to Genesis and Pink Floyd and then I got into heavy metal and punk to be against my sister. Then I wanted to be in the music business, being a drummer or singer or playing in heavy metal bands, but even when I was fourteen I knew that I wanted to take care of the structure.'

Philippe's whole family played a role in fanning the flame that his sister had lit, unintentionally. His mother worked in a nightclub and his Dad, boss at an establishment owned by the Cerboneschi family in the snowfields of France, was the man who brought the noise.

'One day my father called me down to listen to the PA, the big speakers, it was like *Message In A Bottle* by The Police and I was like, 'WOW! What is happening! What is this?' This is what I want, I want to do this!' Through his teen years, Philippe held onto this spark, discovering a recording studio in Paris that was his dream destination, one he eventually made his reality. 'I spent one year as a tea boy, making tea and emptying the ashtrays, then assistant mixer and engineer, but I could never not say anything! I was always saying, 'This should be like this or like this,' and I was always with people who were open to what I say….although…' he says with a giggle, 'I was never allowed to touch anything. But he kept me there for the good vibes.'

The 'he' was Dominque Blanc-Francard, studio owner and father of the man who would become Philippe's brother-in-arms.

'One day he came by to see his Father and instantly I had the same relationship with him as I had with his father, but the guy was my age. In five minutes, we were brothers.' Dominique's son Hubert (*pron: oo-bear if you are a Frenchie*) and Philippe would almost immediately join forces. 'I mixed a track for French hip hop artist MC Solaar and I told Hubert to come by, and we start to say things and then we became a little team.' Together they would work with Solaar on three albums over six years. During this time, on a song called *Obsolete* from MC Solaar's *Prose Combat* album, Philippe would touch on the goal of his sonic life; to have big bass, nice highs and good compression. 'You know how, sometimes in your life you have particle accelerators; songs that make people call you for years. At this time in my life I was listening to lots of Public Enemy, it was so big, and I was thinking, 'Fuck, how will we ever do that?' I went to London and rented a Fairchild compressor and I ran everything through it. It was my best moment in MC Solaar life.'

Before long Zdar and Hubert started collaborating on their own stuff under the name La Funk Mob, a project deeply bass driven and slow in tempo. 'At first it was me mixing and opening my mouth and him doing the songs. It was not until I went into a rave and discovered techno that I wanted to do music too.' So with La Funk Mob well under way but rave in his veins, Philippe was ready to turn up the production as well as the pace, kicking off a new era for himself and Hubert (who was by now known as Boom Bass), defining them as legends of house. 'I was really into techno, raving, going out and making music for this. Hubert was still doing hip hop tracks and we were making music as La Funk Mob which was very slow. James Lavelle called us to do music for Mo'Wax but me, I was getting very frustrated because I wanted to go fast, we went to New York, started making music that was more fast, more club and I said we should change the name. That's when we became Cassius.' By 1995 they were solidly working on both their own music as well as that of other artists such as MC Solaar and Sinclair. It was this straddle between artist and producer that made Philippe's skill spectrum so special: he can produce in a rock sense - overseeing the tracking, engineering, mixing and performance of a band or artist - as well as in a dance and hip hop sense by making the actual beats. But if that were not enough, Philippe completes the trifecta of talent with his skills as a DJ; in fact, the room where he keeps all his vinyl is in clear view through the glass of the production booth, ready to be called upon for inspiration at any moment.

'I don't want to do it as a job,' he says of production, 'I want to be a DJ *and* an artist *and* a producer. It's difficult sometimes, because I have to say no to many things, but people call me because I am honest and I will never go behind the desk for something I don't love and will not fight for until the end.' This passion has garnered him a reputation for immense enthusiasm and a level of quality for which he became legendary.

'It's a hard job being a producer,' says Philippe, 'because you have to keep your focus and go into your deepest strength, so if the music is not good you will not dig deep enough. Liking the people is great, but sometimes there are great musicians who are not great people. But I have been very lucky - Sebastien Tellier, Phoenix, I just worked with Kele from *Bloc*

Party - they are all great people. You can never know this before. Luckily, I like crazy people and I like moody people too, I only hate mean people. But as long as the music was incredible I could probably work with someone really, really bad.' In 1999 Cassius had their first big commercial success with the track *Cassius 1999*. 'I think this track is a great example of what I think is the key of being a producer and musician, that there are no rules. I did this song first and it was very underground and we ask our friends to do a video and we think the video is a hit but the song was not a hit. So, we redid the song for the video and it became a hit.' From here Cassius became a dedicated project for the pair as well as a solid contender in the world of dance music with their second album *Au Reve* being released in 2002 followed by *15 again* four years later. On mention of this latter album, Philippe sums up it's fun-times dance-floor vibe with a little tale that tells mountains about the timeless-looking man before me. 'I spent a summer in Ibiza with friends of mine who don't want to be old, and we will never be old, so we were at seven in the morning going out every night completely like *pfff*! And one girl looks at me and she says to me, 'Oh, today I'm fifteen, she is 29.' It's seven in the morning and she looks into the glass and she says, 'I am fifteen!' And it's true, we are like kids going to the club, to the beach, never sleeping. If I go back to my hometown and see people my age they look a hundred years old. Tomorrow I go to a club in Florence and DJ and half a dozen young guys who are like seventeen years old come up to me at the end and say, 'Man, the music is great thank you so much!' It keeps me young.'

Alongside the success of Cassius and his DJ-ing schedule, Philippe continued to commit to the balance; maintaining work as a producer and mixer whenever he heard things irresistible. One such project was for Australian outfit *Cut Copy*, 'I heard in it new territories, the influences colliding, which is what I'm looking for always,' says Philippe. 'Plus, Dan (*Cut Copy's* main man) is a great guy and when I met him I loved him more than anything. When he told me his favourite band was Fleetwood Mac, I thought, 'A guy who is doing dance music who loves Fleetwood Mac, I must meet him!"

The love affair went both ways, with Dan Whitford admitting he was quite taken with (and possibly a little terrified of) Philippe's extreme enthusiasm.

'When I first met Philippe I was quite blown away, just the idea of going to Paris, hopping off the plane and going to meet this producer who I'd never met, it was all quite overwhelming. I remember him picking me up from the airport and me thinking he was some kind of maniac driver, I remember being a bit white-knuckled as we went flying through these Paris streets. Yeah, I thought he was a bit crazy perhaps, and I think he still is but not in the way I thought he was crazy in the beginning. Now we're just great friends.' Until Dan met Philippe, he confessed to me some weeks before, to having had somewhat of a low regard for sound quality, recording their album *Bright Like Neon Love* quite lo-fi. But Philippe wove his mixing magic and took the album from the bedroom to the club. 'When you are mixing you have all these speakers in front of you,' Philippe explains whilst pointing at all the speakers in front of us. 'It's very important to understand why. We have this little one for when I listen to mono, then I have bigger speakers and bigger than enormous. It's like when you look at a house. You can look at the house one millimetre away, but eventually you have to look at it from a hundred metres away if you want to paint it. One hundred metres away is the little speakers - you see the whole house at once, and if you want to go and paint the lock you go to the big speakers, you zoom right into the lock. This is how you mix an album; to make sure you have looked at it all as a whole. This is what I did with Dan, this is what I do for everything.'

When Dan brought the album back from France and played it to the rest of Cut Copy, they responded with cries of 'Holy Crap!' As did the nation, with the Zdar-touch helping to give non-mainstream Australia one of its finest dance albums of 2004.

When it comes to discussing Philippe's production with both Phoenix and Cut Copy the words 'enormous' and 'magic' are thrown about liberally. For Philippe, it's all about enhancing the 'goosebump' moments.

'I want the sound to be big,' he explains, 'because when I was younger, I was listening to lots of American music - it was big! British music, it was big! Motown lots of bass but French music, lots of nothing! I put a lot of very old EQs in chains and on each one, I know what they're going to do and I make it extreme. Even if it's a slow and very romantic track that could be whispered in your girlfriend's ear, it has to be enhanced. It's like in Japanese theatre; they paint enormous eyes because they know people are going to be watching from seventy metres. Even the emotions should be enhanced, not all *big* but enhanced. When I mix, I go into three dimensions.' He continues to explain his larger-than-life sound by making an analogy with story writing. 'If the legend is better than the fact, print the legend! This is what I have in my mind when I am making an album.'

Fast forward through the release of Cassius's *15 Again* in 2006 and a thousand dark, sweaty mornings on a stage behind the decks, and we arrive at another of Philippe's 'particle accelerator moments' - the making of Phoenix's album *Wolfgang Amadeus Phoenix.*

'They will never let you mess with their albums, they are completely protective,' says Philippe. 'Which is why this is the first time they used a producer.'

Philippe's role on the record was very impromptu. When Phoenix entered his studio to begin work on *Wolfgang,* they were intending, as always, to do it all themselves. It would have remained that way had Philippe not walked by each afternoon and just casually dropped off little moments of genius. During the recording of the track *Lisztomania* the lads from Phoenix confessed to being a little stumped, until Philippe cruised by and dropped four magic words, 'Double up the chorus.' Which, according to Chris and Branco, was a small trick, but one that without, the song did not work. *Lisz-*

tomania was transformed from a stumbling block into the first official single.

These snippets of throwaway genius, along with their mutual love for each other, were enough for Phoenix to bring him on board as another pair of committed hands on deck.

'Honestly, I don't think they really need me though,' says Philippe. 'They are four very good producers. But that's good with my way of working because I don't want to be the daddy. I don't want to be the guy who comes in the morning and leaves in the night and checks *everything*. I want to be, like, in a boat, the guy who says, 'We have to go north.' And if we go a little bit south, I say, 'No no! The north!"'

Having heard nothing after the sexiest version of the word 'Daddy' ever heard, I realise it's time to leave this den of genius-ooh-la-la if I'm to make me next flight upward and onward.

With a hug and a so-Frenchy-kiss-kiss on either cheek, Philippe bids farewell. I pull sunnies down and step out onto the cobblestone street, pondering yet again the diverse components of the great producers as psychologists, nerds and eccentrics. I adjust my thoughts and lock course for the next leg of the pilgrimage: Charles De Gaulle airport here I come.

8

The Alan Moulder Assault: When More is More

*Fly to Heathrow. Once there, jump on the tube to Willesden Green (Jubilee line). Turn right, walk downhill until you get to bakery, buy pale comparison of croissant because you have withdrawals and would inject one if you could, proceed to a large junction - High Road - turn right. After about 10 minutes turn left into Maybury Gardens. The studio, called Battery, is on the right hand side ... two large gates. Press entry phone for Assault & Battery 1. Can you be here by 11?
(Slightly embellished email extract from Alan Moulder's manager at Fundamental Music.)*

Despite the lengthy chat with Philippe, his tardiness *and* a brief patisserie stop afterward for a fruit bun that bordered on orgasm, I manage to catch my flight out of France back to England. Following the above directions precisely (apart from a quick stop to take a photo of Ranga Real Estate to send back to Clare Bowditch and any other redhead who would find it nowhere near as funny as I), I end up where I should be, bang on time. The entire outside of the building is blue, so blue that if London weren't so grey you'd run smack into it. There are big black metal gates, which swing quietly open upon my buzzing. Alan's assistant greets me; his relaxed manner makes me feel immediately at ease and I hope that the assistant is reflective of the man who hired him. To be completely honest though, I've already made up my mind about the palatable nature of Alan's personality: if you can produce records by My Bloody Valentine, Nine Inch Nails *and* Smashing Pumpkins, then you're obviously not a man with a short fuse or a controlling disposition.

'Hi there, how are you?' a gentle voice says to my left. There's a hand outstretched.

'Really well thanks', I say taking the hand and shaking it. 'And you?' I ask Mr Moulder.

'Oh, can't complain. Would you like to follow me?'

We wander past the front desk into a room with walls unexpectedly plum-coloured - on them hang gold records for the Smashing Pumpkins and The Killers - the couches in the middle of the room are shockingly sunflower: if Van Gough had done interior design during the Bauhaus this space would've been his showroom. This space is where bands can take a moment to rest, to restore, to forget about recording for a moment, clear their jumbled musical thoughts and instead ponder the merits of utilising shades from opposing sides of the colour wheel.

For Alan and I, today it is a place of interrogation, a room where Mr Moulder for a change will be the one behind the microphone. And so it begins.

It was at London's famous Trident studios - where Bowie produced Lou Reed's *Transformer*, his own *The Rise and Fall of Ziggy Stardust* and where The Beatles would record *Hey Jude* - that the foundation of Alan's career would be laid.

'The work ethic,' He states, when pondering what he most took away from that time. 'They really beat you down, hours wise. There's no way I could have worked longer hours and physically survived. And that's a good lesson in life. One, it sorts out whether you want to do it or not, and two, it gets your stamina up and puts you under pressure which is a good thing to learn. They were very on you about being professional and not, because nothing had to come back to them. And also, the staff that were there at the time - we had a remarkable time where the in house staff was Flood, Spike Stent, Cenzo Townshend, Steve Osborne, others - a lot of people who have all gone on to do well. And we were all friends working together, so the creativity in the building was really high and everyone was very supportive, but obviously there was a bit of a competitive element there going on. So that was pretty healthy.'

As Mr Moulder sinks more comfortably into position, his relaxed lengthy body, which spans well in excess of 6ft, makes the chair on which he is draped look like an undersized novelty prop as he continues reflection on those tough, rewarding times at Trident.

'Yeah, there were times I'd think 'What the hell am I doing?' When you used to go out Friday afternoon, Friday night at about eight o'clock in the summer and everybody's stood outside the pub and you're walking to fetch yet another pizza, knowing that your weekend involves long hours and no daylight, you did think, 'Have I picked the right thing here?''

It was here at Trident, during those long hours that Alan found in fellow producer Flood, a kindred spirit. For two decades they walked somewhat parallel paths until more recently when they merged those two paths into one.

'We had very similar tastes in music, and similar attitudes to what we thought was right about music. We were young and opinionated about music and we used to go out and get drunk and make these master plans and we just seemed to get on. Very similar attitudes and similar ideals really.'

With both of them now working here under the one roof in their own studio, it's a great stable of skills and passionate minds for any artist finding themselves here.

'Well, it's funny, we cover each other's weaknesses. We have different strengths and we challenge each other. We'll argue about songs and what they should do, and funnily enough that's the part that we enjoy the most, because it's never personal. It's a bit more like a game of chess, where you argue your points and he argues his point and at the end of it you always get something better out of it. And, you know, nobody minds, it's good to see something from a different point of view and from that it's worked well and we've come up with the right result.'

The first big project we did together I think was the Pumpkins' *Mellon Collie*. And I'd worked on *Siamese Dream,* the album before. I'd mixed that with Billy and Butch Vig and Billy was interested in me working on the production on *Mellon Collie* and then, I think he loved *Zooropa*, the U2 album which Flood had done, I think he saw comparisons in how he wanted to take *Mellon Collie* on from *Siamese Dream* to the experimentation U2 had done on *Zooropa*. So, they approached Flood and then they said that they'd like me to be involved as well, so we came up with the co-production. So that's how that happened, and then The Killers… I just thought that would be a brilliant opportunity for us to work together because I think what people don't think about either me or Flood is that we're actually quite pop in our tastes. So, I thought that would be an ideal project for us to do together.'

It was alongside Flood that Alan would experience his career's first watershed moment.

'Yeah, the first one was being asked to engineer *Automatic*, the Jesus and Mary Chain album. I'd worked with Flood on a single at Trident, Flood was asked to engineer it and I demanded to be the assistant because I loved the band, got on with the band and they asked me to do some live work.

So, I did some ill-fated live engineering; I'd never done it before, it was a completely different world. I think we did one gig at the Hammersmith Palais and in the last song I blew eight midrange in the PA, which wasn't too good. So, I thought that would be the end of my live career - leave it to somebody else who knew what they were doing - and then they asked me to do *Automatic*. Before that, it looked like I was doing a lot of dance work, dance mixes, and it looked like I was going to go down the dance mix route, which I didn't mind, I enjoyed it. But really alternative music or guitar rock was my thing, so when I was asked to do that I was ecstatic. Then once I'd done the Mary Chain, Alan McGee who used to manage the Mary Chain liked the sound of the album, so he got me to work with a lot of the Creation bands, then of course I did a Ride single, then I was asked to do *My Bloody Valentine* which then triggered the Pumpkins and Nine Inch Nails 'cause they were interested in both the Mary Chain and My Bloody Valentine.'

By the time recording began on My Bloody Valentine's *Loveless* album in 1989, Alan had already worked with the band once before on the track *Soon* for the *Glider* ep. Once frontman Kevin Shields worked with Alan, there was no going back, entrusting only Alan with specific duties and loathing all other engineers who came with the studio. 'To be honest, my input on that album was quite minor.' Alan says humbly despite all other reports, even those from the band themselves. 'I was the longest serving engineer and Kevin runs the show with that band and he's the brains behind it, and my job on that album was to help keep him sane because he is cursed with the most incredible hearing, he can hear when anything's going wrong. He's worked in the past with a lot of the studios where the studio owner had been the engineer, so he wouldn't believe when Kevin said he thought something was wrong with the equipment. So when I came onboard, if Kevin had any fears, he'd leave the room, I'd check it all out and most of the time he was right but he gave me the trust that if I said. 'No, it's ok,' he'd forget it and carry on. Whereas before he'd get bogged with it and he wouldn't be able to work, he'd get distracted and lose any thread. So, my job very much was… that he trusted me.'

And as all six-foot-something of Alan moulds further into the softness, his body language does indeed declare, 'Nobody panic, it's all just fine.' Combine that with the technical skills to pay the bills, and in Alan Moulder there lies a producer able to facilitate creative genius and creative unrest. Enter stage left: Billy Corgan.

'I went to their… I think it was their first gig in London,' Alan explains when I ask him how it came to be that he would mix The Smashing Pumpkins 1993 album *Siamese Dream*. 'My wife was in a band called Curve and Pumpkins had the same manager, so I went to their gig in Camden, and after the gig we were talking and he said he loved the Ride, Valentine's and Mary Chain albums and then he went off to do the album with Butch and he realised that the songs they'd recorded were going to take a bit of mixing, it was going to take a while, and Butch felt that I would be the right person to mix it cause I'd have the patience to spend five days on a mix. Which some took. So that's how I got the job. Patience I think.'

Siamese Dream ended up taking a total of 36 days just to mix. After Alan showed Corgan that he did indeed have the level of calm approach required to work with *The Smashing Pumpkins*, he brought both Alan and Flood in together to record the abundant double album *Mellon Collie and the Infinite Sadness*.

With time being an issue in the past (Billy often played guitar and bass parts just to speed along the recording process) Alan and Flood decided to have two recording rooms going at once. This allowed for time to keep on ticking and for the two producers to stay ahead of the torrent of Billy's ideas. 'Billy's not good when he's not doing anything. He's got to be kept occupied otherwise he gets twitchy. With two rooms, Billy could always be working, and in the other room work would be getting done too, so double gain really. It didn't matter how long anything would take in our room because work was always getting done in the other room, and vice versa.

There was ... on a track called *Ruby*...78 tracks of guitar! But we did them all in an afternoon! He just was on fire and we just were going next, next, next; all different sounds, just like, 'How many have we got?' And I remember counting them up, there's fifteen tracks of e-bows and it was ... yeah it was crazy!'

'How did you know when to stop?' I ask, mesmerised.

As level as ever, Alan reveals his own deep thirst for

exploration that sits below the calm. 'My philosophy is more is more. When you're making records like that, there's something charming about the ridiculousness of it all. It's like, what the heck, you know? Leave minimalism to somebody else.'

As we take a moment to sip our now tepid cups of tea and I scan quickly over the discography scrawled on the notebook in my lap and decide where to go next, Alan suddenly pipes up. 'I seem to do a lot of double albums, I hate double albums,' he comes out with. 'I always, as a kid, hated double albums, and I seem to just get cursed with them.'

Seems like a good moment now to segue to Nine Inch Nails, a band that Alan has worked with on every album since 1999's extraordinary *double* album *The Fragile*.

'It's funny actually,' says Alan when recalling his first meeting with the powerfully built and powerfully minded Nine Inch Nails frontman, Trent Reznor. 'I was working with the Mary Chain and doing an album with them, and they'd been on tour with Nine Inch Nails. Nine Inch Nails had just done Lollapalooza, and were coming over to do I think their first gig in England at the Astoria I think it was. And so, we took the night off and went down to see them and I saw their show and it scared me. Actually, it was ... I was used to working with Ride and all these nice English bands and there was this band ... it looked like a warzone, and I thought, 'Christ, it's quite scary.'

'I went to the aftershow and Trent was being looked after

by Roz Earls who was Flood's manager and I was talking to her at the aftershow and she said, 'Oh, here's Trent,' and he came up to meet me, and he said, 'Hi, pleased to meet you, I like the records you work on,' He then asked me if I knew a particular person (who I won't name). I told him I did, but that he was quite rude to me. Within thirty seconds he was just ripping (the unnamed person) apart, so he seemed like my kind of guy really. Later on, I don't know if it was a test to see how we got on, but he had just signed Marilyn Manson and he'd sent him off to record his first album and he wasn't totally happy with the way the recordings came back, so he wanted me to do some work on that first. So, we did four tracks, remixed four tracks and then rerecorded six, so we got to work together without it being on his stuff and we got on really good. Then we moved straight onto *Downward Spiral.*'

After Alan had wholly proved his genius on that album - the second record for Nine Inch Nails, which was released in 1994 - the pair would team up to co-produce the epic, double album from Nine Inch Nails *The Fragile*. Two years of their lives that album would chew up, and test all of Alan's skills as both an engineer and as a supportive, patient producer, to their limits.

'The greatest engineer in the world,' is how Trent Reznor would describe Alan to me. 'I don't remember there ever being a struggle,' he said, 'Alan never dominates the room when he comes in, he doesn't dictate how things are going to go. *The Fragile* is still the biggest project that we've worked on together - almost two years of seeing him nearly every day, and I don't recall a moment of raised voices, or a confrontation of how to do things.'

Alan does recollect one moment of slight tension though, but one that actually ended up transforming itself from annoyance to genius. 'We were coming close to the end of the album *Wish*,' he says with the memory of exhaustion entering his tone. 'We were starting to hone it down and Trent came in one day and said, 'I want to work on this track,' which was a loop of a static-y noise. And I just think, 'I can't ... what are you doing? We've got so many things on the go, why do you want to work on that?' It's just this bzzszsz noise. He says, 'yeah I got an idea for it. Let's do some drums.' And I thought 'Alright ok, we'll do some drums, this is going to be a B side at best, it's never going to see the light of day.' So I went in the room, we didn't have any techs or anything, I'd built a space to do the drums that was totally dead, it was all carpeted it was like a box and you could only just fit the drum kit in, so I said, 'Ok, we'll do drums in there.' I thought, 'Let's have a big snare.' I tuned the snare, it was ringy and the most ridiculous snare drum sound I could get, almost through anger that we were doing this track. I got the drums sound in like, fifteen minutes and I thought, 'OK that'll do, let's go.' And he started playing and I thought, 'Oh this sounds good, actually.' And then that became the album's first single, *We're in This Together*.'

Even in gentle tension the partnership between Trent and Alan formed brilliance, and had the smooth nature of the relationship not been what it was, *The Fragile* would not have stood a chance at life. It was a laboriously heavy load, an album of sonic genius where the listener is privileged to a record made with rarely-possible meticulousness: where every single sonic millisecond has been shown the greatest level of care. Of all the instruments on that album - guitar, marimbas, violins, cellos, ukuleles ('Never recorded so many ukuleles in all my life!' Alan declares on their mentioning) and a range of gadgets that only the gods could now identify- it was Trent's voice that showed the greatest resistance.

'At the time I think he was having a fear of writing lyrics,' says Alan reminding me in that moment that beneath the perception of ego there nearly always exists the undertow of insecurity. 'He didn't want to write lyrics. I think it was somewhere that he didn't want to go. And he's a great one at creating a smokescreen to get himself out of things, so he just buries (himself) doing all this work, making all these amazing instrumentals, just recording and making sounds and having fun really, and I kept saying, 'We're really going to need some lyrics, we've got forty songs now, are you sure that's not quite a lot to be taking on?' 'No, no I'll be fine,' he was going. 'How's the lyrics coming', then months later, 'oh got some ideas…"

When I ask Trent about this later, from his hotel room in Amsterdam, he showed a glimpse of that vulnerability nodded at in the album's title.

'I need to look to Alan in terms of - is this good or not?' he confessed. 'Particularly when it comes to my vocals that I know I'm not objective about. I'll be thinking while I'm singing, 'I don't know if this lyric is good or not,' and I'll be fighting with him to turn it down, turn it down, hide it behind this thing and at the time it's not even conscious but looking back on it I go, 'Why am I trying to hide this, oh because I'm unsure.' And when it comes to vocals - maybe I have great lyrics or a great melody - but if it's not delivered properly or convincingly, it's pointless, it's just academics. That's when I really dig into Alan, that's when I'm at my most impatient, my most baby-like, my most unpleasant to be around, but Alan is and certainly was during that time very good at milking the best performance out of me.'

Back on the yellow couch, Alan is quiet for a moment, I can almost hear the faint amazement that still exists in his memory ten years on, of all that they did, for as long as they did, to make that album. 'I always wanted to make what I call my *Dark Side of the Moon*,' he says cautiously, 'and that was my *Dark Side of the Moon* moment, if I may be so bold.'

9

Alan Moulder: Into The 21st Century

> 'The strength to me of Alan, is that he never lets a situation in the studio get desperate or turn down a bad path and continue in a way that's going to be terrible at the end of the day. He keeps things positive, he's willing to try whatever you throw at him, he's got the patience of more than anyone I've ever met in my life, his tolerance level is much higher than I can ever imagine having myself and his endurance is immense - I mean, if you've worked with me and My Bloody Valentine, that's saying something. There the strengths that I need as an artist, I need somebody who can follow me down a path that we may never see the end of.'
>
> Trent Reznor, from a hotel room in Amsterdam July 2009 - mid-final-Nine Inch Nails-tour.

Alan, having proved his willingness to be led into the unknown at the risk of both he and Trent vanishing forever into the wilderness of creation, made him the only choice to take on duties for the next Nine Inch Nails album *With Teeth*.

'It was the perfect follow up to *The Fragile*.' Says Alan, still poised, relaxed and unmoved in the chair he's been sitting in now for 45 minutes, calm stillness emanating from every cell. 'I thought *The Fragile* was such a long big album and so landscapey and experimental, I thought that he needed to do something that was a bit more direct, song-based, hooky - poppier, you may say. So, when I heard what he was doing I thought it was perfect. I really liked the songs, he'd got over his ... he'd been working with Rick Rubin on this. Rick had been encouraging him to send him two or three songs either a week or every two weeks, which got Trent over his fear of writing lyrics and he just realised, you know, every line doesn't have to be Tolstoy or something amazing. Start it if you can, finish it later or just ... just do it, you know? So, that was a brilliant thing that he'd gotten over that. I heard the songs and I just thought it was exactly what he should be doing.'

With Teeth was also recorded in New Orleans, in the old funeral home that Trent had bought and converted into a big recording space - the two viewing rooms providing sound that Alan describes as 'very distinctive'. A new facet to this album, though, would be the introduction of Atticus Ross, the man who Trent would go on and win a Grammy with in 2011 for the soundtrack to *The Social Network*.

'The three of us just really got on very well,' Alan reckons of the addition of the new kid. 'There was no threatening. Everyone (was) striving for the best result, everyone appreciated what everybody else was doing. We'd feed off each other, and how it works now with Atticus and I is, we'll to-and-fro, he'll do some programming and I'll think, 'That's pretty good, I better step up to the plate and do something here.' So then he'll hear what I'm doing and he'll go, 'Well, I've got an idea,' and he'll step in and do stuff.'

In 2003, the year before work started on *With Teeth*, Alan's relationship with *The Killers* began; in much the same way as it did with *The Smashing Pumpkins* - in that Alan was brought in as mixer on one album and as producer on the next.

Sam's Town is a very different sounding record for The Killers compared to their debut album *Hot Fuss*. I wonder what Alan's first impressions of those songs were.

'When I first heard them, they were demos from their rehearsal room and they sounded…well…you had to kind of get beyond the demo sound. But, once I heard them playing them in the rehearsal room I realised how strong they were. I realised it was very different, but then *New Age* is very different to *Sam's Town*. What I love about The Killers is their boldness in moving on - wiping the board clean and starting again. The songs were different but it's still Brandon.

'It was odd though, for the Killers to do their 'American' album with a couple of Brits,' he muses. 'Maybe that was a reaction to the fact that on the first album they were like, seen as the best English band from America, everyone seemed to think they were English, and I think it made Brandon go back and listen to some American classics like Springsteen and Tom Petty and things. He wanted to do something that was a bit more of a nod to where he came from.'

Of Brandon's musical likes, Alan states that he's never worked with anybody who's got the musical taste that Brandon has.

'He loves all the cool stuff like Bowie and stuff, but he loves some uncool stuff too, which is great. He teaches you to realise, just cause it's not cool or whatever, doesn't mean it's not good. Everyone's got guilty secrets about what they've got in their record collection. Brandon's just incredibly honest about his. All their musical tastes are pretty different,' Alan reckons, and of their personal dynamics he says, 'They probably wouldn't hang out if it weren't for the band, but it works - you take one of The Killers out and it's not The Killers.'

It was during the making of *Sam's Town* that Alan would develop an affection for Australian band Wolfmother, using their debut album to amp him up for the day ahead. 'Funnily enough, when I was doing *Sam's Town* there was a long period of time where I used to put their album on, when I was getting ready in the morning. And then I went to see them in London. I think it was one of the few times I've been to a gig where it's not work related. I just went as somebody who liked the music. I mean, I grew up in the seventies, I loved all their reference points, and actually I'd gone to Australia and we were looking to move there at one point. My wife and I were driving around looking at houses listening to triple j and we heard Wolfmother, and I thought, 'Who's this? This is brilliant."

And still they cropped up. While Alan and Flood were working on *Sam's Town*, Wolfmother had a show at The Palms where The Killers were recording. Wolfmother wanted to use one of the rooms they were in to mix the track they had just recorded downstairs, so The Killers vacated for the day and let the Aussies in. At the beginning of 2009, Alan got asked to do a mix of the Wolfmother track *Back Round*, that was going to go on *Guitar Hero*. Andrew liked it and subsequently said to Alan, 'Do you fancy making a record?' He soon got sent the demos, thought they sounded great and off they went.

Fast forward to the future for a moment, not long after my chat with Trent Reznor, I tracked down Andrew Stockdale; curly wurly Wolfmother frontman. He's at the triple j radio studios in Brisbane, wearing a pair of headphones in a booth all alone, talking down a satellite line to me in the Sydney triple j studios. It's a weird set-up, but it works: it's the magical illusion of radio. Of that mix that Alan mentioned, Andrew reckons he was impressed with Alan's bravery to embrace the classic rock sound that's made Wolfmother famous.

'One mix I got back for *Back Round* was stripped back, stylised for American rock radio, which is a sound that I've never been able to relate to entirely, although I know a lot of people do because they think it will open doors for them. But

Alan's? Well, I liked the way he did the vocals, it sounded like a simple, loud, seventies band he wasn't afraid of. Well, he just wasn't afraid.

'He's a classy guy!' says Andrew suddenly, and laughs in that distinct high-pitched, full-force way, before continuing with the praise. 'He brings out the best in people, he's a good moderator, he's humble, he's very patient, he's highly intelligent, he's got a great sense of humour! He's just one of those people that's easy to spend a lot of time with.'

It was at the beautiful Rockinghorse Studios on the outskirts of the Byron Shire where Alan and Andrew's recording adventure for Wolfmother's second record *Cosmic Egg*, would hatch.

Alan's recollection of that time involved the compulsory first date and discussions of risk-taking.

'I turned up in Byron,' says Alan, 'where they were in the studio doing pre-production or working on the songs, we went out for a long lunch. First thing we did. I said, 'Well? What are you looking to achieve with this record?' And he filled me in on the background. He wanted to make it a bit more adventurous and he wasn't too concerned about the hit single, he just wanted to make an album that was enjoyable to make, and at the end of it was the best album he could make at the time. He said, 'I don't want to make a record where everyone's thinking at the end of it, 'Am I going to be able to move house into the next big house, am I going to be able to get the big car?' You know? I don't want to see it as a career move, I just want to see this as a great record. I mean I wasn't even aware really that, until I started working with him, that the other guys had left. So, I just thought it sounded like Wolfmother to me cause, his voice I suppose. And he said, 'You know it's my second shot, I'm lucky, let's just have some fun.' You know?'

These words were a soft magic to Allan's endurance-ready ears.

'It seems a very obvious thing to say, but really I hadn't thought of it that way. I mean, I tend to go into the studio, and, it's like, put your helmet on, strap yourself in, we're in for a bumpy ride. So, I thought yeah, that sounds like an idea!'

Arguably the defining factor of the Wolfmother sound is Andrew's vocals; the distinct whole-body projection of high notes responsible for some terrible karaoke moments. 'Andrew *performs*!' says Alan, of Andrew's time behind the mic. 'I mean, when he sings, you can't make him do it a million times because his head will fall off, you know he's *up* there. I mean the thing is, when he's singing the parts that everyone else would find difficult, they just come out of him. The lower ones, it's more difficult for him because he's so used to screaming at the top of his head on these incredibly high notes which is fun to see but he performs every line, you know.

'What we tried to do on this record was not labour over anything. If it was happening, go with it, and if it wasn't, work on it a bit and then come back to it. So, he was still writing a lot of lyrics and songs were all evolving still. I mean, this band's only been together since late January and we began recording a few months later, so we were suddenly in the studio recording an album, and it's kind of all very fresh, one of the songs was written a week before we went in to track. It was great, you actually get to record things when they're really fresh and they're still being created, really. So, we'd just try stuff, and move on. That was the philosophy. Andrew doesn't work well under getting bogged down. He's much better at getting the right mood. When he's in the right mood.'

And clearly from Andrew's recollections, it was simply Alan's genteel and encouraging nature that allowed the somewhat skittish frontman, the space to breathe and simply to be. 'If I had any idea, he'd just say 'try it'. There was no, 'That's a crap idea! I've been in the industry for this many years, if you wanna make it big you better listen to me!' There was none of that. I can't tell you how much of a relief that was!'

After an hour and a half drifting on the warm plains of Alan's level intonation, I turn off my recording gear somewhat hypnotised and slowly thank him for all his time. 'Ah, that was no time at all,' he says, with that famous measured patience.

I say goodbye and as I walk back to the tube I realise that Alan is my last stop on the European leg of the hunt, it's time to jump on a plane and spend some time in the homeland and see who, and what, presents next.

10

Dave Fridmann: Friends and Follies

Soon enough and sure enough, I find myself in a golf buggy with a man so laden with enthusiasm, that this little trip on these tiny four wheels may as well be on a convertible hovercraft made out of honeycomb, floating on a chocolate sea, for all the fun that Mr Coyne is having. 'This is great! I feel like Lil' Kim!' he declares with trademark enthusiasm.

'I chatted with Dave Fridmann a couple of weeks ago,' I coyly drop as we pass Kele from Bloc Party and wave to Sarah Blasko.

'Truly? What's he like as an interviewee?' He exclaims curiously, whilst saying a quick g'day to Neville Staples from The Specials, who's just stuck his head in the buggy on the way by.

'Amazing.' I say, referring to both The Flaming Lips' frontman's question and the sudden appearance of the legendary Mr Staples.

'Yeah, he's so gracious,' Wayne says returning back to the topic of Dave as we scoot through the backstage area of *Splendour In The Grass* in Byron Bay, Australia. 'He's almost embarrassed that people think he's so cool!'

'I'm including him in a documentary series I make called *The Producer Series*,' I say loudly over the back-of-house volume of the mainstage with the wind in our ears. 'He'll have his own episode, cut together with the music that he's worked on...mainly yours... and Mercury Rev's, of course.'

'Well, you better talk to me then too...I think I'll be in Sydney this week can you make it down there?'

'Of course,' I respond. 'That would be perfect.'

With interview arranged, I drop Wayne off at the Channel V caravan where he'll start a run of interviews he's committed to as part of the *Splendour* festival, as I make my way over to the triple j media area to meet more folk touched by the unorthodox hand of art-rock producer extraordinaire Mr Dave Fridmann - Ben and Andy of MGMT. Their first album, *Oracular Spectacular*, produced by Dave, and their second, *Congratulations,* mixed by him a few years later. *Oracular Spectacular* went absolutely gang-busters here in Australia the year after its release, reaching number 6 on the ARIA charts and making its way into the Hottest 100 three times, the highest pozzie being *Electric Feel* at number 2.

'Have you actually had a chance to speak with him?' Asks lead singer and guitarist Andy, as I set up my recording gear.

'I have, yes.'

'Wow that's great, he doesn't do many interviews.'

'Well he certainly should. We spoke for two and a half hours and I got the feeling that there were a lot of tales he'd never had the chance to tell. He was amazing. So why did you choose him to produce you?'

'He was someone that we'd been tossing around as an idea for a while,' Andy explains. 'We didn't even want a producer at the time, but I think we started to realise that for a band like us that was completely unknown, signed to a major label and not have a name to back it up, we were kinda throwing ourselves to the wolves. Then our label guy said he could put us in touch with Dave Fridmann, so we spoke with him on the phone. We were kinda nervous, not really knowing what kinda person he was at all, and it turned out that he was a really likeable amazing person. Musically it was probably *Soft Bulletin* that I loved most about his work and I'm a big fan of Mogwai too.'

When Andy and Ben made their way up to Dave's studio in the relatively remote Cassadaga village in the south of New York State in 2007, they felt vulnerable and nervous. They didn't have a manager but they had a huge label behind them as they drove into a situation that they knew very little about.

'He did such a great job making us feel comfortable,' Ben explains. 'He was good at mediating between us when we were arguing, and with the label, giving us advice on how to deal with a major label. For someone who's as well respected as he is, he doesn't have any kind of ego about it. He would never impose on somebody, he always puts the band's vision before any egotism or his own beliefs as to how he thinks something should sound. It's definitely set some standards for us in those terms. He recognised that we like music that is strange and subversive in very subtle ways and he would have full-mix distortion on some of the songs and we would all just be laughing…'

'Yeah people still don't understand that that was intentional,' adds Ben. 'We still get comments like. 'Oh, this album wasn't mixed right, the whole mix is fuzzed out,' and a lot of people just don't get it. It was almost a joke in a way, to mess with people, and Dave gets that.'

As the boys wait outside the triple j media camp waiting to be interviewed for the radio, Ben recalls a specific example of Dave's handiwork. 'Take the song *Pieces of What,* that we wrote pretty much in the studio. We took this old reel-to-reel tape machine up there with us and it had a tape on it that was broken and Dave's technician fixed it. It turned out to be this high school band or something playing popular orchestra pieces and so we spent an afternoon in the studio recording it backwards and at different speeds all this weird stuff and just laid it under the whole song. It wasn't a specific thing that you could have in mind before you did it but it was a fun experience doing it and then the end result sounded really cool.'

The two gents describe Dave as a humble, family man

whose kids were a bit skeptical of them at first, but reckon they succeeded in cracking them nonetheless; going out for pizza with them all and playing video games together. 'Dave cares so much less about what a band sounds like then how they are as people,' finishes Ben, 'and his whole family is like that, they judge the bands he works with and it doesn't have to do with their music or if they have cool style it's just whether or not they can hang out with them.'

As I wave farewell and race (at five kilometres an hour in a golf buggy) back to the artist compound to collect the Bloc Party folk, I pass The Flaming Lips's costume guy.

'Hey!' he shouts. 'We're one person short, can you be a gecko?'

'Can I!' I say, ditching my clipboard quicker than a bag of powder at a sniffer dog convention. Before I know it, I'm standing on stage in front of twenty thousand people dressed as a very green reptile watching a man climb through a giant digitised vagina, float about in a big ball above the crowd and singing songs about robots and jelly. As I boogie alongside about eight other geckos and a dude from Danananakroyd, I can't help but wonder if my awesome moves really are as lizard-like as I think they are and at what point this became just another day in the office for a little girl who grew up in the ghettos of Goodna.

A few days later I'm plonking into a seat once again beside Wayne Coyne - lead creator behind The Flaming Lips and all round sage of enthusiasm. This time we're on a couch in a hotel room in Sydney, rented just for the purpose of interrogations. He is swathed in a woolly poncho, his hair is wild and dishevelled. There's confetti in it. How does someone get confetti in their hair on a *Tuesday*? This is what I imagine Moses would have looked like after returning from his dealer Jesus with those ten giant tabs of acid.

To say that Wayne Coyne's energy is infectious is like saying that heroin is hobb*y*-forming. His outlook is worth basing a religion on. 'Often times I've thought - I'm not a very good musician,' he says with his usual humility. 'If it wasn't for punk rock I wouldn't have been able to form The Flaming Lips. You didn't have to be the greatest musician you just had to go for it.'

And just going for it is Wayne's mantra for life. The key, he says, is in the doing not in the thinking. 'If you just keep doing, eventually an idea will present itself. Often, I go into the making of a song with an idea but through the process of 'doing', an even better idea will present itself and we'll end up with a song that sounded nothing like what we started with. So, the thinking just gets you off the couch and you start doing, but it's the doing that then really gets you thinking.' It's a philosophy impossible to debate when the living breathing proof sits before you at 48 years of age with tinsel in his beard.

'I think Dave's greatest quality,' says Wayne, leaping in, eager to discuss his collaborator and dear friend, 'is that he wants to help you make the record that you want to make. And when a group is focused and sticks to their guns and keeps being brave and moving into the unknown, I know he loves that.

'Working on a song like *Race For The Prize,* there is a certain energy, a tempo, there's something happening with the drums, we all knew there was something pretty good there almost as if we didn't make it, it happened and we stood back and said don't muck that up. We tried to do songs after with that same style, that same intention and none of it worked. You just get lucky through trying, by just going for it and Dave is very good with that kind of thinking.'

In The Flaming Lips' camp (of which Dave is an executive member having co-produced with them since 1990) they have a term for when things are not going well in the studio, as they had first believed they would. It's known as Code Blue. It's when the band whole-heartedly knew they were going to do this thing and it was going to be great but everything they've done, has made it boring and normal and no-one in the room is excited about it anymore. This is when Dave steps to the fore. 'That's the moment when he turns to me and says, 'It's your art, make it work,' Wayne explains. 'Dave is very intense, which is why I think we like working together, he believes when he can make something work and I believe it as well and sometimes what we believe isn't the same thing. But what he will do is say. 'If you believe in your idea you will fight for it and if you believe in it enough you will keep fighting for it and if you don't, it doesn't deserve to win.' And if he gives you a fight he's kinda looking at you like, 'Come on it's your idea, make it happen.' He makes you question how much you believe in it.'

It's rare to see a band stick with a producer for so very long, I'm curious as to the possibility of this limiting the channel of ideas and wonder if Wayne ever thinks about changing producers, of the possibility of uncorking a whole new generation of ideas.

'Well, I do, and I know Dave would encourage it, if I said to him, 'Oh I want to go work with Rick Rubin or whoever,' He'd say, 'Go do it, and we'll steal their secrets!' We don't know if what we're doing is a just an incestuous repeating of our same dumb subconscious ideas, but I can say for certain when we finished *Soft Bulletin,* the record company wanted us to go and do a couple of remixes with this guy out of Chicago called Peter Mokran. We were all open to it, and Peter was great, one part of our minds thought he would think. 'What is this silly indie freakout orchestral rock?' But the minute he heard it, he thought, 'This is great, this is not like R Kelly at all!' What we learnt from it all was that there are endless ways still of doing things. I sort of feel like we are making these records *with* Dave, so I don't think I would ever say, 'Oh I don't want to make a record with Dave,' I'd say. 'I'm making a record with Dave *and* with somebody else.' I feel like he's given us the best part of his life already. I've known him since college, I've seen his kids grow up you know - he's really become a master of making the kind of records that we make, he still pushes us even after all the tricks we've already tried!'

As the afternoon Sydney sun streams through the window behind us, it tinkles off the silver streamer still caught amongst his facial hair and now matches the sparkle in Wayne's eye as he recalls the penny-drop moment of his and Dave's relationship.

'We'd always have different friends come out with us and mix our front-of-house sound. We were playing what we thought at the time was a very prestigious show, opening up for Jane's Addiction in Los Angeles, so we thought we should get a real sound engineer for this thing. And he flew out and we told him we didn't want it to be just a standard just-turning-up-the-faders type gig. We wanted him turning up guitar and turning up the effects, we wanted it to be a really visceral, dynamic show and I think all this utterly appealed to him. He told us he wanted to wear a hospital smock with nothing else on, so he's out there, mixing sound, with some giant ponytail on the top of his head, wearing just this hospital smock with no underwear or anything, and I think half the audience were just watching him. So, after the first show we thought, 'This is our guy.' He's willing to be a freak along with us without sacrificing any of the quality.

Dave is intense and he is very kind. As a human he's really one of the greatest people I've ever met in my life. Even if he made *horrible* records, I'd still hold him in very high esteem because he's such a great person. So, in the end, all that skill and all that fighting and all that determination, *that* gets us to the sounds but the reason I want to be with him and want to be around him is because he's just a cool human. If more humans were like him, the world would be a very cool place.'

11

Dave Fridmann: The Man Behind the Awesome

Hunting down Dave Fridmann some six weeks earlier was somewhat easier than most, with his management company able to be found simply and boldly online and only about fifteen email exchanges needed to pin down a suitably pleasing time for us both.

It's 8pm New York time on June 8th, 2009. I've come to the triple j studios straight from the airport, fresh off the plane from Heathrow. For the past three weeks in Europe interviewing Diplo, Philippe Zdar and Alan Moulder, and after 21 hours in the air, I'm as sharp as a ball of wool. Luckily Dave is as easy to chat to as he is to find and when he picks up the phone at his home in Chautauqua County, he's all comfy and ready to reveal.

He's had a rare day away from the studio controls, instead doing the laundry and other domestic chores necessary in a room that is often filled with musicians. He is sitting in the basement of the house beside the Amish barn - the famous Tarbox Road Studios. 'It actually is a barn,' he says of his special studio space. 'For the Amish, there's absolutely no structural difference between a house or a barn. They actually came and put a new roof on it the other day so it looks more Amish than ever.'

To choose to record with Dave Fridmann is to choose a certain degree of desolation; you've got to drive a couple of miles just to get to a candy bar, let alone civilisation and the nearest neighbours are a couple of acres away. It's a space that offers no distractions but those in one's own mind. 'It was a deliberate choice to be set up like this,' explains Dave of the remoteness. 'I'd worked a lot at a place in upstate New York called Sweet Fish Studios after I came out of college and it was the same - a barn with a bunch of gear plopped in it - and the guy gave it to us real cheap and let us go in there and record for weeks on end, so I knew that it could work. I've broken recording time down right now though to two-week segments, that seems to be about all that anybody can take, but that doesn't really matter if you're in the city or anywhere else, after about two weeks, people are just about crawling out of their skin and just about out of ideas.'

Much like the one out to his beautiful property, the road in life that Dave has taken is the one less travelled. Dave was a successful muso who chose the studio over the stage.

'Like many people I liked music as a kid - I found myself

very affected by it and interested in it, and like a lot of people I thought it sounded like a great idea to be in a band…then as a back-up plan I found out about this recording program that was at the University about an hour away from where I grew up and I thought it would be a good place to meet other serious musicians. It turns out that I wasn't as serious as they were, but it was there that I met members of Mercury Rev and through them, members of The Flaming Lips.

'I'd already done a lot of production and mixing on the first Mercury Rev record, which we did while I was still in school over three years. By the time we finished the first Mercury Rev record, I'd already produced and completed the first Flaming Lips record and I was really getting a taste for it. After being out on the road and playing shows and all that stuff, I think it was obvious to me as a musician that I was able to do more by NOT being in a band. It actually gave me a lot more creative possibilities and freedom to explore any style that I wanted. And I love the machines…they don't talk back, which is good. I'm joking, of course! I like the pure elements of music, I like the actual listening to music, in some ways more than creating. It's great when five years later I can listen to something I've worked on and be like, 'Wow that's really cool somebody should do something like that on…oh wait that was me, I did that.' I love also sitting in a room with a bunch of people that have a momentary suspension of all outside forces. There is nothing else apart from what is coming out of those speakers.'

The common thread in Dave's reputation is that as a producer you can throw anything at him, he'll catch it, run with it, enhance it and throw it right back. I ask him what his thoughts are on this perception of his production mindset.

'Sure.' He agrees with a knowing yet humble laugh. 'Through whatever osmosis that I have learned to be an engineer, if people have some kind of musical or sonic problem, chances are I can help them achieve what it is they are trying to achieve, and that is extremely gratifying.

'Not at all to knock what he does but the Steve Albini school of 'you guys come here, perform the first week, we'll mix the second week, that's it bang, the record's done', that's great, he's done a million great records with a million great bands, but it's boring to me. I much prefer to get my hands dirty and the people I work with always seem to have this difficult, intangible sonic dilemma that no-one will know the answer to until we stumble upon it and that's a lot more fun for me.'

'Is there part of you that is that Rick Rubin philosophical type producer? A bit mysterious in your ways?' I ask.

Dave chuckles. 'I'm not really sure what Rick Rubin does, I'm not sure that anyone knows what Rick Rubin does. I guess my basic operating philosophy is, 'Let's get in there and do something unknown, not just to you guys as musicians but also unknown, hopefully, to anybody.' For whatever reason, a lot of bands that come to me are fairly established in their careers and it's at a time in their career where they are saying, 'We want to destroy all preconceived notions of what we've done before, and we want to break out of our own box that we've painted ourselves into, and we want your help doing it.' I think a lot of their fans end up hating me as a result but to me that's fun. Some sound is coming out of the speakers and we're all looking around the room and going. 'OK, we've all just left our comfort zone are we going to retreat or are we going to rush forward into the void.' Philosophically, usually I'm successful at convincing people to rush forward into that void.'

Listening to the beautiful madness of The Flaming Lips, one could be forgiven for thinking that Dave, tucked away in his little Amish barn in the wilderness, is potentially rated high on the oddness scale; a nerdy wizard with a penchant for the teachings of Timothy Leary and an aversion to coherent thought.

'Wayne will often say that he'll talk to people and they'll think there's going to be this crazy drug-taking nutjob wearing robes when they come out to the studio and it just turns out that I'm a normal guy wearing old navy clothes with a straight military haircut - there's no physical aberration, no affectation. People I think are vaguely disappointed when they meet me.'

The very first album that Dave ever produced in its entirety was The Flaming Lips' fourth record, *In A Priest Driven Ambulance*. It was through his own band, Mercury Rev, that he would end up behind the controls of that album.

'We'd already been working on the first Mercury Rev album, *Yerself Is Steam,* for a coupla years, and Jon Donahue from Mercury Rev was actually their (Flaming Lips) tour manager *and* live soundman, so when they could afford a live soundman at some point, Jon called me and I went and met them out on the road and did their live sound. After a couple of months there was discussion that they were going to make another record, and one night I finally got up the courage to sheepishly ask them well…maybe …I could produce the next record? We did a two-week test run and nothing horrible happened. I also managed to book the college studio for three months for a price that would've gotten them two weeks somewhere else, so it enabled us all to explore how crazy we could get in there.'

Of the way that Wayne Coyne works in the studio Dave says he 'twists and turns everything that he touches'.

'He'll take a hammer and turn it into a saw and turn a saw into a snare drum and turn it back into a hammer. It was so crazy,' he says of working on that first record with them. 'I'm trying to explain like, the circle of fifths and some really basic music principles - they do a harmony and I'd say, 'Well, that's not really the right note.' He'd say, 'Why?' He's got a crazy filter on him. No matter who he's working with or what he's working on, *everything* always gets twisted upside down and inside out.'

After Dave finished *In A Priest Driven Ambulance* he returned to Mercury Rev's *Yerself Is Steam* a somewhat changed man.

'Yeah there was definite effect on one album from the

other. We actually used - for the song *Frittering* - Wayne's guitar and his setup. I knew the sound I wanted and it was on Wayne's gear. These similarities and affectations continued throughout most of the Mercury Rev/Flaming Lips albums coming back quite strongly when *Deserter's Songs* and *Soft Bulletin* were being recorded simultaneously, seven years later. All the people all played on each other's albums, listened to each other's demos and gave each other ideas.'

The second album for Mercury Rev was *Boces* and according to Dave, the recording of it was of the salacious stuff that gets books published.

'That album was a *nightmare,*' he shudders. 'There was a lot of personal stuff going on that I don't really want to go into, but it was very crazy interpersonal relationships within the band, and by the time we went out to tour that record, I personally had made up my mind to dedicate x amount of time to make my own records and everyone else was like, 'I do not want to work with any of these people again for the rest of my life under any circumstance."

Dave laughs a little now, time turning the intensity into just another one of life's oh-so-endearing challenges.

'Jonathon came by though at one point, to pick up the band's gear and I said to him, 'I want to keep this one guitar,' and he said, 'On one condition, that you keep recording us'. And I thought, 'Yeah, right. Like you're ever going to want to work with me again,' because I completely blame myself for how things went down. I was a complete tyrant in the studio, it was my worst performance behind the desk ever, and as a member of the band and the producer I took it upon myself to say, 'Well, I'm in charge here, and if I don't like it, I'm not recording it.' It was completely asinine on my part ... this is how chaotic it was - we were mixing the record, which we did up at Sweet Fish and it had a giant console, all six of us were at the board and literally turning up our favourite parts as they went by, still trying to make it sound like a song by the end of it, punching each other at the same time. Yeah, it was total chaos.'

As Dave readjusts himself in the basement where he sits, talk turns to the engineering of Weezer's second album *Pinkerton*. 'What was strange for me about that album was that I'd never worked with anyone so successful in terms of album sales, so that was a lot of pressure. Going out to LA following in the footsteps of famed producer and member of the Cars, Rick Ocasek, I mean, I know I wasn't producing, I was simply engineering, but still they were big shoes to fill. I was definitely very nervous. What was great for me was that it really gave me an impetus to up my professionalism, to really become what I am now.'

On top of their success and talent, Weezer's broad approach to technology stood out to Dave as a revelatory and skill-building approach that would broaden his mind to the possibilities of production.

'They were very early adopters of technology, having a very strange marriage between old and new school. I think we went through thirty reels of tape just in the two weeks that I was there, and that alone represented four entire record budgets for me. They would record each song nine times and it would be completely different each time, then they'd sit down with a list of where they wanted me to make all these edit points. We'd edit it, put it all together into one song, and they'd decide if they liked that or not. If they didn't, they'd go and record nine more takes and we'd do it all over again. Then the new school part was like…they had this one song that they'd recorded with Jo (Baresi) in Boston and they had hired this guy to drag in this pro-tools machine to work twelve hours a day for six days, just to lengthen one of the songs - that's like four buttons now and you're done. All that stuff seemed crazy to me, it was very interesting and eye-opening to me seeing how other people were doing their records.'

Of the tracks that Dave worked on the one that stands out the most is *Butterfly*.

'Rivers (Cuomo, lead singer/guitarist/songwriter) kept telling me the whole time we were working that he had this other song, but we're just going to wait until the time is right. Apparently, the right time was at four am on the last night. He finished the first take, and it was the first time I heard it, and I got on the talkback and said to him, 'Are you sure you want to say that to people?" laughs Dave. 'I'm sure', he said, so I was like ok, good. I mean it was amazing but I couldn't believe he was being this open and honest and unguarded.'

All of it paid off with *Pinkerton* going on to sell more than 850,000 copies in the US alone.

After Weezer, Dave returned to his life as the other member of the Flaming Lips, helping cement their position as one of the most curious bands in the history of music-making with The Parking Lot Experiments. The experiments were a pre-twitter version of a flash mob, where Wayne encouraged 40 lots of people to turn up in their cars, where he would give them each a cassette tape and conduct them all as to when to press play. The result was an elastic and unpredictable composition that would lead him to make the *Zaireeka* album.

'*Zaireeka* consists of four different CDs, all to be played at the same time across four different stereos,' Dave explains of the album that would almost certainly take out the title for Most Ballsy Release by a Major Label. 'Wayne had a weird idea at the time…words like interactive and multimedia were beginning to be thrown around at the time and that drove him crazy. He was like. 'That's not interactive, that's sitting in a room staring at a screen by yourself. (*Zaireeka*) will mean that you've got to get at least three other people in a room with you experiencing music at the same time."

'The other strange thing to happen with *Zaireeka*, much to the credit of everyone at Warner Music at that time, was that they said, 'Yep, we'll put out your crazy stupid art idea *but* we're not giving you any more money to make it. You've got to make both records with the same budget that you've been given for *Soft Bulletin.*' So we got to do what we wanted, which was great. Probably the hardest thing was readapting back to two speakers - we'd be recording *Soft Bulletin* after that and someone would say, 'I wish this speaker could be *all* bass,' but then you've got no room for the drums. With *Zaireeka* it was like. 'Nope, this speaker is now all bass and this one is all drums, this is *awesome!*"

When work commenced on The Flaming Lips' *Soft Bulletin* album in 1998, following *Zaireeka,* production also began on Mercury Rev's acclaimed album *Deserter's Songs* - at the same studio, using the same gear.

'It was still not a great time for the band,' says Dave. 'They were still having a lot of personal drama but um, I don't know how to say it right…I think you can hear a lot of the desolation, a lot of the longing for simpler times, a lot of the need for companionship and hope that somehow the future can be better. I think you can hear that in the songs. That record is very accurate to how particularly Jonathon was feeling at the time.'

Deserter's Songs formed into a desperately delicate and ornate album, a leap from the rowdier sounds from before, revealing an emotional state for the band that was impossible to miss.

'Yeah, it could be argued that Mercury Rev were trying to do that stuff from the beginning but we were hopelessly – myself amongst them – unprepared or incapable of making an album like *Deserter's Songs* before we actually made it. Building the studio had a huge part in that. The truth is, it was the best studio that any of us had ever worked in, so we finally had these really great tools at our disposal. We spent a long time in the nineties, me, Wayne and Jon, saying, 'OK, if we have to choose between gear and time, we'll take the time.' As it turns out, aah, the gear actually matters.' Dave laughs at the memory of their youthful naivety, and of all the years spent crafting genius with second-rate tools.

'I'll tell you a short story – The Flaming Lips' drum sound. We had an idea of this kind of Zeppelin-y, crazy, roomy kind of sound that we liked, but it took us sometimes a *week* to get the drum sounds right for a single track. That's why we'd always say we need the time, but there was a time where I'd just gotten in a new microphone – this new very expensive U47 – and we were like, 'OK, let's do some drum recording here.' So Wayne goes out to the kitchen and makes himself some coffee. At the time he still smoked, so he got himself the ashtray, came into the control room sat down. We're going to be a couple of hours before we even figure out the kick drum. While he's out there though, I'm setting up the microphone and we opened the mic for the first time on the drum kit, and Steve's out there playing and we were like, 'Okay, well the drums are done, now what are we going to do?' So, having that $8000 microphone does make a difference as it turns out.'

For more than an hour already, Dave and I have been gasbagging and we're only up to 1998! I don't know about him but my bum is getting sore, my mouth is getting dry and glares through window from other presenters into the much-needed studio are getting icy! So, we fast-forward to 2005.

'I actually talked to them on the phone a bunch before I met them, and they were good but difficult conversations, where I was like, 'I don't actually like any of your other records, but if you guys are interested in doing something different then I'm totally on board and if you're interested in doing what you did before I'm totally not interested."

It's a boldness that few folks would dare with all-girl punk contingency Sleater-Kinney, but in approaching their seventh (and what would be their final) record, the ladies were glad to hear it.

'They specifically told me, 'We want you to cut our audience in half - people who've liked what we've done in the past hopefully won't even like what we're doing now, we want to do something utterly different.' And of course, that was completely appealing to me.'

It was during the couple of days of pre-production that Dave really got to see just how much they meant what they said, and for him to witness first-hand the sheer skill of Sleater-Kinney doing what they do best.

'We just stood in a room and they played and I was like, 'I gotta tell you, this already sounds nothing like any of your other records, this is totally intense and amazing and I'm totally excited about what I'm hearing. I don't know how I'm gonna get it on tape but I love it.' When I was sitting in the room while they were playing, amplifiers blaring, I was like. 'This fucking rules!'

'It felt like a great success for me personally just to have none of the pitfalls – everybody's personal relationships stayed together and I'd never been so direct with any band, ever, that was the first time I felt, ahh, soooo like I'd put myself out there so much. That was a great, big difference for me.'

With just minutes to go of our chat time together, we move on to MGMT and I wonder if Dave's accomplished ears had been able to detect what was going to happen commercially with their album *Oracular Spectacular* when he first heard the demos.

'No not at all,' he states firmly. 'I've completely given up on pretending I know what might work or might not, all I can do is enjoy what's coming out of the speakers and move forward.

'I think I saw the potential in it, but being here where I am, living in a small town, I'm quite distant from it all. It doesn't seem as big as what people tell me that album has become. You know, people might call me and tell me they heard it on K-Rock in LA or some other big radio market, but out here it strangely doesn't have any basis in my actual reality.'

When MGMT came out to Tarbox Road, they were just babies compared to the majority of other bands that Dave had worked with. It was a new dynamic for him in both his studio as well as in his home.

'There was this one funny scene,' he says chuckling. 'I've got two sons and I'm married, and we had the fellas over goofing around one night playing video games with my children who were at the time 12 and 9, and my wife and I were like, 'I think these guys might have more in common with our children then with us!' They're really great guys and just seeing them be young and having a good time was great. They grew up a lot during the making of that record, having to deal with the realities of being signed to a major label. I had to talk to them a few times and say, 'Guys, you didn't really think they were just going to give you the money and not ask anything in return, did you? You know they're going to want what they want as well."

I explain to him the enormity of the record here, particularly the single *Electric Feel,* which took out the number two spot of the Hottest 100 behind Kings of Leon's *Sex on Fire* in 2007.

'Oh, that's funny,' he says, as if I've just shown him a vegetable shaped like part of the male anatomy. 'They're both such great musicians,' he says matter-of-factly of the talent-saturated duo. 'They can both sing any part, or play any part on any instrument and go, 'What if the keyboard solo went like this?' and then play some crazy-ass thing you'd be totally impressed with if a classical pianist was playing, and then the other guy'll step up and go, 'Well, what about like this?' and does the same thing only different, and you go, 'Holy crap! You guys can really fucking play."

Nearly two hours since he first picked up the phone, we agree to wrap it up. I blame the extent of the chat on him and his extensive career. As he laughs with that good-natured joviality that Wayne Coyne champions, he leaves off with one final generous tip for young players looking to a career in production.

'I actually teach at the college here and I've told the kids many times, the ideal double major would be sound recording and psychology. There's a point as an engineer or as a producer where there's a technical proficiency you need to get to where you're as good or better than ninety percent of the guys out there. Once you're past that point, it's all about your personality and your problem solving skills - musical, technical, psychological.'

'What another amazing, marathon chat.' I think happily as I gather teacups and papers and check to see that those 6000 words have gone onto tape. Thankfully it's all there and as I leave the studio, suddenly incredibly weary, jetlagged, hungry and talked out, I wish that I too was in New York right now and it was bedtime, rather than midday with a three-hour drive ahead to get me home.

Bit of Trivia*: According to Dave Fridmann most people's eardrums start distorting sound at 90db; the point where the human body can no longer send a clear signal along the nerve endings. Sleater-Kinney played at a volume higher than this, which is why their album* The Woods *is fuzzier than a bear in an electrical storm.*

12

Mark Ronson: Touched by Angels

It's the year 2011, nearly a year and a half after the last producer series aired on triple j and the urge to speak with another sonic magician has pushed its way to the front of my cranium, leading me yet again through different landscapes and in this case, through different sub-cultures. The road to Mr Ronson has leap-frogged through punk, metal, hardcore, Brisbane, Sydney, Melbourne, Adelaide and Perth, a sea of flouro and ending in the back room of a dance festival, where I stand with one very sweaty man and too many free servings of chocolate cake.

Mark Ronson's name had been bouncing around in the Producer Series research realm since about 2006 when he popped up in conjunction with Lily Allen. Lily's debut album *Alright, Still* exploded, gathering up everyone attached to it and sending them hurtling like shrapnel into the atmosphere. One of those shards was British coolio Mark Ronson, who'd worked on the track *Littlest Things* and later on, *Oh My God*. Already Mark had released his own album *Here Comes The Fuzz,* worked with Macy Gray and Ol' Dirty Bastard as well as making a name for himself as a fashion-clad celebrity DJ. Whilst the genuine desire to share and produce great music was definitely there, Mark's connection with the superstar set, his obsession with style and his privileged background had him struggling for credibility within the music world. His connections though, and his skills, always kept him strutting just one small step ahead of the heel-biting naysayers.

On his first album Mark brought on board some impressive names - Jack White, Sean Paul and Rivers Cuomo - but his most significant guest was Nikka Costa, a lady who had been his doorway into the giant, soundproof booth of production two years earlier. Mark co-produced Nikka's first record in 2001 alongside her husband Justin Stanley - an Australian record producer who was in the bands Noiseworks and Electric Hippies. Of that time in studio, Mark says he 'literally just learned by staring at the back of Justin's head for six months. I just would stay back and just learn and stare and it was like an apprenticeship.'

Five years on from there, and only months after meeting Lily, Mark would align with the woman who proved to be the most significant of all he would work with: Amy Winehouse. Being a man not to miss a single moment, Mark bashed out his second album *Version,* whilst all eyes were still on him, landing a number 2 possie on the UK charts. Despite the commercial success, the British press still didn't know quite what to make of him. An album of covers is not the best way to prove your breadth on the creative landscape. But whilst it mightn't have cemented his place in the annals of song writing, it certainly highlighted his skills and diversity as a producer who could hop genres and hang it all cohesively on beats that were fun, dusty and stylish enough to lock into the frequency of even the most fashionably unamused.

By the time I got to Mark, he was three albums in and trendier than dumpling soup in the East Village. He was also on a national festival tour in Australia, and so was I. Unfortunately, though (from a logistical perspective) not the same one.

In January of 2011 I got an email from Sony Records asking if I had any interest in writing a story on New Zealand songstress Zowie who was just about to be announced as the support for Mark Ronson on his Australian tour through March. I did have interest in Zowie and I had interest in Mark also, it was a double-deal of negotiation that saw interviews with both the rising star and the risen, approved. Locking down a time with Mark though, was quite the mission for all parties. We were both moving our way around the country, part of different musical juggernauts. The only way to intercept required pure luck and tenacity. I was on the *Soundwave* tour as the National Media Manager with Iron Maiden, Slayer, The Bronx, Pennywise, Slash and sixty other bands from the worlds of punk, metal and hardcore. Mark was on *Future Music* with Pendulum, Ke$ha, MGMT, The Presets and thirty other artists from the domain of all that glows in the dark.

On my run, Perth was the last show on a five-day capital city tour, on Mark's it was the second. I was flying in on March 6th from Adelaide on a travel day, for Mark it was a show day. Generally, things like this are locked in at least a few weeks out - preferably before all parties even land in the country so the intricate scheduling required for touring can be taken care of well in advance. But due to both of us being on tour, this was simply impossible. On March first, I received the below email from the lovely Therese from Sony,

'I just don't know how it's going to work time wise. He's on stage at 4:30pm and you land at 1:30pm and need an hour with him. There is no other way to do it unless it's on-site at Future and you can go straight there from the airport. What time do you think you'd get there?'

On the morning of March sixth, just before I was due to get on the flight to Perth from Adelaide, Bron from Sony gave word that she'd heard back from Mark's management in the UK and all was good to go. I was to meet Mark at 6pm on site at *Future Music* half an hour after he got off stage. Bron had organised laminates to be left at the gate for me to get into the festival, a West Australian Sony rep for me to contact once I got on-site and details for the event media person to take me through to the backstage media area. At my end, the *Soundwave* crew organised a driver to get me out there and hold my hand as my blinded eyes adjusted to a crowd full of fluoro kids after so many weeks of nothing but black. It was a beautiful ballet of music industry professionalism that enabled me to walk past security backstage into this room of a very sweaty and hyped up Mark Ronson. I'm surprised that with all it took to get us here that when we finally shook hands, something odd didn't happen to the fabric of time and space.

Mark's manager set us up in a steamy little office room beside the dressing room, with a couple of bottles of water and some booze for Mark. Mark's energy was pretty high - he had just come off stage but I get the feeling that it wasn't too many pegs above normal - I thought it best we settle into chats about the easy stuff first, nonetheless, and headed back in discussion to Mark's colourful childhood.

'Although my stepdad Mick was a big influence on me growing up, my Mum didn't marry him until I was six or seven and I do have much earlier memories of music,' Mark says, talking of growing up with Mick Jones from The Clash and his own discovery of music. 'Like, my Dad was super into soul. He was like a lot of English guys that grew up in the sixties, a proper soul boy, and he played all these records around the house and I remember waking up in the middle of the night, my parents were… I think they were kind of like a wild young couple. I don't want to delve into specifically what they were doing but they would have lots of people over and I'd wake up at three in the morning and walk out into the living room and there'd be all these people and loud music and I would sit down in front of the speaker and I would play air drums. I would pretend like I was playing a drum kit. My mum says it was Keith Moon that said something, but I feel like that's a typical Mum exaggeration. I think he was dead already, but she said that Keith Moon saw me playing air drums and said, you know, 'Ah, get that kid like a set of drums.' So, my earliest memory is really like three or four years old, playing along to the radio on this children's trap kit. And then I also remember getting one of those, it was called like a Sony My First Record Player and it was this big plastic thing in primary colours, like blue, yellow, red, and I loved the actual process of watching the needle, like lifting the needle and putting it on the 45, and I guess it kind of makes it seem a bit obvious that I would end up somewhere down the line as a DJ.'

Mark somewhat humbly reckons that his path as a DJ was also born from having no one obvious talent. He had a crack at playing in bands on rhythm guitar and as a voluntary music writer for *Rolling Stone* when he was fourteen, but it wasn't until he discovered hip hop in the early nineties in New York that he found a little niche for himself.

'That was the first thing that I sort of grabbed onto that seemed like I was good at or had some kind of promise, you know. When I think of people like my contemporaries like Errol Alkin or Brian Burton (Dangermouse), we're all kind of these musical sponges that are all that nerdy trainspotter-y type. Whether it came from working in a record shop or being a DJ. All that knowledge you amass in the back of your head, that's what I think makes us ... I don't want to say *good* because that's a matter of taste and judgement, but that what makes us the producers that we are, because you have this kind of like virtual record shop in your head, and you think, 'Oh, I'd like a bit of that record and that one.' Well, the only difference when you're a producer, you're just supposed to use your talent and your ear to figure out how to apply all these things. I mean, Stevie Wonder, too is arguably one of the greatest songwriters-vocalists-talents of modern music, I think he's probably being overly modest but he used to say, 'Everyone thinks that I'm some kind of genius but all I knew was where to borrow from.'

In how that translates in hands-on terms for Mark as a producer, he admits that he's constantly learning, but that the technical application of his ideas has definitely come a long way. At the beginning of this road, his producer-aspirations sat comfortably with little more than a drum machine, a sampler and the ability to make a loop. All Mark had really ever wanted to be was a hip-hop producer, just like his idols DJ Premier and RZA. That all began to change when he was working with Nikka and he started to discover the more organic way of creating and wielding audio. But it was during a search for a specific sound for Amy Winehouse's *Back to Black* album that Mark's small world broke through into a whole new universe.

'When I met Amy, we started doing these demos in my little studio and I was using every sort of digital plug-in in the book, to try and make it sound old. Then I heard these Dap King recordings and I was like, 'Holy shit, I cannot believe this record was made, like, two months ago. This sounds like golden-era Motown."

Out of the blue, with the confident audacity of a kid raised with money, Mark called Gabriel Roth - the miracle minimalist engineer of Daptone records - and told him flat out that he had to record Amy there in his studio with his mad-Motown skills. Despite Gabe not knowing Mark from a blade of grass, he agreed to let the cocky little fella come on down and play him Amy's demos.

'I remember the first day that I walked in to the studio and he was getting drum sounds; Homer (Steinweiss drummer for the Dap-Kings) was playing and I walked in and it was like one of those, it sounds so cliché, but one of those moments where it's just like (*angels singing*) Aaaaaahhhh! Homer was playing as Gabe was eq-ing the mic, and it sounded like every gorgeous beautiful, but like dirty, like hip hop, break I'd ever loved in my life. Every hip hop producer in New York would go into a record shop and try and find a new drum break that no-one else had. But we were all searching for the same sound, this sound that sounded like this sixties fucking heavy break, and I walk into this studio in Bushwick Brooklyn and there's a fucking dude on the other side of the control room playing it, and it sounds like every break that I've ever wanted to use or would pay fifty bucks for in some East Village record store, only there it is, like a live human playing it, who can play fills and speed up and slow down and bring the song to life '

The demos that Mark took to Gabe that day were the very beginnings of what would be her biggest and last studio album; *Back to Black*. It was an album that spawned five Grammys and five massive singles, including the autobiographical *Rehab*, a song she wrote in New York, where she would also meet Mark for the first time thanks to a label guy called Guy, at EMI records who thought the pair should meet.

'I'd listened to her first record *Frank* quite a bit,' says Mark, explaining his first impressions of Amy. 'There was one song called *In My Bed* that she reworked this Nas beat that I really liked. I just had a feeling she was a bit too special and a bit above doing the typical thing where you play a bunch of tracks, 'd'you like this one, d'you like this one?' I didn't even want to play her something that I had and just risk ruining it. So, I said, 'What kind of record do you want to make and what do you envisage?' And she said, 'Well I like all this ... this is what I like,' and she just started playing me a bunch of shit from the Shangri-Las, sort of like sixties you know, juke box pop music to R&B bands like the New Birth and there were things that I knew and things that I didn't, and I was like, 'All right, well listen, I don't have anything like that, but go back to your hotel and come back tomorrow, like let me see what I can come up with tonight."

Mark put his head down and his creative hat on and came up with a 'minor-y' chord progression, a touch of percussion and a soaking of reverb that he describes as 'insta-Spector'. He came up with the beginnings of the album's title track.

'She is just so, like, deadpan and she doesn't give anything away,' he says, thinking back to those awkward moments as he played her what he'd come up with. 'She was like, 'Yeah... er, I like it.' And I was like, 'Ah, this is fucked, she's leaving.' Then she went out of the room. It's so goofy but I called my manager and was like, 'I don't think Amy really liked this, but anyway it was cool,' and he was like, 'Oh no, no, I just got a call from her manager saying she loves the thing you just did and she's staying another two weeks and she thinks you're the guy to make her album."

Almost all of the bones of the tracks were written by Amy, Mark fleshing them out to her nod or shake of the head, except for *Rehab,* which appeared as an unexpected gift. 'We were walking down the street in Soho, and she wanted to buy a little shirt from Ben Sherman for her boyfriend and she was just telling me about some shit she's gone through in her life and there was a particularly low point and she said, 'Yeah, my Dad came over and I was fucked and they tried to make me go to rehab and I was like, 'no, no, no' and she put up the hand, and it just instantly sounded like a song, just the way she said it: 'They tried to make me go to rehab and I was like no, no, no'. We went back to the studio and she kind of wrote it in about an hour.'

How Amy originally wrote it was much more down-tempo, in a twelve-bar blues style. It was Mark and what he credits to the DJ 'side of mind' who felt that although the content definitely sat well with the blues, people should still be able to move to it. So together they upped the tempo, put some soul-swing in there and created a track that would win three Grammys.

As Mark pours himself a dark spirit, he admits that that album changed everything. 'I had been making records for ... well trying to make records for a good ten, eleven or twelve years, and then maybe my first thing that saw some kind of light was the Nikka Costa record and a little bit of my first album, but nothing that really, really registered. I had made my name as a DJ in that New York scene and I knew Kanye when he was coming up and I knew Pharrell and Chad from The Neptunes and they would always be like, 'This is Mark, he's our favourite DJ.' In the back of my mind I was flattered they said that, but I was also burning a little bit because I was like, well I don't want to be known as a DJ, I want to be like you guys, I want to be known as a producer. But you can't get mad about that if you haven't had a hit. You can't go running around saying, 'Why does no one know I'm a producer?"

And then the last person I saw really just blow by me was Brian - Dangermouse. I was DJing these little clubs in London and he'd just done the Grey Album, so obviously his name was kind of known, but he came and he was in New York one day and he said, 'I just produced this Gorillaz record and I just want to hear it on some speakers, and I don't have anywhere to go in New York can I come to your place?' And I heard it and I thought it was so brilliant, and I was just like, fuck it's so good, what am I doing? I don't even know how you would make those sounds listening to that record and I just thought you know maybe my thing's never gonna blow up. I was thirty at the time and I was just like, maybe it's just cool to just admit that I gave it a shot and it's not really going to happen."

It was at that time that Mark met Lily Allen. The pair making *Littlest Things* and *Oh My God*, and then about two months later he met Amy. Over two records, Mark Ronson became one of the most well-known producers of the new-school in the world.

Mark suddenly gets a look on his face like a private school boy who's just given the local green grocer a wedgie. I turn around to look behind me to see one of his mates behind the glass in the other room doing one of the most dismal versions of the escalator I have ever seen. Acting like a twelve-year-old is awesome but you've got to at least add some thirty-year-old panache to it.

I play the stern librarian face and Mark comes back to the conversation, I ask him about towing the line with Lily Allen, a woman who very much expects full creative control.

'Lily's a tough, independent woman and no one's more at the helm of the Lily Allen ship than she is,' he acknowledges. 'There were always these articles in England for a while that said, 'Mark Ronson the man behind Lily Allen and Amy Winehouse.' A) it's such a bunch of bullshit and B) I understand why it would drive her crazy because she had her whole record and her vision.

'The reason I started working with her is cause I met her at a club when I was DJing once and she gave me these demos of her album and I heard *LDN* and *Smile* and I was like, 'This is amazing!' And I called her up and I asked her to come up to New York. and at that time the label wasn't going to pay for her to fly up to work with me because I was a no-name, so I've got her a ticket like on my air miles and put her up at the Howard Johnson's Hotel, this really budget hotel in New York, round the corner from my studio that happened to be in

Chinatown at the height of the avian bird flu scare. So Lily fucking lands, she's like twenty in New York all by herself, shows up to this weird hotel and there's just all these Chinese business men walking around with these facemasks on and she's freaking out…I love that fucking band, they are so fucking good!' he says, all of a sudden with seemingly no context but for the comic strip of his mind.

'Who?' I ask, looking around for clues.

'Tame Impala!' he says as they walk past the door. 'That's my absolute favourite shit.'

My heart swells a little with Aussie pride, I wanna yell out to them and tell them what Mark has just said, but figure that might be weird for everyone. Hopefully Tame Impala you are reading this now…or word has at least spread.

Getting back to Miss Allen:

'I could listen to her sing the phonebook,' reckons Mark enthusiastically. 'There's something instinctually melodic, even though she doesn't give herself enough credit for what a great singer and what a melodic brain she has. Everything she said, I'd just go like 'googoo gaga', you know what I mean? It was right on the money. At the same time, she was kind of in the beginning stages too, so if I did ever say, 'Oh what about this instead?' She would have been like, 'All right.'

'When we were working on *Back to Black* though, there were much more tense moments, but I learned so much from Amy because she doesn't suffer any bullshit either ... sometimes in a studio you'll play an idea for a singer, you'll have an idea for a track and you'll go, 'Do you like this?' And it's such this game of diplomacy and everyone's so afraid to hurt each other's feelings they go, 'Oh well er, not crazy about it.' And then you go, 'What if I change this?' And then you change this and all you do is end up spending half an hour making something that no one really liked in the first place. Whereas Amy, as soon as she heard something she didn't like she goes, 'No, I don't like it.' And I go, 'Well, what if I change like that?' She goes, 'No I'm not gonna like it, it's not gonna make a difference if you change that thing, it's shit.' As much as it hurts a tiny bit at the beginning, it saves so much fucking time.'

It's nice to hear that Mark has been shaped in the studio somewhat by two powerful ladies - justifiably or not, there is a bit of a naughty rich boy vibe about him, but there's also an obvious desire to be a decent guy. A swarthy man sticks his head in at this point and says, 'Long interview, man!' It's like someone has rung the bell, Mark and I both realising we've been chatting for a long while and we've both got tours to continue on with. He wraps it up explaining his perception of perhaps why people come to him for production.

'I don't think there's a sonic reason, because it varies from record to record and I remember around the time that *Version* (Mark's second album) was at its peak, I would see things described as a sort of 'The Mark Ronson Sound' in quotes, and that's when you wanna fucking change it up pretty quickly, cause means that there's something about your sound that's predictable. I think the thing that you just want to do is make records that sound somewhat timeless and I'm not saying that I've achieved that, but whether I'm working with Duran Duran or Black Lips or Ghostface, whether it's a hip-hop record, a garage punk record, you know a synth pop record, you want to hear it in fifteen years and feel it hasn't dated. And I think that that's what I think I try to do the most.'

Shaking hands and saying adieu, I grab one last piece of chocolate cake off the catering table, imagining as I do the dynamic between Mark Ronson and the formidable force of Amy Winehouse, with no sense that in just four months times, Amy Winehouse will be found dead from alcohol intoxication. The news transforming *Rehab* from a catchy single about rock n roll rebellion into an up-tempo eulogy of a young woman as at risk, as her family had painfully perceived; a soulful ditty morphed into a song of sorrowful 'what ifs'. I slide my way through the fluoro sea, with me Soundwave wingman Ben Steele in tow, we maxi van it safely back to our familiar ocean of black.

13

Steve Albini: Sleep Before Money

The following night as I sit in my makeshift office at the Claremont Showgrounds in Perth, the exhaustion washes over me. The final show of the national *Soundwave* tour 2011 is coming to an end outside these four little walls. Only those who have worked this particular festival know what that means physically and psychologically. This tour intensity over the years transformed the *Soundwave* crew from colleagues to family; there's an enormous amount of looking out for each other, which often includes much drinking when the job is done, paralleled only by the level of ranting about the level of job done. Sitting in this donga, with only a few final tasks to go to wrap this tour up and before the final party of the tour begins, I start thinking about the chat I'd just had with Ronson yesterday, and it dawns on me that it has been almost six years precisely since I'd spoken with my very first producer. So much has happened between then and now, so many interviews, so many tours, so many albums listened to, so many personal challenges and so many tales told.

Through it all, the rich bounty of high-calibre chats, it's Steve Albini - the very first producer I ever spoke with - who remains up there as one of the most straightforward and unique people I've ever spoken with. And although I didn't have the privilege with that first series to travel to Chicago to meet him face to face as I've done with others these past few years, the chat was so poignant it really was the propulsion that got me to where I sit with the series today. To every interview that came after, every kilometre travelled, every moment away from my babies. Steve Albini revealed the story-gold that producers and producers alone, guard. Perspectives on artists and albums unique as invested, intimately involved but slightly detached third parties, looking at it all from an elevated perch with a clearer, less emotionally obstructed view of the whole.

One of the reasons that Albini is so famous and why he took that spot as the first Producer Series participant, is because he has an easily defined approach - something you may have realised by now is very rare in the oh-so-tangible realm of attempting to define production. He also has some very unique philosophies, the kind that haven't made him rich but allow him, as he put it 'to sleep at night.' Albini could've been one of the richest producers around having worked with The Breeders, The Pixies, Nirvana, Urge Overkill, Mark of Cain, Jon Spencer Blues Explosion, McClusky, Joanna Newsom, Joan of Arse (I have no idea who they are but what a name!), Iggy and The Stooges and on and on the list goes, into the *hundreds*. As a musician himself, Albini has also released countless records in bands Big Black, Rapeman and Shellac.

It was 10pm Chicago time when I called him all those years ago and he'd just finished up for the day. When he's not being interrogated by the likes of me, he said he grabs just a little bit of relax time before bed, and then gets back in the studio in the AM to do what he's done for thirty years - make music.

Albini's foray into production began where it often must for many a self-supporting muso - necessity. 'All the bands that I was in from a teenager on, whenever we wanted to make a recording, we would do it ourselves.' He explained. 'Once you've done it a few times you have a facility for it and then you, just by default, end up being the guy that records your band. Then when your friends need somebody to record them, you end up recording their bands as well. It was just an extension or parallel to being in a band; figuring out how to make a recording of that band and making myself available to other bands to do the same thing.'

In 1987, after Albini had saved a little bit of cash and had enough recording work booked in to last him about three months, he quit his day job and embarked on a full time life in the studio. Still, Steve keeps himself booked out about three to four months ahead. Astonishingly, he admits that about once a year something will blow out causing enough of a hole to actually threaten the existence of the studio. I was shocked to hear that this man with the mad skills and the metre-long list of production credits written in twelve-point font, battles along like the rest of us.

'There's two ways to go about it,' he explained of his monetary stance. 'You can either make one record a year and charge a fortune for it and subsist that way, or you can make fifty or a hundred records a year and don't charge very much for them, and I'm more happy working than I am sitting on my ass, so I generally try to find myself busy.'

It's not just the work ethic, it's the ideology that's kept Steve mingling with those in the trenches. 'I do prefer working with bands that are on the same mental plane as I am, bands that think of things in a realistic perspective. I do prefer working with younger bands and bands that are independent-minded, but having said that, I don't actually get approached by that many famous people. It's very rare, actually, that a famous person will call me and ask me to work on his record. I think there's a hierarchy of famous producers and engineers and those famous people tend to work with other famous people. I don't qualify as famous, I'm considered more of a working-class engineer, so working class bands are the bands that call me. And I'm happy with that, because they think like I do and we communicate easily and we all have similar life experiences.'

At the point where I was at, back then, when I spoke with Albini, I didn't have a large map of producer stories in front of me like I do now, to formulate any authentic opinions or accumulate stats, but I do remember having the theory that most producers must be failed musicians forced into another direction to make some coin. Albini did fit into that category, somewhat, but with the midline success of his bands, particularly Shellac, without all the studio overheads he may well have been in the same financial position with or without his producer trade.

I've learned over the years that there are many producers - like Nick Launay and Rick Rubin for instance - who have gotten along as producers just fine without being musicians themselves, but for Steve Albini, he considers it one of his most necessary attributes.

'Oh yeah, I don't think I could do it otherwise. I think part of the reason that I've been able to stay in business so long is that I'm sympathetic to the way the bands function as a social entity. And the reason that I'm sympathetic to that is that I've been in bands my whole life. I'm in a band now, and I know the sorts of interactions that band members have with each other and with the outside world. And because I understand that, and it's familiar to me, I can communicate effectively and I can avoid causing problems for them. Similarly, because I've worked on my own music, I understand how important certain aspects of it are to people and how you can feel completely exposed when you're making a record for other people to listen to, and I try to remain sympathetic and sensitive to that sort of thing. Whereas, if I was an engineer that had no musical background or experience of being in a band, I might not grasp any of those subtleties, it might just be all about making killer tones or whatever.'

This was one of the first comments made to me that started my brain ticking about the complexity of the producer role and the intensity of the creative process. Inside those studio walls was a big bang - the creation of something out of nothing but the thin air of ideas and the use of incredible inventions able to make the sound of those ideas and then capture them for near eternity. An incredible process as it is, but even more so when there is more than one deity, one that may be saying, 'Let there be light,' and another saying, 'No. Let there be fish.' For this reason, Steve does his best to be nothing more than a facilitator.

'The number one biggest mistake that anybody that's not in the band can make is telling the band they're wrong about their own music. If the band wants to have a five-minute-long guitar solo in the middle of the song and the producer or manager or whoever is telling them that that's a mistake, whoever that person that's not in the band is, should completely shut the hell up. I feel like being in a band is such a rare and perfect thing, that the band should be allowed to conduct its affairs the way it wants to, and everybody else should follow their lead. And the biggest mistake that I see other people making is trying to tell the band what to do with their music. The band made it up out of whole cloth, it's theirs, it's nobody else's, everybody else should just shut up and stay out of the way.'

Whilst statements like these would have the fists of musos punching the air in agreement, it probably goes a long way in also explaining why 'famous' people - or rather, the people who look after famous people - avoid Albini like a rattlesnake. His complete lack of 'hit single' focus would unnerve any record exec who looks at music as naught more than a gyrating money machine. Imagine my shock those years later, when I sat in that booth with Beinhorn, hearing the tale of him *firing* Anthony Keidis - another enormously pivotal moment for me personally in realising the breadth of what it meant to produce someone's record. No record label is going to hope that when they send Courtney Love in to make a new album that the producer turns around and says, 'You do what *you* want honey, let those creative substances flow.' But perhaps for someone with such a large profile, being dictated to prevents a floundering in false ideas of one's own grandeur, whereas for Albini, who prefers to work with those at the beginning of their careers, a boost of confidence is exactly what is required.

One of the consistent questions I have enjoyed asking producers over the years is 'What's the first question you ask musicians interested in working with you?' The tradition of this question, which has spawned so many diverse answers over these past 6 years, is because of the straightforward response of Albini.

'How many minutes of music are we trying to record?' he responded before laughing for the first time - a subtle, sincere chuckle that reinforces that what you see (and hear) is what you get. I could tell by that breathy sound of humour that if you were to tell Albini a joke, you'd want it to be funny because he ain't about to laugh politely to fill the awkward moment.

He continued in earnest to explain the joke that turns out wasn't a joke at all. 'Depending on how much time they have in the studio will dictate a lot of other things. And then I grill them about what their production aspirations are: are there going to be extra musicians, do they want to have really complex orchestration, do they want to have real simple presentation, is it supposed to be stylised, what are some of their favourite records, what kind of sound do they imagine for their songs, are there some songs that they want to sound big and some that they want to sound tight? Just go through the list of conceptual decisions or aesthetic decisions that they would have made and that way I find out what they want and I can adapt the techniques and the studio session to facilitate their expectations.'

In getting a clear picture, Albini said he's more than happy to speak in the vocabulary of rock fans, using examples they may like such as 'Led Zeppelin bass drum and Killing Joke guitar sound.' I found this latter an intriguing example and took it as a sign to move onto Steve's work with Nirvana. The segue in my mind being that Killing Joke (claimed to have) filed a lawsuit against Nirvana for ripping the guitar riff to *Come As You Are* straight from their track *Eighties*.

It wasn't *Nevermind* though, that Albini worked on (that

being the crowning moment of Butch Vig's career) but *In Utero*, the third and final studio album from Nirvana - a record that the band deliberately wanted to shift them away from the polished sounds of its thirty million-copy-selling predecessor.

The most astute step to achieving that? Go from a dapper gent who rarely leaves the house without a suit, even to sit in the somewhat solitary confines of the production desk, to Steve Albini - achieving in one fell swoop the rawness Nirvana were after as well the one contradictory moment of Albini's career where the famous people *did* come knocking. 'That was a very straightforward session actually,' Albini said, unsurprisingly untheatrically. 'Not significantly different from any of the other records that I'd been doing up until that point.'

I distinctly remember internally sighing at this point... where's the drama? The drug use, the *emotion?!* I remember thinking, 'This is Nirvana we're talking about!' A band whose frontman proved too fragile for this brutal world when he took his own life in 1994. Surely there was masses of substance use? Mental delirium? Theatrics?! It was another good lesson for me, that things - particularly in the world of music - are not always what they seem. But perhaps that even if the in-studio antics were of Mötley Crüe proportions, Steve Albini would retell them in such a way that one was left with the impression that all was very much in order. Albini spoke in exactly the same tone about the biggest band in the world as he did about every other band - Albini's picture would not be out of place in the Oxford dictionary next to the word 'egalitarian'.

'The band set up and played live,' he continued in regards to Nirvana, as if he were talking about what he had on his toast that morning. 'There may have been the occasional overdub on a couple of the songs, but everything was basically recorded live, the singing was done remarkably quickly, the singing wasn't done live with the band but the singing was done…' he paused slightly rearranging his thoughts. 'Kurt basically sat down one evening and sang the whole record. That was pretty impressive to me. He had it paced out so that he wasn't gonna strain himself, he sang the easy songs first and the hard one last, that kind of thing.'

Possibly another reason why Nirvana came to choose Albini was that while the world spun on its head off the back of *Nevermind*, Albini remained indifferent. 'I have to admit I wasn't really a fan of Nirvana before I started working on that record but,' he continued in the same steady tone, 'I developed a respect for them and the way they worked as a band and I developed considerable respect for Kurt as a songwriter and as an intellect…as a thinker. I think he thought about music in an abstract and sincere way and he tried to embody that in his band. I developed quite a respect for that band while we were working on that record. And I'm sure that I never would have had that kind of perspective on them just from listening to their music, which up until that point really didn't mean anything to me.'

When I tried to discuss the mark he may have made on the record, he swerved wide from the suggestion. It's ironic in the case of Albini really because his 'anti-production' as it were and the desire to wholeheartedly just 'capture' the organic nature of what is happening, has probably led to a more distinctive signature sound than for many other producers less shy of leaving an imprint, but more elastic in their approach. His position on it all almost painfully humble.

'Well, to be honest I don't think that I'm responsible for ... the good records that I've worked on, I don't think me working on them has actually been a definitive factor in why they were good. I feel like I get away with murder in that respect. I had the good fortune to be there when The Jesus Lizard made some amazing records and the same with PJ Harvey and The Breeders. They were making records that were really remarkable. So, I get a lot of credit that I don't really deserve. I do feel like my working methods and my techniques are conducive to a band. If a band is capable of really knocking it out of the park, then the way I normally do things doesn't interfere with that. If a band is really firing on all cylinders and they're playing well as a band, I feel like the way I go about recording them is probably going to be the most sympathetic way. So, in that regard I guess maybe I can be pleased that I didn't cause any trouble.'

And here he serves up one of his famously unexpected but on-point analogies. 'But it's sort of like cooking a fish, if you don't do anything stupid to the fish it comes out fine. It's only when you start trying to really get fancy with the fish that you end up destroying it.'

The way that Albini approaches production in order not to mess things up - which is also the thing that has made him famous (regardless of his belief that he is not) - is that he encourages bands to record live. The band sets up and they play. They play exactly how they are as band, they sound as they are as a band, leaving Albini's role simply to encourage and then capture the best performance.

'There are about a hundred reasons why it's a good idea to record the band all playing at the same time.' He explained. 'The majority of the time it's very good for the budget, because it takes much less time to get one solid performance from three guys than it does to piece together three individual solid performances superimposed on each other and try to create a simulacrum of an ensemble sound.'

Another reason he said that recording live is a good idea is that 'it sounds normal'. He explained that if you're recording the band separately, one player at a time and piecing it all together, not only do you get a fabricated version of the band, but you can also be a long way into the process before discovering there's a fundamental problem you missed right at the beginning. The only 'problem' as such with Albini's technique - is that if your band is no good, there ain't nothin' to hide behind.

'Some bands have an expectation of their record that isn't

really substantiated by their abilities,' he stated with stone-cold reality. 'They go into a studio and expect that something magic will happen and make the record better than they are. Given enough time and enough money, you can fake it to a large degree, you can make a band sound like they are more competent than they are. But mercifully I don't work with that many millionaires. And the ones that I occasionally do work with generally have higher standards than that. You do run into situations where a band is not playing well but they still expect their record to come out well, and it requires more work, but I've never had to send anybody home without a record.'

As well as being renowned for his live recording approach, Albini has quite the reputation for his thoughts on the music industry. His views are socialist in the sense that he attempts to regard all humans (or more specifically muso-sapiens) as equally deserving of respect, so much so that within that respect he believes in a band's right to make the decisions that best suit them, even if that concludes that the record company beast is the way to go.

'My position with regard to major labels is they are ruthless businesses, and there are some things that a ruthless business can offer that nothing else can offer you. So, if it's important for you to behave in a manner that can only be satisfied by the ruthless entertainment industry, then you really have no choice. You have to deal with the big, mainstream, show business record labels. If your main concern is just keeping your band's head above water and providing yourself an outlet for music and means of distribution, of an international presence that would allow you to do touring, well you can do that on a shoestring now. You really don't need any kind of a record label at all. But if you do get involved with a record label, my only advice is to understand that the record label is not doing it for your benefit. If you walk into a relationship like that with open eyes and say, 'All right, well they're fixin' to take advantage of us, but in the process we'll get to have a couple of crazy experiences that we couldn't have otherwise and that's ok with me.' Well then, I really can't criticise that kind of decision.'

Even via the phone I could hear the sound of Albini's thought engine winding up a gear, he's taken a turn off the picturesque sanctuary of production lane and headed out onto the chaotic highway of the music industry metropolis, where shiny skyscrapers gleam with promise, but on every corner lurks a robbed musician hustling their creative ideas for a blow job and a dime.

'I never fault the bands for making a decision with regard to their own best interests,' he continued. 'But in a lot of cases their best interests are actually hidden from them, because there are a lot of secondary and tertiary people who can make a living in the music business without ever playing a note, those people have, as part of their vested interest, making sure that bands don't understand where their best interests lie. A booking agent will want a band to play a bajillion shows because he gets a percentage of every one of them. Now, a large percentage of those shows might be meaningless, they might be playing to an audience that isn't receptive whatsoever, and the travel time to get to the gig and the gas money and hotel and food might eat up whatever profit would be generated from the gig, so there's literally no reason for the band to play such a gig whatsoever. But the booking agent gets his percentage out of it so there's a reason for the booking agent to ask the band to play that gig. That's the kind of decision that I'm talking about. It's not the case that every band needs a team of professionals working on their behalf. Those professionals are doing it because it's in their best interest, not because it's in the band's best interest.'

I couldn't help but wonder though, how willing Mr Albini is to put his money where his mouth is. How truly different he is from many others who are willing to take the sickle to capitalism in theory but potentially not in practice?

'Well that's pretty simple,' he summated without hesitation. 'You just don't charge too much. If you price your services according to your clientele and your own needs rather than trying to maximise your income, well then, you're behaving honourably. If you're just trying to squeeze every last nickel that you can get out of everybody then you're trying to take advantage of people and I don't see that as a particularly honourable way of earning a living.'

'Do you think there's ever going to be moments where you think about the maths and you regret the amount of dollars that you've turned your back on?' I asked.

'My girlfriend regrets the amount of money that I've turned down,' he said. 'I don't. I sleep pretty well knowing that I haven't been a part of this system of exploitation, of constantly bleeding the band until they're pale and then patching them up just long enough to get their red blood cell count back up again. I'm not a part of that. And I feel good about not being a part of that. And I know that every dollar that I don't take from a band is another dollar that they get to keep themselves, and I feel pretty good knowing that other bands that I'm sympathetic with have their lives a little bit easier because I haven't tried to screw them.'

Albini Wisdom

Discourages the use of a metronome. 'If you go see a band play live, there are exciting parts and there are mellow parts and there are moments of anticipation and that sort of thing. So, there's quite a bit of elasticity in the timing of any good performance. And when you take that into the studio and iron that out so it completely disappears, well it's no mystery then that the performances sound less exciting, because one whole aspect of the performance dynamic has been removed, the elasticity of the time.

Forces himself out of the box. 'I try to do something new on every session, on every session that I do I try to do at least one thing that I've never done before, if only just to force myself to think of something that will prevent me from being completely hide bound in my tastes; even if it's just one stupid thing, like one microphone that I've never used before in that application.'

Believes a layman *can* tell the difference between

analogue and digital. 'Digital systems were invented to manipulate sound. And so, as a natural function of their implementation in recording, sound get manipulated a lot more than it does using analogue techniques. And I think the cumulative effect of a million of these little manipulations is discernible to just about anybody. In the same way that when you're in a movie theatre you can tell when you get to that CGI moment where there's an impossible crane shot or a physically impossible space alien just walks in, something like that; they're kind of jarring moments where you're suddenly aware that what you're looking at or what you're listening to is not a real event.'

14

Steve Albini: The Pixies, The Breeders and a Fletcher

Along with Nirvana, another of the big 'nineties' bands that Albini worked with were Pixies, taking on production duties for their first album that came out in 1988, *Surfer Rosa*. In fact, it was the recording and the song writing on this record that led Kurt Cobain to Albini five years later for *In Utero*. What's most interesting about this record is that the mere mention of Albini's name in a Pixies chat room is enough to send a forum into frenzy. Albini, not one to shy away from his own plain and simple truths, made it rather known that he didn't think Pixies were too much chop. He's since apologised for some of the more powerful remarks but his feelings remain the same.

'I have to admit, the Pixies as a band never really meant much to me. I know that they mean a lot to a lot of other people and I can only be happy that other people get something out of it, but their music never really meant anything to me. I felt like they were sincere and nice enough people and I was glad I got to work on their record and I felt like I did a good job. But their music didn't really resonate with me in any of the ways that my favourite bands do,' he said matter-of-factly, before continuing a little deeper. 'As a very simple comparison, Kim Deal who was in the Pixies, was also in a band called The Breeders. She started The Breeders, and I feel like The Breeders' music is orders of magnitude more interesting and more unusual and, I don't know, more charismatic than the Pixies music. So, given my druthers, if the Pixies didn't exist maybe The Breeders would never have had a chance to make a record. So ,we owe the Pixies that at least. But I feel like The Breeders are twice the band that the Pixies were.'

In contrast to his thoughts on Pixies, Albini praises the joyously clever Welsh outfit, McClusky, whom he worked with on the recording of their second album *McClusky Do Dallas* and the fabulously titled follow-up *The Difference Between Me and You Is That I'm Not On Fire*.

'Oh yeah, what a terrific band. A really, really fantastic band, great people, super funny.'

'From a musical perspective McClusky had (they broke up in 2005) an energy about them that was strangely both in-your-face and deadpan. They were intellects as well as delinquents and it made for quite the rapturous combination.'

Albini's job was to capture all of this and one of the techniques he did employ was simply where he placed the vocals in the mix.

'Andy had a real stentorian delivery and John had a more ironic delivery and it seemed like if the vocals weren't thrust at you then you wouldn't feel the intensity of their personalities,' he said. 'There was a kind of crazy energy to McClusky that sometimes obscures the content of the music; you can exaggerate the hyperbolic sonic elements of a band to emphasise the craziness and in the process of doing that you lose a lot of the content. In some cases, that's actually a good thing because there's not much content there to deal with, there's more of an intensity and an attitude than there is actual music and text, but for them, the music and text was also quite important. So, I guess the idea was to have a really supercharged sound, a really exciting, really electric sound but not to interfere with the fact that the music was also quite innovative and the subject matter was also pretty funny.'

Albini went on to admit that he was quite surprised when they broke up a year later from his time with them in studio - not because they didn't have their tensions but because they'd already experienced tensions and remained together. This led us to talk about the concept that studio time can exacerbate pre-existing cracks in a band's internal functions.

'I think that whole mythology of this studio psychosis, that's all quite exaggerated from my experience. I've found that if the band is functioning normally and if they're comfortable, making a record doesn't have to be any more arduous than making a dinner date.'

He reckoned that maybe only once or twice a year did he ever witness those awkward moments of artistic stand-offs that turn personal and when they happen, does he play referee?

'Oh no, hell no. I'm not in the band.'

'What if they asked you though? To be part of that vote?' I pushed.

'Well, anybody can have an opinion; you can grab some dude off the street and ask them. Somebody walking through the room could have an opinion. I don't necessarily think uneducated opinions like that really matter very much. It's kind of a truism that people who aren't in bands say, 'Well, maybe you're too close to it, maybe you should get an outside perspective?' Screw that! Outside? Why do you want an outside perspective? The only perspective that matters is the perspective of the people who are in the band, who have to carry that record around for the rest of their lives and say, 'Yeah this is our record.' I'm not a proponent of the outside perspective at all, I think the outside perspective is an uneducated pointless one. Screw the outside perspective!'

The last album I remember touching base with Albini on was Joanna Newsom's *Y's* from 2006. It's yet another of many records that Albini is listed as engineer on, not producer, himself shying away from the term in general, preferring instead the more modest hands-on title of Audio Engineer. He described his role on that album as 'a really straightforward one; I recorded Joanna singing and playing her harp and that was it. And I gotta say, she *tore ass on that thing*.'

This last sentence came with possibly the most amount of emotional elevation I'd yet heard from him and it really made me sit up and pay attention.

'She's one of the best musicians I've ever worked with,' he continued passionately. 'It's a really unwieldy instrument, really difficult to control and she has that thing *down*; it was a joy working on that record. I think she's a terrific player, she sings like an angel - everything about it was great.'

And although Albini had recorded a harp previously, it had only ever been as an accompaniment never the centrepiece, so he tried a few things a little differently to give it the sonic spotlight it deserved.

'There's a classic technique for recording an acoustic instrument, which is to have a microphone some distance away at about mid-height on the instrument. And so, I did that but I also know that she has a tendency to play in a non-traditional style, a lot of her music is not in harp idiom, it's more like a piano idiom. So I wanted to get more detail out of the notes, so I put microphones right next to the strings along the length of the harp, I put four microphones right next to the strings so that there'd be a more direct plucking sound, and then balancing those with the ambient microphone and microphone that was more classic technique, that all worked out quite well, I was pleased at the way the harp came out.'

And so were many others. *Y's* received vast critical

acclaim, with the raw, organic nature of Albini's part in capturing the harp being lauded as a key component to the depth achieved in that album, alongside the otherwise heavily orchestral arrangements.

As we wrapped up our hour-long conversation, I couldn't help but ask if even this frank, lay-it-bare man has had his zany recording moment; an idiosyncratic decision where sound was achieved through some strange and unexpected process?

'There was a thing I did for a Jesus Lizard record,' he began slowly. 'David Yow, the vocalist, wanted at one point in the song to sound like he had just walked into a big empty room and then also a very claustrophobic-my-head-is-in-a-bucket-sound. And so, what we did was we physically mounted a microphone to his head and in the part where he was supposed to walk into the big room he walked into a big ambient room and then for the part where he was supposed to sound like his head was in a bucket we stuck his head in a bucket. It worked pretty well. I have to admit that was a nice little engineering decision there.'

I couldn't tell if he was being sarcastic or not. Suddenly the door to my office at the Claremont Showground opened, heaving me from my deep reminisce. It was Byron from Pennywise making little sense; highly agitated. What I gathered is that the band's guitarist, Fletcher, had just done something spectacular and Byron was not happy.

I walked over to Pennywise's dressing room and found a

couple of frightened-looking paramedics standing outside. In the doorway was big Fletcher, covered in blood from head to toe, with a nasty gash from nipple to navel, arms outspread, looking for a bear hug. As his band mates relate the details of Fletcher's decision to glass himself with joy, so overcome with delight and excitement at watching LA band The Bronx perform, he thought they might appreciate a blood sacrifice!

The after-party for Fletcher turned into a trip to the ER and my reflections of Albini vaporised in the surrealism of yet another rock and roll tale that required, for the moment, my full attention.

15

Scott Horscroft: In the Halls and the Corridors

Mr Horscroft greets me in a black suit. The kind most only get out for funerals or organised crime. He wears it so comfortably it may as well be a chenille tracksuit. His white shirt is unbuttoned loosely around the neck and it's not so much tucked in as it is accidentally falling behind his belt. He's got an edge that keeps him planted on the right side of dignified, but a gentle breeze could very well teeter him over into the precipice of the dishevelled.

At 10.30 am on a cold grey street in Sydney's inner city, standing out front of Big Jesus Burger studios, Scott Horscroft - hair slicked back, tortoiseshell shades on - looks like he's either in a film clip or seeing the morning from the side of a very late night. This place he stands in front of has fast become iconic, Scott Horscroft along with it.

The road that led me to this one, in the ghetto-chic suburb of Surry Hills, actually started on the other side of the world.

I'd gone to Barcelona to stalk My Bloody Valentine, in an attempt to get their voices on the Alan Moulder episode. By sheer luck of knowing some very great people connected to other really great people, I ended up in a beautiful Spanish apartment right in the heart of the Gothic Quarter, with Wally Kempton from The Meanies; Darren Hawthorne, the notoriously furious national tour manager for Soundwave; Dave Benj, co-owner of Speak n Spell Records, and his lovely lass Tanya Horo from Sherlock's Daughter. Even though my reason was slightly more specific than the others, we were all there for one purpose, well two really; Primavera Festival and a good time.

During the five days that I had there, we all spent a fair bit of time together as a group: waking up at eleven, going for Spanish omelettes and sangria, meandering down the beach getting gelatos and then heading into the festival. Day in, day out. There were many moments of conversation, hilarity and synchronicity. On one particular evening, Andy, the gent who owned the apartment, arrived from Melbourne and took us all to the oldest restaurant in Barcelona - Can Culleretes, the second oldest in all of Spain. The place is amazing - opening in 1786, generations of famous folk have dined there, many of whom took the time to scribble on the walls. At one point, I turned to talk to a friend, Ben, who was sitting at the table behind me, noticing the lovely doodle next to his head, signed - Mr Picasso. I am digressing further from my point but before

I pull back, I have to tell you that to this day I've still put nothing in my mouth as good as the plate of peas I feasted on that evening - yes, peas.

Joining us that evening was Simon, a friend of Ben's (Ben lives in Barcelona in Andy's apartment - so each year at Primavera time he gets invaded by riff-raff like us). Simon was a music producer and had his own studio set-up in the heart of the gothic district in Barcelona. We got talking about all things production when Mr Dave Benj sidled up out of nowhere and starting talking about Scott Horscroft. Turns out that Speak n Spell records were just about to take on the management of Australian record producer Horscroft, after they were blown away by his production/mixing credits on all kinds of albums that aligned with the Speak n Spell flavour: The Presets, The Panics, Sleepy Jackson, The Scare, Yves Klein Blue, Brous, Silverchair and on and on and on.

The arrangement wasn't official yet, but well and truly intrigued, I grabbed Dave's details and those of his colleague David Shrimpton, who I had had dealings with at triple j and knew I'd probably have a better bet at tracking down back in Australia, and I slotted Horscroft into the space in my mind reserved for The Producer Series. Oh, and by the way, my attempt to snag My Bloody Valentine failed.

The only guidelines I really had when plotting out a new season of The Producer series is that I cover a span of genres, techniques, nationalities and that there'll be at least one

Australian and as many women as possible (this last proving nigh on impossible after completing the first two seasons). The rest is left up to fate and synchronicity. So, when ten days later I bumped into Dave's colleague David from Speak n Spell at the Tate in London, despite David coming from Sydney, the synchronicity was signed pretty clearly about Horscroft's inclusion. David remarked immediately that they'd just picked up management of him and I thought, 'Well, that's that then.' I didn't even really know anything about him at all at that stage, but I did know that his presence in this next series could not be ignored.

So, here we are. Back in Surry Hills with Scott shaking my hand and taking me up a steep, narrow flight of stairs. Straight into the mixing room we go, with its massive Neve console in the centre, and the tour begins. He points to his left, to an area where bands sit, rest, put their heads in their hands, weep and generally do the things that artists do when painstakingly mixing all the thousands of tiny components that make up one cohesive, beautiful, singular song. The Mess Hall had been in the night before, and by the looks of all the fast food wrappers over the ground, they are by nature as they are by name.

'Okay, should we start from the beginning?' Scott asks, plotting out our path for the morning. 'Right then, let's go next door. We'll start there, 'cause that was the first studio that we ever had here at BJB back ten years ago. So, let's go through these doors. So, here we are walking into the quad eight room at BJB, which was originally set up ten years ago by Chris, it was a lot smaller in those days and had this great old 1977 quad eight mixing board which has kind of become the back bone of BJBs sound. I think he did a lot of stuff with Australian eighties punk band Celibate Rifles and a lot of more avant-garde stuff, a lot more experimental bands, and then Portishead came into town and rented the studio for a long time and just did a lot of sampling and so on. That really gave the studio a kickstart in terms of developing from being Chris' home studio into being more of a professional place.'

BJB aka Big Jesus Burger, has become renowned for producing off-kilter records that have something a little different to offer, as well as for the thick, warm sounds that can only be genuinely achieved through the big ol' desks like the one in this quad eight room, which all sound runs through to get to its end result.

With its high ceilings and walls put up here and there to create a multitude of different spaces, the place has a New York warehouse atmosphere about it. It's kind of ramshackle, like a small universe of creativity, where the entire process of developing an idea from its very inception may occur, as opposed to a space with a specific, focused purpose - a place where artists simply come to turn their well-formed arrangements into polished, sellable tunes as quickly and efficiently as possible.

Scott reads my mind. 'The big positive thing about BJB is

that it's not a corporate studio, it's a place that's run by two musician-producers who love the idea of creativity and allowing musicians to run a-creative-mok here and do whatever they want, and still have really amazing equipment to record on. So it's that great juxtaposition between better gear than a corporate studio, and more (a) vintage, unique variety of gear, and the ability to really make the place your home and spread out and make a mess. But also, it's become such a hub. We've got this great kitchen, and throughout a day you'll see ten people from the music industry just pop in, just come to say hello to Sam the manager or me or Chris, so it's just got this developing vibe where a lot of the younger musicians who come in here want to be in the kitchen, just to see who they'll see spending the day here, which is a really great thing. Just to know that people keep us in their mind when they're thinking, 'What should I do when I'm in Surry Hills?"

From the quad eight room, we enter the live room it's attached to. This is one of the rooms where the real magic happens, where the true test of a great producer comes into play. How well can they capture performance? If they're not ready, don't have the room set-up right, can't get the artist in the right headspace, no amount of tweaking later is going to make up for the shortfall.

This room is like the lab in Get Smart, where Max would go and pick up all those kitschy gadgets meant for spy-type combat and comedy. There are suspicious looking bits and pieces everywhere. Dangling precariously from the ceiling is a large timber board, clearly a giant acme-bad-guy-squisher, until I notice there's no X painted on the floor and a distinct lack of pesky Russians. Scott, however, believes it to be a 'sound reflector'. Apparently, you bring it up and down to close off the room size, so you can have smaller, more intimate acoustics, or be big reflective and hall-like instead (likely story, Mr Horscroft, if that even *is* your real name).

There are what look to be stainless steel colanders hanging beneath every light globe. Radar dishes, circa 1977 perhaps? (For American spies, of course, who may want to steal the BJB secrets!)

'Well they're, umm, colanders.' Says Scott, upon inquisition. 'We put them up there because it makes little sparkles come out of the lights. Again, makeshift home jobs, it looks really fantastic at night - BJB really comes to life at night, which is mainly when it's used.'

Dissolving my eighties pop cultural imaginings of this place as a secret spy den of slapstick, I envisage instead the range of characters and outfits that must spend their time here, with little care for night or day.

'Yeah, you can smell it. Can't you?' Scott says, making me suddenly aware of how delightfully Old Spice and anxiety work together.

It's worth mentioning too, that, quite uniquely, there are skylights in this room - a fantastic anomaly for a recording room, which are nearly always dark little caves where musos can stay holed up for weeks. Not only does this lovely touch of sunshine prevent vitamin D-depleted musos from getting scurvy, it also serves to highlight four large paintings that appear to be the canvassed embodiment of someone's fragile emotional state, hanging on the far wall. They are heavily weighted with paint, colour and collage. Scott tells me they were done by Luke Steele of Australian band's Sleepy Jackson and Empire of the Sun, during the making of the *Personality: One Was A Spider, One Was A Bird* record. 'They took him eight months to paint, because it took eight months to make that record. You can see how they changed over time, how thick the paint is. I think that's great because it's just like the record. There's so many layers of him thinking and his ideas coming out and I think some people go, 'God, look at them they're over the top,' and I go, 'Well, have you heard the record?"

As we start to wander into the second live recording room and I ponder the richness of that Sleepy Jackson record and the interest it received here in Australia, I ask Scott which albums he thinks are the ones that have been the biggest door-openers for BJB?

'Definitely initially it was *Beams* by The Presets, their first record. And then *Apocalypso* their second record, that's done a lot for opening up more of the electronic avenues for the studio. But I think definitely Sleepy Jackson's *Personality* was a massive one, because I think that big, open-room, psychedelic, fifties/sixties sound that he went for, is a big part of these rooms - that big, open sound and the vintage gear that we've got, he really took advantage of it all.'

As we push the heavy, soundproof doors open through to the second room, the first thing I notice is the mass of instruments everywhere. Pianos, organs and keyboards, amplifiers; new ones to old ones, there's Wurlitzers, Rhodes and most impressively a giant Hammond organ - a monster of a thing made to be a self-contained universe of sound.

'That's a big C4, I think they call it,' begins Scott with pride. 'I'm so terrible with names, but it's the big performance Hammond, it's got a big Leslie attached to it, so you can get all your tremolos and all the crazy bits, but it's really well looked after, we keep it serviced, but it's an old beast and it's extremely loud, so people really love getting on there and haunting the whole of BJB with it. It was made in the days when that was what you had on stage, so it's extremely loud but a gorgeous sound.'

He turns it on. I press one note and nearly wee a little. Wowsers.

Apart from the instruments, there's little bits and pieces all over the place – paintings and odd ornaments. A little miniature carousel that in this setting looks more eerie than quaint - like an empty swing set swinging all by itself.

'Chris and I are hoarders,' Scott admits. 'But I guess it's just over ten years we've been here and you see something around and you pick it up and somehow everything just tends to stay here. It's got a little bit better. I tell you, we used to have lots and lots of stuff hanging around, but as we've gotten more professional over the years and have things coming in that actually work, and are useful, rather than little kids carousels and funny looking weird sculptures and stuff, we've had to remove them.'

Scott says the word 'professional' as if he's just discovered it.

'The big thing,' he explains of his tingle of disdain, 'is that we're not a corporate studio, this has been built up and it really has been over the last six years that the studio has become a really hard working studio, whereas before it was me and Chris making our own music, doing a few bands here and there'

Scott explains his definition of corporate as being attached to and supported financially by an external subsidiary company.

'Building studios is very expensive,' he points out. 'Most studios are multimillion-dollar fitouts, and multimillion-dollar gear lists and stuff, and I suppose for us, just being more hands-on, we've just slowly built that up, but never had multi-million dollar backing to get it all going. And I think that's the feeling of BJB, is that everything's been hand-picked and everything's useful and everything has some type of esoteric value, not just to us but to everyone. So again, just that feeling of being able to do whatever you want, I think that's anti-corporate in itself really, isn't it?'

The smell of DIY ethic breathes thick from these walls, it's like a teenage boy's bedroom on a grand scale, but with no parents around to get in the way of a good time. And so the good times roll. Every Friday afternoon apparently, with BJB bubbling to life; working artists and friendly drop-ins gathering around the enormous kitchen table that Scott and I now stand before. We've strolled into the true heartspace of BJB; the giant, sunny kitchen where running right through the centre is the most impressive table ever to be seen outside a Viking feast. It's about five metres long, maybe six. As a small child, this would be the vast ship, the floor the wild waters and the Kermit-coloured walls the imaginings of jungle-covered islands filled with castaways and rapscallions. As a cooped-up recording artist and ever-faithful producer, this imagining is probably not far from mind either.

'It often gets called the catwalk,' says Scott drifting into my little sea-faring fantasy. I turn to look at him, he's really lit up. This is a room of good energy and even better memories, by the look on Mr Horscroft's face. 'There's a great sound system in here so people tend to get up on the table and dance and it's a really great space. Lots of room, vinyl floors for the hose out in the morning, it's really good fun.'

I stop myself from thinking too much about the 'hose out', pondering instead all the other studios I've been in around the country and around the world. Philippe Zdar's stunning, clean-lined space with its warm downlights and pale polished timber floors. Alan Moulder's industrial feeling stronghold surrounded by its big black metal fences. Harry Vanda's opulent fit out at the new Alberts with the biggest recording console I've ever seen and many others. There are none, though, quite like this. This is a place that invites you in, makes you feel like you want to be part of this secret little community hidden in the heart of Sydney city.

'What green would you call this, Chris?' Scott yells out to co-owner Chris Townend, who's standing at the sink washing up his well-worn looking coffee cup.

'Squashed Caterpillar green,' says Chris, clearly having spent a lot of time thinking about it.

'It goes with the vibe of the kitchen.' Scott shrugs in defence of the interior design, which is also laden with beautiful sailing pictures, abstract paintings and wacky little ornaments which Scott says, 'Just go with the open and experimental creative vibe of BJB.'

'Do these have a story?' I ask of the eclectic artworks nailed to the open belly of the squashed caterpillar.

'They've been collected over the years from all different places. There's this painting by Gabrielle, when he was a young, young boy, which is Chris' son, and a lot of these more experimental ones have just been picked up on my walk to and from the studio just from galleries around. I'm a mad sailor as well, so all the yachting and pirate-style stuff is mine. Which keeps me inspired.'

Turns out that Scott has spent a lot of time in the Whitsundays, sailing around in the emerald green seas, the wind becoming the product for his slicked back hair. I try to imagine him in a shirt of an orange, floral persuasion, white tailored shorts and deck shoes. The picture comes surprisingly easily and I see him differently now. I pull my attention back to the room in which we stand. 'So, who do you think have been some of the best catwalkers that you've seen on this table?'

'Well, Daniel Johns is very good on the old catwalk here.' (I can instantly imagine the seductive sway in the Silverchair frontman's tiny hips) 'I must say I do it pretty well,' Mr Horscroft admits with pride, 'and often inspire other people to do it too.' His true colours are unfolding like a rose.

'I see that there's still a bottle of booze on the table?' I say in that drawn-out questioning way mastered only by mothers and highway patrol.

'Well that's The Dirty Secrets',' Scott says, dobbing in the West Australian synth-loving rockers. 'They enjoy their rum, so they got through a bottle last night. For some people, it may sound horrifying, but it's really just an everyday thing that people are recording, then coming out into the kitchen where usually all twelve chairs are full with the different bands from the different places and people sharing stories of the industry.

So, Jet are in town this weekend to do their shows, so I'm sure they'll pop up and they don't mind a drink either. *But* this is definitely an after-hours thing, and the focus that the musicians have that we tend to get here, especially those I've been working with, are extremely focused when in the studio. But definitely just as focused when letting their hair down, when they're out of the studio.'

We head back down the corridor we started in, toward the very first room we went into. It's the most spacious place in the building, the big mixing room with a raised lounge area at one end and the giant Neve mixing board right in the centre. There are faders and buttons and fandangly things all over it - it could be the control hub of The Doctor's Tardis and as tech-advanced looking as a Dalek.

The Neve is a huge old beast spanning a couple of metres that must weigh as much as an inner-city hatchback. 'So, what's the story with this ol' girl?' I ask.

'Well this one's fifty channels, so you know, extremely large and it's got automation on all the faders, so it's got a great flying faders set up. I think for us, it was about the sound, and it's the earliest model of the larger style Neves, so it's got lots of versatility with mixing. But, it's also the oldest-sounding version of this type of board. For us, it was always about trying to maintain that vintage feel of BJB, but at the same time wanting a board that had all the bells and whistles with versatility and mixing. It's been great. You know, like any old board, (there's) lots of upkeep and continually trying to better the board. We've had new centre sections put in to fit our style of music and make it a bit more hi-fi for modern music and so on.

'But the great thing about this board,' says Scott as he starts laughing, 'is the story of getting it in here.' Turns out this mini-spaceship came all the way from Paris. After shipping it over here at great expense, Scott and Chris realised that there was no way in hell they were going to get it upstairs without some seriously creative thinking. Their first idea was to have the roof of the building removed - not a small idea, but they weren't dealing with a small thing. After looking into the scenario of peeling back BJB's lid and using a very large crane to get the Neve in over the top, they discovered that on top of the cost of the operation itself, the busy city location and all the surrounding power lines made for a crippling insurance situation. They realised that the only way it was getting inside, without the invention of molecular transference, was to take the whole thing apart, piece by piece. It was a painstaking and heavy operation, with an unexpected cost. Whilst the contents of the crate grew smaller each day, the crate sat out on the footpath, to the ire of the Sydney City Council. Clearly having no regulation for such a thing, they did what any puzzled reactionary council would do: they made this Neve the very first mixing board in known history to receive a parking ticket.

Apart from its criminal history, the Neve also has a sonic reputation that is the distinct thread in all the records made at BJB; from The Panics, to Brous, to Sleepy Jackson. It's a difficult thing to articulate but it's the beautiful warmth; instead of say a crisp, clean sound where you can hear the sharp edge of each sound, everything is just a little fuzzy and gentle around the edges. It's how things would sound if your ears had had a red wine or two. This is as much about the gear as it is the warm fuzzy producers. 'Who wish they were living in the fifties,' Scott adds.

As cosy as Scott's resulting sounds maybe, his background is a long way from warm and fuzzy - geographically at least - having chosen to study his craft in the Arctic regions of Finland and Russia.

'I did 3D sound, so was making experimental soundscapes and soundworks for 3D spaces and installing them in galleries and doing big multi-instrumental soundworks, and very much interested in the avant-garde. I was composing that music - and using Pro Tools in studios which definitely taught me how to use all the gear - 'cause I was using it in such an experimental way. It's often, if you're trying to find boundaries and push things and make things sound interesting, then I think you quickly learn more about what the equipment can do.'

He says his studies affected his ability to get sound out of an artist as well as a room, in the form of understanding the energy of a space and of a song. Scott specialises in immersing the artist in an environment that properly reflects the mood of the piece they are trying to perform, hence the colander lights, the emotion-laden paintings, the velvet drapes and the overall feel of this place.

In keeping that mood alive for the vocalist who's just about to go in and sing, or the guitarist who's about to set the tone of a story with the sound of their strings, Scott says that the secret is in the set-up; doing all the legwork before the band/artist comes in so they don't get bogged down in the machinations. Communication is also key; never letting the artist sit there wondering what to do or how they performed. Keeping dialogue moving so they can remain in exactly the space that they need to be with a song.

As we sit on the couch, feet dancing over the Mess Hall's leftovers, we chat about the intimate relationship between producer and artist: the unique insight that a producer has into someone's vulnerabilities under pressure, their personal hygiene and the bonds that are formed through it all.

'A lot of musicians are crazy people,' Scott says without judgement. 'They're eccentric. A lot of them have this massive ego, it's not easy to be around some musicians all the time. Unfortunately, or maybe fortunately I'm not sure, in this job it's usually getting in at ten, finishing at twelve to two o'clock in the morning, then going and having a debrief somewhere, some dinner at that time of the morning, a couple of drinks or what have you. You're living with these people. But again, for me a lot of my best friends are the bands and the musicians that I work with. I'm constantly hanging out with Paul Mac and Luke Steele and Daniel Johns and the guys from The Scare, they're all my best friends. That relationship of doing creative things together and creating these pieces of art that have come from everyone's soul and life and mind, bonds everyone together to become great friends.'

16

Francois Tetaz: Master of the Minutia

When I was in my late teens searching for self-identity, I read a book called *The Celestine Prophecy* by James Redfield. It was a book that shopped out spirituality in an easily accessible form, talking of quantum physics but for stoned adolescents, the overriding theme being there are no coincidences. One of the book's examples was of strangers who repeatedly cross paths, the suggestion being that this will keep happening until their purpose in each other's lives becomes actualised. Such was the case with Francois Tetaz, who zig-zagged his way through my life, until finally making his way to these pages.

The first time I became aware of him was in 2007 during a panel forum for up-and-coming songwriters entitled The Songwriter and The Producer, put together by The Australasian Performing Right Association (APRA). I was to facilitate the panel and Franc was to be one of the panellists. I knew nothing of Franc at the time, but after a bit of emailing back and forth during the lead-up to the forum, I learned that he was the Producer on Australian singer/songwriter Lior's 2005 *Autumn Flow* album, which was very big at the time on triple j.

I had just recently met Lior. He had swung by the triple j studios to record a cover song for a segment I'd started the year before, called Like A Version, where artists play a cover song significant in some way to their own musical journey, along with one of their own tracks. Lior chose Neil Young's *Needle and the Damage Done*, which perfectly epitomised the style of music that he was pursuing in his career at that time. Much in the same way as Young, Lior's gift was the ability to showcase his heart and talents unpretentiously, in a very natural and raw sounding setting. Again, much like Young, the simplicity in the sound was not accidental; its ease was deliberate; born from intellect and an exact clarity of how the sentiment within the music needed to be presented. Production-wise, the genius was in its invisibility, with the well thought out approach, lying just below the surface of a very 'unproduced' sounding recording. At the time I didn't know any of this. All I knew was that Lior made beautiful yet simple music and that Franc had hit record.

With only the knowledge of Franc's work on Lior's seemingly stripped-back record, the pieces of his musical background came as a surprise. Learning through my research for the APRA panel discussion that his history was based in cinematic soundtracks, having even picked himself up an ARIA award for his aural work on the pant-shittingly scary film *Wolf Creek*.

By the end of the workshop for The Songwriter and The Producer, I was so curious about Franc (whose sonic journey was a colourful pastiche of seemingly different musical directions) that I couldn't wait to hear his life story and discover how he could swing from warm olde-worlde sounds to a profound talent for penning complex cinematic arrangements. After the forum that evening, we all went out for dinner (where, out of pure curiosity and a rebellion of sorts from my own plant-based tendencies, I ate snails). Unfortunately, the escargot took up most of our discussion and stories of his life, his work and his character would have to wait. It was another three years before I would see Franc again. Which, to my knowledge, had nothing to do with the snails.

The next zig in our celestial intersections would take place in Melbourne. At the time, I was Music Editor for Sydney-based women's mag, *yen* and had recently begun writing a section called 'Lunch With…' where two interesting and established friends from different fields were interviewed together over lunch. Franc had recently finished recording an album for Aussie artist, Wally De Backer, whose publicist was a former triple j colleague, the captivating Claire Collins, who organised for Franc, Wally and myself to come together in

Melbourne at a café of their choosing. We spoke in length about the fascinating working relationship of such a creative pair and of the as-yet-unnamed record, under Wally's Gotye moniker, which they'd just recorded, that would go on to become one of the most successful in Australian history.

In August 2011, Gotye would release the album *Making Mirrors* and no-one - not Gotye, not his label nor Frank - could possibly have foreseen the altitude it would reach: number one in Australia, Greece and the US alternative charts, Gold in seven countries, Platinum in two countries, 2 x Platinum in Poland (after just one day of release) and 3 x Platinum in Australia. Also, in Australia it was awarded Album of the Year by triple j and in 2013 it won a Grammy for Best Alternative Album. Its lead single *Somebody That I Used To Know* has sold in excess of thirteen million copies across the globe.

On November 4th, 2010 with the recording of the album so fresh it was still yet to be named, Frank, Wally De Backer and myself met for a lunch date to discuss their working relationship.

Wally had at this stage in his career already enjoyed a large amount of success with his debut album *Like Drawing Blood,* which boasted the brilliant ditty *Heart's A Mess.* I had no idea what to expect of him, but I must confess to a fair amount of surprise when he rolled into sight, a shaggy-haired guy driving a beat up ol' white van that looked like it had done as many miles as the faded blue Bonds shirt worn by its driver. Maybe I had expectations that he would look more polished, that his success would have bought him a crisper tee and a vehicle made in this century. I'm not sure, but the socialist in me is very pleased that he looks more like a busker than the international success he is.

'Jump in,' says Wally to Franc and I, who are standing on the sidewalk at the designated pick up point. Being a gentleman, Franc allows me to ride shotgun whilst he yanks open the sliding door to jump in the rear. The back of the van (of course!) has no seats and Franc happily sits on the floor alongside a drum kit and a keyboard like a twenty-one-year-old bass player off with his band mates to play their first ever show at the local tav. Wally scoots us around to The Tofu Shop in Richmond, where the three of us sit down over bowls of radish and tofu, and begin to traverse topics from Belgium to High School to Danish pop duo Laban and then, mostly, to the new album they'd just recorded which at this point in time does not even have a name.

Frank jokes that the pair met on Victoria Street in Richmond when he was approached by a down and out Wally, 'Asking me if I'd like a taste,' Frank laughs.

'Um…errr…it wasn't too dissimilar to that I guess.' Wally chuckles.

Closer to the truth though, the pair met not long after Wally had done his first record *Boardface*, which was Wally's first album under the Gotye moniker.

'I didn't know anything about what he was doing,' Frank said. 'He called me up, because…I don't know why…why did you call me up?' he asks, turning to Wally.

'It had been recommended to me to contact you, by Georgie and Paris from a Sydney label called Groove Scooter - a little label. They were distributed by Creative Vibes at the time and I'd asked them...they had kind of wanted to sign *Boardface* or they wanted to license *Boardface* and put it out, but had sort of said, 'Oh, you know, it's very low-fi and maybe you could get it remixed or at least remastered?' And I was like, 'Oh, well that would be nice but you're offering me zero dollars so what am I going to do that with?' And they said 'Well, here's someone you could contact'.

So, they gave me a list of people and Franc was one of them and I don't know, I didn't follow it up [laughs]. I think at the time I went, 'Look, I've mixed this record myself. It is what it is. I think it sounds great in its own way and I shouldn't drag it on trying to find money to spend money to make it sound better,' or whatever and I ended up not licensing it to them and just putting it out myself [laughs]. But yeah, that had planted some kind of seed and I'd gone and listened to some of the records that you had been involved in.'

Whilst there was a definite sense of relief that the well-known torture technique of keeping a musician cooped up inside a studio was over, it wasn't yet far enough for Wally from the recording process the two had so recently endured, for all of the psychological bruises to have fully faded.

'One of the things maybe that potentially frustrates me about the process with Franc...well no, not frustrates me, this is probably just my own frustration that I get a lot just making music, at least for my own stuff, is on some level I want to just hand over what I've done and say, 'I've got this one great idea! It still needs five other great ideas to make it great. Can you give me those five ideas?' I want someone like that and yet, I know that I'd probably struggle with someone who had a lot of great ideas, particularly if I then kinda went, 'Aw nah I'm not really into that,' and then that became an issue. Whereas Franc, I guess, on some level is great at being an excellent sounding-board and maybe sometimes just going, 'That's okay, just go back and work more. Just come up with other ideas. Nah you need more ideas or try this, try that,' and sometimes that kind of makes me go away and go, 'Hmmph, I've worked so hard on this song already. I don't wanna do any more work on it.' At which point Franc chimes in with his pom poms and his cheers of 'Come on! Keep going, Wally!' and I just want to say, 'Can't you just do it for me, please?"

'But you know,' says Franc, 'Wally essentially always knows exactly what he's after in that kind of way, and the only person who can really do it; that is actually going to make it satisfactory for him, is him. Unless, of course, it's a deliberate collaboration or it's in a band process, where he's able to give it over. And in the situations where there has been input, what I've watched within Wally, is this frustration that he has with those other ideas, where he's like, 'Argh, that's not quite what I wanted it to be. I actually want it to be more like this.' So, in the end it's got to go into his swirl or his filter in the way that his sound works because as soon as it's someone else's idea you can tell it's not his aesthetic and it's not the way he would do it. So yeah, it's an interesting process.'

'Basically what Franc says to me is. 'Take a good look at yourself mate."

'Ha! That's exactly right!' Franc agrees.

I ask him to describe their process of working together on the Gotye project, Wally chuckles and simply says '*extended*'. A lot of this comes down to both gents being incredibly busy but for the most part it taking time due to the way in which Wally painstakingly builds entire songs around tiny fragments of sound.

'It is very lengthy,' he admits in reference to how he works. 'Bitsy. And revisions and ideas, and coming up with what I feel is like, tonnes and tonnes of shit ideas that I kind of scrap or shift through until something works.'

'The songs that are sample-based,' Franc elaborates, 'Wally's taken samples and manipulated them in various ways with small loops, small things from many, many sources, fitted them all together into a…you know…a concoction which has a logic to how it works….some of the songs are made up of, you know…they might be…I don't know like 120, 150 tracks throughout a song say a five-minute arrangement of lots and lots and lots of different sounds put together that sort of fit together in certain ways.'

From there, Franc's work begins. De-noising loops, taking out the clicks, creating a cohesion to the EQing with the sole intention of adhering the plethora of different sonic aesthetics together, without losing Wally's original intention.

'The trick of it is that because Wally has constructed it in a particular way, it has its own logic, and if you change the vibe or deconstruct it, or whatever, it actually all of a sudden falls to pieces and it doesn't make any sense. So, a lot of the job is actually trying to push it so it will work the way it kind of will work, but not, you know, make it fall to pieces like a house of cards. It's a very tricky thing, cleaning things up cause you're wanting to keep the vibe, but also make it translate so when you put it on next to something else your listening to…I always listen to Katy Perry and then put on whatever I'm listening to next, and then you go 'Katy Perry sounds great and Wally sounds great next to it', rather than going 'Wally sounds a little bit low-fi'. But it doesn't always work like that, sometimes you want to hold onto that dusty aesthetic.'

'Yes,' Wally pipes in enthusiastically, 'If you want a turd, you don't wanna go polish that turd too far.'

'Yeah that's right. Exactly,' laughs Franc.

'You don't want to polish turds. It's a bit weird anyway, it should never really be done. Instead accept perhaps the turd was just fine in the first place.'

Never in the thousands of interviews I've done with musicians, scientists, actors, authors, producers, has it ever taken me so many conversations to get to the pith of someone's makings. With Franc, I was loving this slowly-evolving process of getting to see what makes him tick; in complete opposition to the rocket-speed of live radio interviews where the revealing of someone's heart needs to happen with surgeon-like precision within a 4-minute deadline. But this third and final time I will speak with Franc is the extended window to get the goss, from go to whoa.

It's July 2012 and I'm in the ABC studios on the Gold Coast. That once nameless album we'd chatted about two years ago in Melbourne, has since been titled *Making Mirrors* and has served up the highest selling Australian single of all time called *Somebody That I Used To Know*, effectively changing both Franc and Wally's lives forever.

As soon as we begin chatting again, I remember what I enjoy most about catching up with him - his enthusiasm for the topic. Which topic? Any! Franc doesn't mind a chat. He took me by surprise in many ways. I thought he would be straight-up traditional almost, an old-school producer who simply loved to capture the honesty of performance without all the fuss and fiddling. But Franc was nerdy and complex, incredibly artistic but as approachable as your favourite schoolteacher, although far too naughty to be one. He *loves* what he does; the diversity of personality, along with the different ideas and approaches to making music that such diversity brought with it. So, let's go to the beginning of Franc's journey and follow him from the drought that changed his life to the streets of Richmond, then onto the USA where the story reaches thus far.

'My parents were both really into music, so as a kid there was always a lot of music around our house even though we were on a farm,' says Franc speaking to me from the Melbourne ABC studios on his early childhood years. 'My dad listened to a lot of music. He only really listened to classical music at that stage. But when I was about five, there was a really bad drought on the farm. We had to sell most of the cows and everyone was really suffering. My mum started thinking about moving to Melbourne to work for a while and for dad to look after us on the farm.'

Luckily, for the richness that future Franc would bring to the world through music, his parents made the decision over time to leave the farm and give the boys more options than being farmers

'They thought, 'We'll send them to a school where they'll have choice about other things to do'. So, my mum went. She didn't have a uni degree but she always wanted to teach music and she'd always played violin and piano. She enrolled in uni when she was about 45-46 and went and studied music. Through that process she was introduced to a whole lot of new music, you know, doing a funky 70's music course there was lots of art music, lots of electronica and whatever, so there was lots of music that came into the house, lots of Kraftwerk and I don't know, Tangerine Dream, all the European electronica that they were really into, and my dad adopted that too, so that become very much a soundtrack to us on our car journeys from the country to the city and that was the beginning of that for me.'

This diverse spectrum of sound that Franc thought little of as a youngster is one of the key things he attributes to the genre-less way in which he hears music today. As a child, Franc never thought, 'Oh, this is classical and this is German electronica', it was just sounds and textures he heard. All of it was simply music.

It wasn't just the drought though that changed the direction of the Tetaz family and saw Franc's world expand. Beneath the dry, unyielding soil, there was a much sadder tale.

'I had an elder sister and she... she got leukaemia when she was six and I was four, she died very soon after being diagnosed. So, part of it...all those things happened in one big sort of whammy in my family - a drought, my sister dying - it was pretty dark and that was a catalyst in many ways I think for my parents. They thought, 'Well, there's so many other things going on in the world and we would dearly love to be part of that but we haven't been. We've been on the farm and farming, but there's so many other things we'd like to do.' And they loved it! I mean, my parents are real...I kinda class them as ... like...life enthusiasts. They loved discovering new things and doing things and part of being on the farm was that you're really tied to it. You can't really go anywhere or do anything without making a huge effort. So, for them, moving away from the farm was like a real, new beginning in a way.'

As the family was firming its plans for the relocation to the city of Geelong, south-west of Melbourne, Franc took up study of the violin and discovered the Geelong Regional Record Library, a magical place where common folk could go and borrow vinyl.

'My brother and I would go in every Saturday and just borrow all the records we could on recommendation,' he recalls with the same enthusiasm that the story invokes in me as both a lover of vinyl and perhaps even more so, of libraries. 'Or we'd just find things from reading the record sleeves, and of course, we'd take them all and we had this big tape collection too. So, I sort of did that from the age of about, I don't know, ten or eleven, through to when I started earning money and could afford to buy records when I was about fourteen or fifteen.'

Not long after the injection of his own cash supply, Franc started playing drums and other percussion pretty seriously, stating, 'That's pretty much all I did.' He lived out the teen dream by dropping maths at school to take on a second music subject and made the decision that everything he would do in his life from that point on would be centred around music. All he had to do was decide what aspect he would find most interesting and most sustainable and like many of the producers who's stories we've already heard, part of Franc's journey to producer-dom was discovering that he wasn't the greatest player, and sustainability wasn't likely to be found in being a rock star.

What Franc did discover as a genuine talent, however, was the *creation* of sound. 'It wasn't really specific.' He explains of that discovery. 'I wasn't into writing songs or lyrics, I wasn't interested in that. I was more interested in electronic music. So that's what I started doing. After I left school, I couldn't find a course that I really wanted to do, so I just sat in on friend's uni lectures and found a bunch of teachers to work with and took lessons. My brother was nice enough - he had a job, I just had part-time teaching jobs, teaching drums and percussion and whatever, and he had an eight-track recorder and a bunch of gear, so I just started making music at our home studio and it kinda started then, all I needed was the skills!'

Initially Franc found it a little difficult to find people to collaborate with on a sonics level.

'Maybe I was a bit control-freaky...maybe I still am,' he laughs reflectively.

It was at this time that Franc realised that recording music was where his heart lay; having the skills to manipulate sound became his focus and he set out to learn how to mix. His mixing journey took him through the studio of one Ian Eccles-Smith an Australian classical composer. 'He had a studio in St. Kilda and from the age of twenty-one I spent a couple of years working with him. He doesn't do music anymore but he was really amazing...incredible pianist and flautist but he had this amazing electronic studio. He was really into, like, De La Soul...oh god, all sorts of electronic music like English-scented electronic music more than anything else. So, I pretty much apprenticed to him in a way and through working with him I met a Melbourne engineer called Mark Forester, who'd get lots of work because he'd worked with Prince, like remix work. I did quite a few songs with him for things like the singer from Sisters of Mercy and I don't know, terrible things like this terrible track I did with Peter Andre [chuckle]. Most of the music wasn't particularly good, but it was a really great training ground because I was just dealing with a lot of things that I hadn't dealt with before, and Ian was very detailed. He had an amazing knowledge, so I pretty much just soaked up all his techniques and ideas. He was quite a few years older than me.'

Having made the decision to make music his bread and butter, Franc had to find a way to make it sustainable, so instead of setting up another recording studio in Melbourne, he set up a mastering studio. Ask many a musician what mastering is (irrelevant of how many albums deep they are in their career) and most will say they have no idea, but do know it's something that has to be done. So, for those of you like me and the vast majorities of others who may perhaps feel that not much happens through mastering, Franc explains the process.

'When you're mixing a record, you're looking at the elements within a single song, how loud particular elements are - the vocals, the bass, the guitars, or whatever, and when you've mixed a whole record and it has ten or twelve tracks they can all sound a little different to each other or they don't necessarily make a story as a collection, so mastering does a couple of things. It makes it flow as a whole thing, so it will tell you the story of the complete project; it's about the order of the songs but it's also then about individual tone and the loudness of each song and its intent and you can change that quite a deal in mastering. It can make a difference between a record really feeling like a whole piece of work, or it being a bunch of separate things.

'It's a really interesting, way of looking at music because you aren't looking at just a song, you are looking at what an artist was trying to do with a whole record or a whole bunch of ideas. So, it's the other end of the decision-making process.'

At the same time as Franc was discovering that he wasn't going to break many hearts as a musician, setting up instead the mastering studio, he began writing soundtracks for student short films as well as for choreography. 'The mastering work would help support the other projects that weren't well paid at all or *not* paid because, you know, they don't have budgets. But the short films, they were very much a training ground of a kind, learning how to apply sound to a narrative and understanding the structure of a film and then collaborating with the person making the film. Films are much like records in that they are just large collaborations between people and you have to find a way of being able to know what the film needs and then communicate what you think it should be so people can understand that and then you can actually do that. There's a lot of navigation of communication to be able to collaborate on an idea - whether it be for film or for a record.'

I wonder if it were simpler to put music to a film because that early question, 'What is the purpose of this', is already answered by the visual representation.

'Well yeah,' Franc laughs. 'As long as everyone agrees! There's all those great YouTube clips with the Shining re-interpreted with different music to make it into a comedy or...

you know, you can really do anything with a score and quite often the thing is to try and find what a scene is about, or try and communicate it because it can be *trying* to communicate all sorts of different things, depending on where it is and what it is. So, to understand that or to actually get the director to tell you what their idea of that is, and then for you to understand what that is, that's the real craft. And it is related to learning the purpose of a piece of music, yeah very much so. If you don't really know that, it just becomes a sort of scattergun thing where you apply something and you say, 'That's kind of cool,' but it doesn't necessarily get to the guts of what an idea is. In film, that's certainly something that I'm really interested in…is trying to find the core of what this idea is actually about.'

The biggest accolade in terms of film that Franc had received to this point in time was the Australasian Performing Right Association (APRA) / Australian Guild of Screen Composers (AGSC) 2006 'Feature Film Score of the Year' Award for the score to the terrifying, outback-tourism-destroying flick *Wolf Creek*. The unique thing about the film, musically, is that rather than implement sonics of fear i.e. *Jaws, American Psycho* style, the *Wolf Creek* soundtrack taps into the terribly desolate and lonely side of the characters' experience. It makes them more human, more vulnerable and therefore much more deeply disturbing.

'The director, Greg Mclean, wanted to make a film that was unusual, and so he wanted to do the opposite of what you would expect to happen in a film like that. It has a very slow beginning, nothing much happens and there's no dialogue for the last thirty minutes of the film. It's just people wandering in the wilderness to music [slight chuckle], looking scared. There are lots of editors who use it for temping and lots of people who like that soundtrack, which is really nice, and independent to the film itself, but the thing that I get comments about the most is that people find it really emotional. The music is really, really emotional.'

Franc's aim was to score it as an emotional component of the film as opposed to merely frights. Through the music his intention was to tap viewers into the desolation and feeling of loss as a direct internal experience.

'I was thinking of it, instead of being an Australian slasher film, as being a European art film, and so the score I was trying to make was this luscious thing with tinges of Australiana about it. I certainly tried to make it into something that got to the core of the emotional journey of the characters and of course, because of that journey, it is quite chilling.'

Apparently, after the movie was complete, Greg confessed to Frank that several times he'd wandered into the booth to see what he was up to, 'And he had no idea what the fuck he was doing.' It was no wonder - Frank spent long, long days after days experimenting with piano, untuned piano, elbows, at one point scoring with nothing but bits and pieces he had lying around the studio. But despite Greg's bewilderment, he trusted Franc, so rather then get overly involved in changes or corrections along the way, he was happy to wait and see what Franc came up with and listen as it was intended - up against the film.

'We would have spent days talking about the film conceptually,' Frank says of the conversation he and Greg had about the film's score leading into production, 'I would have had to be an idiot not to get it fairly close!' The result was, that bar a thirty-second piece of music in the middle of the film that got the arse, everything remained exactly how Frank presented it.

17

Harry Vanda: Willy Wonka & the Rock n Roll Factory

During the initial Producer Series on triple j radio, Mark Opitz was amongst that first round of luminaries, included for his role as an integral corner stone in the solid guitar rock era of The Angels, AC/DC and Rose Tattoo. Opitz was the apprentice of Vanda & Young, so it seemed fitting that with the series itself having grown into an internationally renowned platform for the voices of producers to be heard, it was time to move from the apprentice to the master.

George Young had moved overseas some years earlier, once the long lasting and rich partnership between the two gents had come to its natural end in the late nineties. Harry Vanda lived in Australia for four decades. After more than twenty years at Alberts Studios, he took some time out from the music industry. It wasn't until 2005 - the precise year I would find myself seeking him out - that Harry would set up a brand new studio with his son Daniel in Sydney's Surry Hills.

Whilst Harry was a true legend - both as a producer for AC/DC and as an acclaimed songwriter on such 'mum and dad' hits as John Paul Young's *Love Is In The Air* - it was his work with young Melbourne band British India, that threw him onto the radar for the Producer Series. I caught up with British India a few weeks before my interview with Harry was scheduled, to get a sense of why they chose to work with Harry, and as a heads-up as to what that interview may have in store.

'Harry, he's a great guitarist, but he's got such a huge range vocally,' explains lead vocalist, lyricist and guitarist Declan Melia. 'Towards the end of The Easybeats he was singing on records more than Stevie was, and it's really crazy to see him working in the studio with harmonies, just how good of an ear he has for it... and how high and low he can go, it's insane.'

Harry's talent for singing and his deep love of polished song writing had the effect of hypnotically switching Declan from being a vocalist who shouted to a singer who lullabied.

'I don't know how he did it,' Declan laughs. 'I think it was more on the first record he kind of injected, all of us, the band mentality with a love of pop music and I think singing comes from that, being more inclined to sing rather than just bellow and shout.'

Guitarist Nic Wilson agrees. 'I think you can sort of see that development hugely between the *Outside 109 / Automatic Blitzkrieg* EP and the first album, *Guillotine*,' he says to Declan. 'He let you do your thing on the EP, and when it was time to come to the album, it was like, 'Okay this isn't going to fly. There's no more of this screaming crud.'"

'I only screamed because I couldn't sing at all - he must have just taught me how, through osmosis,' says Declan. 'There wasn't a particular time when he sat me down and said, 'Well, you know son ... ' There wasn't anything like that and that's the great thing. There was never a tense moment throughout the whole recording of either of the records, it was always teaching through osmosis.'

'He really just, sort of pushes you in the right direction without you realising that he's doing it,' says Nic. 'He's just so diplomatic.'

'He's like a horse whisperer.'

'He's like Robert Redford.'

'Except Dutch.'

'A Dutch Robert Redford. It's like a nightmare.'

I imagine Robert Redford with either the sweet Dutch accent of my gentle Pop or the thick Dutch yell of my terrifying Nanna, as I walk now along this definitive Surry Hills back alley, lined with back fences of urban backyards, made mostly still from corrugated iron sheeting. It was much like any other back alley in this part of town and its non-descript nature made it feel like a hidden entrance JK Rowling would have approved of. At the end of the lane stood the (as yet unfinished) entrance to Harry's Flashpoint Studios. There was a tradesman working away out front and bits and pieces of building materials still lying here and there. After years of working in someone else's studio, Harry wasn't holding back. I take a moment to take it all in, waiting for the usual combination of excitement and nerves to reach my belly and steady myself with a few slow breaths, to meet one of the most well-known names in the production world. I remember, when it came to securing Harry for this interview, that the response wasn't as instantaneously receptive as I had hoped, and ponder how that may influence the interview we were about to do. Upon my initial request, Harry's assistant, Chris, emailed to say, 'Sorry for the delay, I had to track Harry down and unfortunately he is unable to make himself available for this. It's a shame because it sounds like it will be a great series. I'll let you know if the situation changes.'

'Fuck!' Was all I remember thinking at the time. Every series needed a great Aussie, and there were few names as well known as Vandas when it came to Australian producers. In the past I'd interviewed Tim Whitten, who lent his ears to the sounds of Architecture in Helsinki and The Panics, the wildly loose Tony Cohen who stood (sometimes horizontally) side by side The Birthday Party, through the wild whiskey times of the seventies and Harry's own apprentice, the aforementioned Opitz.

There were few around of this profile, and they were getting less and less with the completion of each new series as the new up-and-comers continued to cut their teeth with more and more successful artists. I was determined Harry should have his place. I emailed back in deeper explanation, and of the appreciation if anything could be done to bring about a change of heart. I wrote, 'This will not just be good for him (Harry) but great for British India as well. Is there anything I can do to have him reconsider?'

I can only presume that mention of British India must've been the key: the knowledge that this would assist a band he had taken under his wing and who were still in the early stages of their career. Three days later the email reply came from Chris stating that, 'I've managed to talk him into doing it.' In other words, he's agreed to do ONE final interview. Just five days later, I was back in Sydney, finding myself wandering through this ordinary back alley in the inner-city suburb of Surry Hills, wondering how Harry's initial hesitation would translate, once the interview began.

He came out to greet me from some far-end of the still-in-construction studios. He was much taller, lankier, longer-haired and eccentric looking than I expected. In a later chat I would have with British India, they would describe him this time as a Dutch Willy Wonka - a more accurate analogy has never been spoken; the only things missing were the top hat and purple velvet suit. He sweeps me up in his slipstream, down the hall and into the kitchen where it is imperative Harry grab a cup of tea - a true addiction of his it seems - a cuppa between takes and a cuppa for chats.

With china in hand, Harry leads us back down the corridor through a large studio, with a proportionately large control room attached to it. Mounted on the wall is the largest computer monitor I have ever seen, the wave files in each track must've been about a palm size in height - you'd end up dreaming in audio waves with the imprint this thing would leave on your retinas.

'You need a screen that size when you've got a recording desk with that many channels,' Harry says in response to my nerdy glee.

I drop my gaze down to the console Harry is referring to, it stretches metres and *metres*, it could record live symphonies with an accompanying children's choir and still accommodate a folk outfit and a barbershop quartet. We wandered through the recording room to a little booth tucked off to the side, nice and quiet.

As I set up my gear and test the levels (always an intimidating thing to do in front of a producer) Harry leaves the room and returns with a mic stand so neither of us shall be left with a tired limb from holding onto the microphone. It also means that the recording levels will remain fairly consistent (presuming Mr Dutch Gene Wilder over here doesn't display the usual terrible microphone techniques, ironically often possessed by microphone-shy producers, who have a tendency to move their heads away from the recording end of a mic it as if it were a cat's bottom).

With teacups on saucers (and mouth so professionally a hand's width away from microphone) Harry begins to unfurl the Vanda story.

His Australian life began when he was seventeen years old, dragged 'kicking and screaming and fighting!' by his parents from Holland. The family, like most migrants of the time, set up at camp at Villawood - not the horrifically infamous place it has become these days - but a transition centre on the oustskirts of Sydney's west, for those *welcome* to set up a new life in Australia. Harry describes the shelters as, 'Old Nissan huts - shaped like a half moon type thing. They used to put the Japanese in there as prisoners of war and all that sort of stuff.'

Two years the Vandas (or the Vandenbergs as they were known then) did in that migration centre before his parents decided it was all too hot and all too hard and that it was time to return to Holland. But surprisingly, young Harry - in contrast to his initial tanty - stayed. By the time his folks were ready to leave, a large Scottish family had arrived in camp. Harry and their eldest son, George, had formed a fast alliance. The rest of the Youngs, along with George, got together and pooled their money to get a house together and left Villawood in a flash, taking Harry with them. Also in tow was another young lad who - along with Harry and the Youngs - would go on to etch his name in Australian music history. That young wild fella was Stevie Wright.

'The place was a mad house. You can imagine,' says Harry of the home that contained the whole rambunctious lot of them.

After all the times Harry has no doubt spoken of these early years, there is still in his voice a surprising amount of affection and enthusiasm.

The main reason that Harry stayed put in Australia was exactly the same as why he didn't want to leave Holland in the first place - he had a band going. Whilst they were still in Villawood, Stevie, George and Harry formed the outfit that would help define Australian music during the sixties. The Easybeats - with their love of raw rock that would carry them all through fascinating careers, combined with the world-class pop song writing sensibility of Vanda and Young - would become the first Australian band to ever have an internationally successful single.

'The funny thing is,' says Harry in reflection of the five short but impactful years of the band's life, 'is that it's more amazing looking back than what it is living it, you see. I mean, as you live it there are so many other bits and pieces that you worry about, it's not all like, 'Ok, hey, wow, this is wonderful' - it doesn't work like that. You're still living a life, which has all its ups and downs. So what you are - a pop star, you're a billionaire, whatever you are - people say, 'Ooh, isn't that wonderful.' It's not so wonderful when you're having other things happening at the same time, which makes you the same as everybody else. It's not really something that means anything in a real sense. And then later on you say, 'Shit, I did that."

Out of that one band, all three close friends would become legends - Stevie would reach new levels of fame with the massive hit song, *Evie,* as well as with his battles with drug addiction and the barbaric rehabilitation 'treatments' that would change him forever. Harry and George would sway more and more to the gold mine that was song writing.

'We were absolutely flabbergasted when we found out that in the early sixties, (*whispers*), 'You get paid for writing songs? Wow! I reckon I could write a couple of million of them!' And away we went, writing songs.'

Harry and George took off overseas, and for three or four years set up camp in London where they felt they'd have a better crack at making some bigger bucks. Whilst they had their share of highs, it proved a tougher market over there than they had hoped. So when Ted Albert, whom they'd been sending songs to back in Oz, offered them place as the main producers and songwriters for what would become Australia's most iconic studio, the two ambitious lads couldn't resist.

At Albert's Studios, Harry and George, better known by then as Vanda & Young, produced some of the grittiest bands in Australian rock history; most famous of all, the band belonging to George's little bros - AC/DC. This is the subject that Harry has had to cover more times than he can remember, and there's a slight trace of weariness as we move into Acca Dacca territory. He knows it can't be avoided.

'It *was* fun,' he says almost reluctantly. 'Look, it was tongue-in-cheek that was always the funny thing about it. Bon Scott really had a way with words that, the guy could say things in two lines that would take anybody else two books. You know, just *nail* it. It was great.'

But for most listeners, tongue in cheek it was not. AC/DC

were the ideological spokesmen for the working-class bloke who loved his beer and loved sex even more. They were the epitome of what Joe Average in his blue King Gees wanted to be. And in a highly conservative Australian radio climate of the time, Scott and the rest of the Young brothers stood out like big balls on a well-manicured poodle.

'It was a funny thing actually,' reckons Harry. 'What we noticed when we came back here from London and listened to some stuff that was coming on the radio, I couldn't get over how sterile it was sounding. And I thought, 'Jesus Christ, there's got to be a problem here. Is that the best they've got?' Maybe it was because having been in London and doing the rounds and all that sort of business, we'd been on the cutting edge of where things were supposed to be happening. We didn't think at the time, 'Hey, I'm on the cutting edge, watch me cut!' It just was a state of mind.

'We came back here,' he continues, 'and it wasn't there, but you go out and when you saw the same bands live, ooh, great band. What happened? What? These guys are fucking fantastic! Listen to this! But listen to the record, it had all been sterilised - no needles could go in the red it was all ooh, very pristine. And that's not rock and roll, is it? It wasn't in my book and it wasn't in George's either. So when AC/DC came along you'd go, 'Hey! The snare drum's rattling!' Because when the drummer plays and all that stuff, the snare keeps *zzzzzzz* and who gives a shit? Let it rattle! So what we basically did was just put a band in the studio, and then mic'd them up in such a way as if they were live. We started to use the ambient mics and all that sort of stuff as well, to pick up the size of things, to pick up the life, to hear things. To make it breathe instead of that really tight *ticky ticky ticky* sound. 'Can't have no spill! Ooohooh."

As the conversation moves along, so do Harry's hand movements, and the highs and lows in his voice. He's morphing before my eyes from legendary producer to legendary producer in animated cartoon form. I can suddenly see the gangly, enthusiastic, anarchic but nerdy kid he must've been those decades ago, who had the skills to turn himself from lolloping guitar geek to music icon. It's a funny thing about the music business; the ones at the top are the ones that in any other industry you'd vote least likely to succeed. But in this artistic, creative world it's the idiosyncrasies and the oddness that propagates genius.

The first six AC/DC records: *High Voltage, TNT, Dirty Deeds Done Dirt Cheap, Let There Be Rock, Powerage* and *Highway to Hell,* all featured the unique tones of Bon Scott before his death in 1980. His vocals were some of the most distinct ever recorded - somehow both nasally, high-pitched and mighty, simultaneously - and Harry and George were masters at capturing it to tape, reckoning it was all in the mic techniques.

'That's what's important,' Harry says. 'Using the right mics, picking up the whole spectrum of the sound, not just a bit of it. We used to spend…I mean I nearly went deaf looking for the right spot on the speakers! We always tried to nail the sweet spots. Now if one thing sounds big on top of each other, you get a big sound. A natural big sound. Then you got to try and fit the voice in in the same way, then it just becomes a question of spacing things. We used hardly any effects on Bon whatsoever. Maybe a bit of reverb, that's all.'

Harry's whole demeanour returns to the animated enthusiast of before, as he chats about studio time, recalling how high-energy the band were in that confined space, making the biggest problem for he and George, trying to keep everything mic'd up while the band threw themselves around all over the place.

Harry remembers Angus being particularly true to form. 'The best way to get a performance out of Angus, was to get a couple of chicks in the studio to watch him. He'd see the glass window, and he'd go and play there and do his solo, and he'd just absolutely bloody go wild. With the earphones flying everywhere and you'd look at it and he's still playing, it's rocking like hell, and you look at him and he hasn't even got his earphones on, 'cause he lost them!'

Alongside Bon's vocals, Angus's guitar tones were essential in defining the sound and the thrust of AC/DC. 'I would have loved to see the duel between Angus and Jimi Hendrix.' Harry says, suddenly giggling and wriggling in his chair. 'Let me tell you that would have been the sight of the century. Unfortunately, Jimi bloody carked it! But it was all Angus ever did - play guitar. He used to sit up, night after night after night after night, just playing the guitar. He was meant to play the bloody guitar.'

Of the overall way that Harry talks about recording AC/DC - from the meticulous study Angus would make of his guitar tones, from the live way that Phil needed to play his drums, to the natural swagger that Bon would bring straight to the mic each and every time - it seems the main focus for Harry simply had to be capturing what was naturally presenting itself: the band were the wild animals and Harry was David Attenborough. Even when it came to the bagpipes, Harry just had to have his audio net ready to capture the ear-warbling sound that would become the most famous bagpipe solo in the world.

'I just stuck a mic in front of it and there it was.' Says Harry ridiculously nonchalantly.

'But it sounds amazing!' I say, searching for some secret technique, 'I was just listening to it again in the car, and they sound absolutely immaculate, they're note for note, I didn't know bagpipes could hold a note so beautifully.'

'Yeah, I mean, Bon could play the bagpipes, but he was not a virtuoso. So, it took a bit to get it right. Look, don't forget, the people that were responsible for this bagpiping stuff, they were Scotsmen. So they knew what they were doing. But Oh Jesus Christ, at first, before he got the hang of it, it sounded like somebody strangling a cat.'

The other part of that song to become legend is the part that Harry can lay committed claim to - the pisstake of the chorus.

'Look if you threw a line in there for them, somebody

would pick up on it. This whole business about *It's A Long Way To The Shop If You Want A Sausage Roll*, (a studio lark that's become almost as legendary as the song itself) that was me standing there pissing around going, 'It's a long way to the shop.' And Malcolm went, 'If you want a sausage roll.' And that's where that came from. I never thought it was gonna be that big, otherwise I would have patented it!'

This type of taking the piss is what Harry actually puts down as the key to a great performance. Making artists feel comfortable in that great Aussie tradition of talking shit.

'Look, I've been to sessions where I really would have preferred sitting there watching paint dry on a door or something, because it was *'so exciting'*. Usually, some paranoid control freak is looking for things that are not humanly possible to produce. But he can hear it somewhere in his head. He can't do it, he expects you to do it. Those sessions were painful, no wonder that it all comes out sounding like *ooooh*. But not with AC/DC, we had great fun sessions even before we started recording, which was very important. Not just AC/DC, The Angels, all the other guys as well, it was really important to put people at ease and put them in the right frame of mind.'

But what exactly, with such raucous creatures, would that entail?

'Well you have great slagging sessions! We were the most balanced people in the world. We hated everyone!'

Not long after AC/DC formed, and while they were still finding their feet to release their first album *High Voltage*, old mate Stevie Wright was busy cracking away at his solo career. In 1974 Stevie broke every law of radio convention by releasing an eleven-minute track that would go on to have huge commercial airplay. Whilst the track was broken up into three more palatable chunks, the sheer anarchy of the decision and the ensuing success, was mind-blowing.

'What do *you* reckon Harry?' I ask, relishing yet another immense opportunity to hear the details of another incredible moment in music history, directly from one of the few people who had any genuine association to comment. Direct from source. 'What was it about 'Evie' that made it able to break convention like that?'

'You know, I still can't figure it out to tell you the truth, because sure it was alright, good rock riff, all this sort of stuff. And obviously it's got a big hammering on the radio now, I always have my suspicions about why they played it: they played the full eleven minutes because it gave them a breather!'

Harry's honesty catches me off guard and I learn instantly that he is a man not afraid to say what he thinks.

'The radio guys could piss outside, have a cigarette, I have my suspicions. But having said all that, it really wasn't the sort of, for me, it wasn't the sort of song that would have set the world on fire. But eleven minutes, yeah it was an interesting image, part of the whole thing. And it did all fit together, and I'm sure the people out there love the tune and all that sort of business, and I think it's pretty good. But so was *MacArthur Park*, you know? That was a good one.'

Although Stevie has left an undeniably potent impact on the Australian musical landscape, his personal tales have captured attention almost as much. The story of a rock star riding round and round the dizzying cycle of the substance carousel is by no means a unique one. For Stevie, it was the controversial use of so-called Deep Sleep Treatment by psychiatrist Harry Bailey, which combined drug-induced coma and electroconvulsive therapy, damaging the malleable and vulnerable human mind forever, that turned his story into a tragedy. Particularly when contrasted against the dynamic nature he once possessed.

'When he was together,' begins Harry passionately, 'Steven, when he was together, Jesus. I can't think of a better showman. I've never seen anybody that can radiate that type of charisma, when he really had his act together. He just had to stick his face in, basically. He was just one of those guys that, well he still is I suppose, he could just generate excitement. It's just something about the way they stand, the way they talk, there doesn't seem to be anything different about people like him except that for some reason or other, they have this excitement and you haven't. It's like people that can tell dirty jokes everyone goes 'hahaha', you go, 'Well, I'll give you a filthy one,' and everybody thinks, 'You dirty old- ' You know what I mean?'

When Harry worked with Stevie, it was paramount to pump him up, to make him feel good about himself and take on that role that every producer has to at some point - the master ego stroker.

'I can't overestimate how important it is that people can relate to you,' he says with great emphasis. 'And feel really at ease, like they can let go. If they don't, you never get the best out of them. No way. There are producers that know fashions and they know that this particular *ding* is now a *zing* this week, because that's so passé, that's last week. And the RPMs are now not 'boom boom' they're (double time) 'boom boom boom boom'. 'Cause that's very important, that's this week. And I'm not taking the piss by the way, because that is very, very important to know what it is you are producing. If you want a classical record done you don't go and see a guy that's great at punk music. So there are many horses for courses. But I think what they all have to do, in the studio, they have to be the person that everyone can turn to and say, 'Is it all right?' You have to be able to say yea or nay. Because who will otherwise, you know?'

So, how then does pride weave its magic in the relationship of two *producers*? Two who've managed a working partnership, ever increasing in profile themselves, for almost four decades? Did Harry and George lavish each other with praise out of habit, or were they so depleted from the unbalanced nature of the artist/producer relationship that behind closed doors, they ended up maniacal big-heads themselves?

'Well...' laughs Harry tilting his head and averting his gaze to the ceiling like a guilty eight-year-old selling his best mate's secrets to the principal for a shot at his own freedom. 'We had our ups and downs,' he admits coyly. 'You know, we got together when we were kids. We went through so many sticky times together, you know what I mean? You get like…a band becomes a family, you know? It really does. It's like you can relate more to the band members than to their family members. It really becomes a bonding type thing. So, you don't fall out over small things. I don't think George and I have had any major thing to fall out over. We fought like cat and dog but it was never serious. It was never insulting, if you know what I mean?'

I can't wait to hear about their scrap-resolution process.

Harry chuckles, recalling how their little fallouts would end. 'By either me feeling embarrassed about it or him feeling embarrassed about it. Then we'd end up saying, 'Oh all right then, we'll do it your way,' then, 'No, no let's do it your way'. Then we'll have another fight over doing it the other person's way…'

Harry's Mad Hatter laughter continues as the soundtrack of my thoughts as I scan the notes in front of me to see where we're at, chronologically, with recordings to chat about. My eyes fall on The Wrights. The Wrights were but a blip on the musical landscape, but one worth noting for the all-star collaboration that it was. In 2005 Nic Cester from Jet, Pat Bourke from Dallas Crane, Phil Jamieson of Grinspoon, Powderfinger's Bernard Fanning, Chris Cheney from The Living End and Kram from Spiderbait released the supergroup's first and only single: a cover of Stevie Wright's famous opus, *Evie*.

Apart from the bringing together of so many prolific young Australians, the most unusual thing about it was that the project was simply born from Nic Cester's inner torment over the tragedies that marked the rock n roll life of Stevie. For Nic, perhaps due to his own band having reached nose-bleed heights of success in a very short space of time, allowing them the capacity to explore any level of indulgence they saw fit, it struck a chord. Maybe there was a small part of Nic that realised that had he lived in a different time, Stevie's story could be his own. He might have seen himself the victim of draconian rehab treatments and never, like Stevie, have been able to find his way back.

'I thought it a bit strange at first,' admits Harry, stumbling over his words. 'But then I met Nick and just had a few beers with him across the road, and he's such a sincere guy, you know. He was so into it. He really wanted to help Steven and all that sort of business, and I thought, Jesus…how sulky can you be if you don't do it?' Harry's words turn once again into snorty giggles. 'So I said, 'Yeah sure.' And then I thought, 'Hang on a minute… [laughs] we coulda picked something easier. Now we gotta bloody do the Evies! They can't be any worse than the originals [more laughs], can they? And that's not gonna be easy! Shit!" He laughs even harder before composing himself, realising perhaps that he's given too much of his true feelings away about the three-part track that he and George had penned for Stevie in the first place.

'I think they did alright actually,' he says much more soberly. 'Nic did a good job and Bernard Fanning did a wonderful job of part two and Phil did part three, he did a great job as well so...'

'It must have been a surreal experience for you Harry?'

'Oh, they all tried so hard, you know what I mean, these guys. And so uh, so I thought 'well shit,' he laughs, 'I better try hard as well.'

It was a perfect scenario to see how production of a song is determined by the people making the music, as well as how the music carries its own demands. I wonder how similar Harry's approach was on this remake to the original Evie,

'Oh, you know,' Harry sighs in a way that indicates he really doesn't care to analyse but responds nonetheless. 'It was a very easy-going session, because you know, like....look, these guys could play. So there was no problem there, it was only a few stylistic little things, you know what I mean? Whether you hold the note of...on riffs for instance [Harry begins to sing a guitar riff 'dow dada dow dada dow dow'], the 'dada' you know, makes a difference. You gotta play it 'DADA DADA' [vocalising in a heavier voice]. Or you know, there's a way of playing it [sings a riff again]...so that it flows. That's the only thing I actually told one of the guys. We...did a few takes. No more than two, three? It was sort of like, 'Well, how much better do you want it?' [Laughs] 'That'll do'.

So, we did part one and part three in Melbourne and we did part two here.'

The band, however, that truly pulled Harry from a generation of *Love is in the Air* fans and into the twenty-first century, was Melbourne four-piece, British India. The band had gentle notoriety in 2005 with their first single *Outside 109 / Automatic Blitzkrieg*, a thrashier, more garagey piece of music than the refined pop-rock that would crack them through the Aussie big time, two years later. When Harry first heard the band, he wasn't that impressed, giving the demo being played to him by a colleague a mere shrug of the shoulders and an unmoved response of ,'ehhh, it's not bad.' But it was seeing the band live that turned him 180, taking the band under his wing, thrusting both of their names into the music news headlines.

'When I saw Nick on stage the very first time in a shitty little place somewhere, just the attitude that was coming off him doing his thing…' Harry laughs at the joy of the recollection. 'It was like 'ohh, hang on [more laughs] there a couple of guys here' and Dec! Dec was so much like Stevie, that sort of…that almost…casual…but intense casual. I thought, 'Jesus, these guys are not bad' because when I first heard the demo…', Harry says, trailing off, reinforcing his lack of initial connection. 'But when I saw them live, I thought, 'These guys got something happening'. And uh, cause it reminded me of myself, you know what I mean.' Harry's voice goes deep and rough, morphing into comedy mode as he says (by way of unsuccessful explanation), 'Argh! Let's get into it. KILL!'

In this moment of Harry's wonderful eccentricity, I remember the Dutch in myself and I think the similarities with some of my own relatives' idiosyncrasies and the way they too deliver their humour. I imagine a few uncles still thick with

Dutch accent and how much more eccentric they would be after forty years in the music business, instead of under the austere regime of my Grandmother who'd been shot at by the Gestapo, mauled by their dogs, lost her husband to for 4 years in a POW camp in Siberia and as a consequence became well-versed at being tough as nails.

Seeing that which is 'Dutch' in Harry, who has lived a life so different to my relatives, is an interesting insight into a culture I've always felt so distant from. Even in the similarities in the textures of their skin bringing back wonderful memories of my Pop, who I had loved dearly and whose story I didn't know even as fully as I now know Harry's. I vow to take the time to sit with my family and ask them questions to the depth in which I have sat with many a stranger.

I return to the conversation as Harry explains the next important step after being satisfied by British India's talents live: making sure they were people worth working with.

'I've learnt my lesson there. I've made mistakes with people who are absolutely brilliant, but they were awful and yes, really, life's too short to be hanging out with vexatious people. You leave that alone and um, yeah so, I met with the guys and it was great.' Harry describes them as being a lot of fun, their sessions full of jokes and shenanigans, then adding, 'They are very well-read people'.

'They are smart blokes.' He explains further. 'I think they were all sort of in the bloody top percent of the state or something like that; in high school sort of thing and all that. You know, you could talk to them as well on different levels. It wasn't just 'hubba hubba hubba!"

In terms of technical production, the thing that British India required most from Harry was a skill at the top of his repertoire - helping them become better musicians.

'The playing together part was something that probably had to be addressed. Like, lots of young guys they still don't... they hadn't quite...they weren't quite *listening* to each other just yet, and by listening, I mean a process of osmosis. They don't even listen to each other but it just seeps through. So they have to be made aware of things like that, once you become aware of these sorts of things, then it becomes second nature after a while. Especially with bands that have got the right chemistry. I can only go by the Easybeats when it comes to that sort of thing. We weren't the best players in town...we probably weren't fuckin' the best players in the street, honestly [chuckles]. But, we fitted together. It really worked. As a team, we did what we did.'

Apart from pulling the band together into a unified playing team, it was Harry's exceptional talent for pop song writing that once again pulled yet another band from the garage to the podium. British India began as a 'shouty' band and by the time Harry got his hands firmly around their vocal chords, the lads had not just relented to sing but were harmonizing - a notion they weren't entirely receptive to straight away. 'No, on the first recording it was a bit of a, 'We don't sing, we can't sing.' Harry explains, his response (buoyed again by bubbles of laughter) being, 'Course you can sing, anybody can sing! Come in with me.' We'd stand around the mic 'arh rah rah rah' [laughs], doing our bit, you know? But, they picked it up pretty fast. They can sing all right.'

Of the evolution of working with Harry, British India had admitted, when I caught up with them some weeks before, that the songs on the first album hadn't really taken much shape before they made their way into *Flashpoint*.

'Harry really helped us with that, and that's quite a difficult thing to do, especially in this band because we've got such big egos and we take our songs quite seriously,' Declan would say with surprising honesty. 'But because, I think, he's a musician, he's able to introduce ideas so gently that you don't quite realise he's tampering with your songs until you can see how much better it is. So after we had done the first album, he'd really injected that sense of song craft into the mentality of the group, so we were able to do that a lot more with our own writing. So after that, the relationship was a bit more give and take.'

By this stage, Harry and I have been chatting for almost two hours - a valuable chunk in the working day of a man such as this. Before we wrap up and say our thank yous, chat returns one last time to AC/DC. I'm curious about the 'oi's in TNT - not only did they make the song what it was, but they set a cultural cornerstone that would have every educated Australian shuddering to this day, as the 'oi' took its place beside meat pies and footy games, as opposed to dreamtime and traditional songlines, when it came to defining Australians for uneducated foreigners.

'It sounds like an Angus thing to me,' says Harry, when looking where to accurately place the blame. 'Yes, OI, OI, OI,' he laughs, 'It sounds like an Angus thing. There's not a lot of pretty singing going on is there? Not exactly what you call the Bee Gees is it? [Laughs] You have this bleeding Neanderthal standing next to you screaming at the top of his head, you've gotta somehow keep up [laughs]. I usually got a splitting headache like 'oohhhh' [more laughs].'

'So was it the whole band that were doing the 'oi's? ' I ask, 'Even you?'

'Oh no, no, no, I think we used Angus mainly. Yeah, yeah.'

'Just Angus?' I ask surprised, 'It sounds like there's a choir of football teams…'

'Yeah, yeah,' laughs Harry. 'There's a *lot* of Angus's.'

On that, I thank Harry and quickly scan through my notes to make sure that, despite the endless amount of little curiosities that could still be queried, I haven't left out any gapingly obvious holes.

'You can always give me a ring if there's anything missing and say, 'Oh by the way, I forgot to ask you this and blah, blah, blah.'' It's a far cry from the reluctance of those initial emails and I can see that Harry is happy to have spoken about an entire career, not just a singular chunk of rock donning a school uniform.

As for me, I'm pulling up stumps for a while. I have to go through everything, but I feel like the interview time is now done. I've got one big glaring task to undertake - the transcribing of an interview I did with Butch Vig some seven years before, but first, to find it…

18

Butch Vig: The Man Who Never Minds

It's been a long time since that moment in the lunchroom. Little did Jordie or I know just how much ground would be traversed, nor how much of my life would pass, how many immense personal mountains would be trudged from that point to now.

The taking of my 14-year-old child from a school bus stop and all that followed from that. Rape, domestic violence, torture, venturing deep into the world of meth amphetamine use on many a rescue mission, discovering the darkest, as well as the lightest, nature of the patriarchy in the justice system, getting married myself, adding another baby to our lives, learning how to parent six children in a blended family, giving up drinking and crawling, climbing - at times even powering - our way to better and better territory where the air is cleaner, some of the rage has been processed and we stand higher than the events that nearly broke us.

All the while, The Producers; endless nights editing audio, penning words, engineering sounds, thousands and thousands of kilometres traveled, conversations had, gems of wisdom captured - all of it becoming a part of the familiar, comforting framework of life's smorgasbord, a thread that became a lifeline amongst the madness. Just Butch Vig to go.

It's now May 2014. I'm in a motel that's second only in dodginess to a flea-ridden cum pit I made the mistake of pulling into in the Californian town of Oxnard, on a mission chasing Josh Homme in relation to the Rancho De La Luna. This time though, the motel is not part of my search but end of the stretch - a place I've run to to reflect on my long Butch Vig journey, to put it all on paper and put to bed The Producer series, for the time being.

Located in a quaint coastal town in northern New South Wales, this motel is surrounded by scenery much more picturesque than its Oxnard inbred cousin, but still the sex-predator vibe lingers. Somehow, it seems a fitting finish, with my surfboard and whatever furniture I can lift or push propped up behind the flimsy hollow door, this red brick palace is the doorway for Butch Vig's story - across two colossal interviews and nine years - to finally step through and for this epic adventure to come to an end. For the most part.

Getting Butch, particularly for that first series - which had no credible history to prove its worth - was quite the coup. I didn't realise how much though, until the research began; ridiculous really that I didn't already know more about this impressive human when you consider his production pedigree. Turned out, this unassuming gent was the producer behind Smashing Pumpkins, L7, Sonic Youth, Foo Fighters, AFI, Green Day, Nirvana's *Nevermind* and one of the brains (as well as the drummer) behind alternative US rock band Garbage.

Do you think it would be fair to say that a) Butch was/is one of the most influential producers of our time and b) that we should all learn about folks like Butch in high school music class?

The first interview I did with him was in the triple j studios in Sydney in 2005. My memory has him being very dapper, in a black pin-striped suit with neatly combed-back hair. I wouldn't swear on some form of important text that this was actually what he was wearing, but in my mind's eye as it squints down my littered cerebral hallway, I even see him with a red silk handkerchief neatly protruding from his breast pocket. One thing *is* for sure, he is as charming as he is amicable as he is debonair. The combination of his relaxed manner and generosity of tale was as big a spark as Albini's moral commitment and obscure analogies, that set the passion alight within me to walk this producer path over a decade.

Which, if I think on it, makes him somewhat responsible for this floral, nylon bed cover/pastel Matisse/brown velour sofa motel nightmare I now find myself entombed in.

Six years after I had done that original interview with Butch, triple j put together a Nirvana special to celebrate twenty years since the release of *Nevermind*. The station was producing a pastiche of all archived interviews with various folks involved in the coming together and the release of that album. I directed them to my Butch Vig interview, which was beautifully catalogued in no specific order, in a cardboard box beneath a desk that hadn't even been mine for two years. Somehow, miraculously, they found the audio, bits and pieces were used for the special, and that was the last time the DAT was ever seen again. Initially I was devastated. It was the last chapter I had to write and now it couldn't be. The book could not be finished and I would not do it without the man behind the buttons behind the album that soundtracked the final decade of the 20th century.

For an entire year I sat with that knowledge, trying to figure out how I could massage my way around the problem - who could take Butch's place at the end of this book? Put simply, no-one seemed as right. Then the gods stepped back in with their wandering hands, delivering me Butch via *Soundwave*: Garbage had been booked to play the festival in 2013 and as the Festival's on-ground Media Liaison, access would come with no obstacle. I got in touch with Butch's people and he was more than happy to redo the interview when he returned to Australia.

Halle-fucking-lujah!

This second meeting took place in Sydney at a swanky

joint called The Darling Hotel, where his record label had arranged for the very hip Sokyo Bar to be opened just for us. Still to this day I never cease to marvel at the power of fame. You could be a Nobel Prize winner and stand in cattle class with everyone else, but make a song that everybody knows and you suddenly have powers of the gods.

As Butch walked out of the elevator, I was momentarily confused. He seemed almost bohemian in his relaxed button up shirt and jeans, his hair longer and hanging unabated by the products of modern man. He was wearing thick-rimmed spectacles and a soothing moustache that said, 'Do not be afraid'. He appeared to me in that moment, not Butch Vig the rock star but Butch Vig: Music Scientist.

We shake hands, make small talk and settle into a couple of opulent black leather couches situated in wherever-the-hell-we-please.

'I'm lucky that I grew up in a house filled with music,' Butch begins in reflection of his childhood musical memories. 'My mother was a music teacher and forced me into piano lessons when I was in first grade, when I was probably about six-years-old. At the time, I remember I sort of resisted, but then we would come home and she was always playing piano around the house, playing music - all kinds of music. She loved classical music and crooners - Frank Sinatra and Tijuana Brass and the Beatles and the Top Forty, it was just part of our lifestyle in our house.

'I started to get into piano and I got actually pretty good at it,' Butch laughs as he gently shifts in his seat. 'I think, when I was probably in fifth or sixth grade, I saw The Who play on the *Smothers Brothers* show. Keith Moon completely destroyed his drum kit and I was like, 'I want to do *that*!' I mean, I got so excited, my parents were aghast; they're going, 'Oh my god, what is this band and what are they all about?' I convinced my parents to buy me a cheap drum kit, like a Sears drum kit or something, for fifty bucks, under the condition that I promised my mother that I would keep playing piano. Well, as soon as I got the drum kit the piano lessons went downhill after that.'

Butch laments not having continued with the discipline of piano, acknowledging it for intellectualising his drumming skills as well as taking him to the top of the high school heap.

'I played in the high school band, and I played in the high school orchestra. Any sort of side projects that they had going on in the school, musically, I got involved in, because I was the only percussionist who could read music. All the other guys in the orchestra or the band were just kind of goof-offs who just wanted to get into the band for fun. And so, even when I was like, a freshman, became the leader of the school orchestra. In the percussion section there was a little bit of uh…hmmm well some of the older kids were a little pissed off because, you know, they were three or four years older than me, and I was telling them what to do…maybe that was my production skills getting honed at a very early age.'

It was around this same time that Butch started listening to and exploring music differently.

'Around thirteen or fourteen, I would get record jackets and I would listen to the records with headphones on and I would comb through the records trying to figure out how they did that, you know? I didn't really know anything about what it was to make a record, what the recording experience or the process was. But I became fascinated with it, and I would look at who produced this, what does the producer do, who engineered it, where was it recorded? And sometimes in record jackets there would be photos of the band in a studio and I would just look at it, look at the microphones and didn't really understand what it was, but it piqued my interest and it was something that I was trying to figure out you know; how exactly that process went.'

While the curiosity of the technical jigsaw puzzle began to unfold for little Butch, he was still a muso first and foremost. Already he, along with the other kids in the neighbourhood, had formed their first band, called The Rat Finx (now there is some winning pub trivia knowledge!) Together they tormented local parties and barbecues with their 'terrible, absolutely terrible' racket.

Eclipse was the next band that took shape for Butch. By this time he was in high school, with a few more skills under his high hat. In his description of that band ,they lost one 'terrible' and one 'absolutely' in comparison to his description of the first band. Eclipse went on to play clubs and venues around Wisconsin, and they would also be Butch's first attempt at recording.

'I had a two-track in our rehearsal space and we made

some attempts at recording live. I didn't know what I was doing. I got some microphones and I had a little mixer and I had to balance it all with headphones, and then we would play a bunch of takes live and then listen back to it and there was always something that was off. Like, the bass drum was really distorted or the vocals were too low or the lead guitar was too loud in the mix, and I remember I was quite frustrated because I never really successfully got a good recording. Because one, I didn't know what I was doing and two, it was live and we weren't very good players, but I was hell bent on trying to make it happen.'

Butch confesses though, that whilst his passion for music was strong, he in fact, came close to being Dr Vig MD. Butch's dad was the doctor in their small town, and of course, this career provided some footsteps worth following. But it just didn't sit right with Vig Jr. Instead he took a class at college in electronic music, which was his watershed moment; a split decision that would eventually lead Vig to produce one of the biggest albums of all time. Life eh? What a grand and unexpected thing.

'The instructor at college didn't give tests,' Butch explains of how this class shaped his malleable young mind. 'He just gave you projects and you had three or four projects each semester. And the studio was a tiny room, like the size of a small bedroom, and there were maybe ten or twelve students in there with me. There were no keyboards. He said on day one, 'I do not want you to try and play *Switched-On Bach*'. He wanted us to learn how to manipulate sound via either recording something or running it through ARP synthesisers or MOOG synthesisers and using the filters and VCAs and oscillators and things like that, to try and really come up with a new sound experience. They had a four-track tape recorder there, so that was the first time I learnt about over-dubbing; where you could actually do right. Well, I took four semesters of that, and it was by far my favourite thing that I did in college.'

Butch went on and got a degree in film and made some independent movies, entertaining ideas of Hollywood, but it was the sound designer bug that got him.

'I just couldn't wait,' he explains of his hell-bent enthusiasm. 'I would look at the free-time sheet for the studio, and anytime that was open, I signed up for it. I spent hours and hours and hours in there recording crazy, weird-sounding bits of music. My fellow film students knew that I was really into sound and they started coming to me and asking me if I would do a soundtrack for them; and I would watch a little seven-minute clip they were editing and I'd go, 'Okay'! I would go into the experimental electronic music studio on Monday night at ten o'clock with a case of beer and some potato chips, and I would come out at eight o'clock the next morning and give them a reel and go, 'Here's your soundtrack'. It was all crazy weird trippy stuff and they loved it!'

During Butch's University of Wisconsin days, he would meet Steve Marker and Duke Erikson, the two gents he would go on to collaborate with in a little band called Garbage. Duke was looking for a drummer and Steve had a four-track. They were a perfect fit. The four-track went into the basement of Butch's apartment and they began recording local bands. 'We'd say, 'Hey do you wanna come down and record for free? Just bring a case of beer and bring a reel of tape and come on down and you can record.' That was the start of Smart Studios.'

Butch shuffles in his black leather chair and takes another swig of the sparkling water that has been lavished upon us. Talk shifts ahead to 1991. This is THE year for Butch; by 1992 his life would be forever changed.

'I got a call from Billy Corgan after he heard Killdozer.', says Butch, beginning the tale on how he and the Smashing Pumpkins singer and songwriter would come to carve the formidable path they did in laying down two of the most ambitious and distinctive albums of the nineties. 'Killdozer were one of the bands that really brought a lot of attention to me and to Smart Studios because they were pretty extreme sounding albums. Yet as durgy and grungy as the band was, the albums sounded really interesting and I always tried to make them sound heavy but also throw in some sonic surprises; just things that would catch people's ear. Things that they wouldn't necessarily do live and the band was always up for that.'

Billy called after he had heard the *Twelve Point Buck* record and I ended up doing a single with him; just two songs. I was immediately struck by Billy and how driven he was and how focused. A lot of the bands I had been recording at Smart Studios up to that point were punk bands, some who could barely play and had no idea what it was to be inside the recording studio and didn't necessarily wanna be pushed to an extreme. Billy was the exact opposite. He was very focused. He wanted to make ambitious sounding records. He was willing to play a guitar riff, over and over and over again hundreds of times until he and I felt like he got it. I found working with him absolutely fascinating, and I loved it because I wanted to work with someone who was driven like that, because deep down inside I think I was just as driven as he was.'

'That must've been dangerous,' I suggest. 'Having two such driven people in the studio? A recording could potentially never end.'

'That's something that I've always had to keep an eye on through all of my career.' Butch admits. 'I have been guilty of that happening to myself in Garbage, where we just keep layering and recording and layering and recording…and then you don't know when to stop. With Billy, we set the bar very high for *Gish* and then we set it way, way higher for *Siamese Dream*.'

Considering *Gish* took thirty-six to thirty-eight days, fourteen to sixteen hours per day, rarely breaking during those times for food or liquids, you'd think a little bit of burnout might have kept Smashing Pumpkins paced during *Siamese Dream*. But Billy's meticulous ambition coupled with a cesspool of in-band dysfunction meant that the completion of *Siamese Dream*, whilst resulting in a masterpiece, was nothing short of miraculous.

Just getting into the studio came with a degree of pain,

with Billy reticent to play Butch the songs, feeling like he didn't have a complete album to show. For four or five months, Butch was put in a holding pattern whilst Billy pulled *Siamese Dream* (almost) together. Eventually Butch got a call to head down to Chicago to the band's rehearsal space and listen to most of what would become one of the early nineties' most defining records. Two rather significant tracks though were not in that mix Butch heard in Chicago. *Today* and *Disarm*, which came together in the studio at the 11th hour, going on to became two of the album's biggest songs. It was the same rabbit-out-of-the-hat trick that Billy would also pull off during the band's third album, *Melancholy and the Infinite Sadness,* with Alan Moulder at the helm, two years later.

'We decided to go make that record in Atlanta,' Butch says of *Siamese Dream*, explaining how they tried (and failed) to reduce the in-studio stress levels. 'We didn't want any distractions in Madison. I had a tonne of friends there and because we'd done *Gish* at Smart we thought we wanted a change of scenery. We didn't wanna do the record in Chicago because they had tonnes of friends there. So we went to Atlanta and found this studio called Triclopse. It had a great old Neve desk, it was a one-studio facility, big large tracking room, and the staff were really cool there.'

Very quickly though the wheels began to wobble on this already shaky machine when Jimmy Chamberlin, the drummer, became friends with what appeared to be every pimp and drug dealer in Atlanta.

'There were crazy parties,' recalls Butch. 'People coming by the studio from day one; and I was like, 'Who are these people?' People would show up and say 'Is Jimmy here? Tell him Sal's at the back. I need to talk to him.' Billy and I were like, 'This is not conducive to being focused."

Early on, Jimmy just started getting completely unpredictable. He was going out and partying to the point where we didn't know if he was going to be able to play or not, and that was causing a lot of tension. Billy Corgan was getting extremely pissed at him. Darcy and James were also very dysfunctional, and Billy was very focused and driven - so the four of them as a band? They were not functioning well and when I say dysfunctional that's an understatement. They could barely speak to each other sometimes. When we would be in the studio, when I could get him in and focus on cutting a basic track, they were all pretty focused. James knew his parts, Darcy was really good - especially with Billy giving him feedback on his arrangements or how the performance was feeling, and Jimmy, when he was focused, is an incredible drummer. But there were days where the opposite would happen. You know, Darcy could barely stand up, James would be playing but would not really say anything and emotionally wouldn't contribute very much, and Jimmy would be so fucked up he couldn't even play. And so…the record started out kind of rough and the whole time that we were there, which was five straight months, I never really quite knew what to expect on a day to day basis. We had an intervention maybe about halfway through where the A&R person from the label came and one of their managers came and we all sat in this room and everyone sort of…screamed at each other. Not me! I sat in the back and sort of…tried to mediate. But Billy basically said, 'I'll finish this record with Butch if you guys can't get up to speed on this."

Somehow this snappy little pep talk did the trick and everyone, for the most part, rose out of their mental duress and pulled the focus into getting the job done. The workload increased, with six days straight turning into seven with even longer hours per day. During a time when Pro Tools was still a game changer of the future, it all came down to performance. Whilst Jimmy played the drums, Billy, according to Butch, played around ninety-five percent of the tracks on the record. 'I think he and I felt,' explains Butch carefully. 'No matter how good Darcy's bass playing was gonna get, or James Iha's guitar, Billy Corgan was gonna be able to play it better; and I think that's one of the things that caused a lot of distress in the band.'

It was during this arduous period of *Siamese Dream* that Butch fully realised that getting sounds was no longer the sole focus of being producer, it was about making big decisions and gently navigating and channelling the complex human condition. A task difficult enough when dealing with left-brain logic. But with sensitive, ego-tormented, art folk? This was neural wizardry.

'As people started asking me for production decisions, I became more aware of what a songs arrangement was and what the song should feel like… but then you find out that the psychological aspect is just as important as anything else, because you have to gauge the temperature of the band. You need to be able to pull good performances and keep them focused. Sometimes you have to console, sometimes you have to push them and shout at them, sometimes you have to leave them alone and let them figure out things on their own. With a band like the Pumpkins, everyday could be different. So, it was a challenge, and when we finished recording that, it had been five months. Then we went and mixed with Alan Moulder for six straight weeks, seven days a week.'

By the time *Siamese Dream* was finished Butch was completely fried, still heralding it as the hardest album he has ever worked on. If *that* album didn't deter him from continuing on as a producer with all the new aspects to the role he'd unearthed, then nothing would. If anything, it cemented his belief in the suitability of his aptitude for the position.

'I'm generally very laid back,' he explains, in a very laid-back manner, from a very laid-back posture on the couch. 'I enjoy people's company and I can engage socially on any different level, but I can also sit there and be quiet and let someone rant if they need to. I don't really like to go in and shout and scream at people unless I absolutely have to, and if I have to, I will. It has happened sometimes. It happened with my band Garbage, it's happened with certain artists in the past where you realise talking logically is not working - you gotta do something drastic to get a reaction and sometimes you gotta tell yourself that you have to do whatever it takes to motivate the artist.

'One of the reasons that I love recording every day and

still do,' he continues, 'is because you think in your head, 'Today is going to go down this path,' and then you go in the studio and something completely different happens. Or the song takes a turn, or somebody screws up and writes a mistake that becomes a brilliant part, or somebody gets into a massive argument with another member of the band and you have to work through that. The process of recording music and collaborating with people is unpredictable and that's what I love. That bumpy road. That's what's still really exciting for me.'

Incredibly, during 1991, Butch would not only be the man at the recording nucleus of Billy Corgan's creative cell but he would also begin working with Kurt Cobain. Injecting himself unwittingly right into the main vein of the nineties cultural zeitgeist. Working with not just one band but *two* in the same year that would define the jaded beating heart of a generation.

Softening into this couch far from home, Butch looks as comfortable as if you were catching him unannounced in his own abode, he sits relaxed and genteel, discussing these things with a level of forthcoming-ness that in a thousand interviews with musicians, I rarely ever reached. Producers sit on the mountain top, seeing it all unfold, every recess of the process observed and considered; many moments that band members will rarely expose, perhaps not having even seen them unfold at all. But whilst Billy and Kurt may have shared similarities in terms of success, when it came to their approach to making music, you'd be hard pressed to find two artists further apart. Butch played witness, as well as participant, in it all.

'Working with Nirvana was…exciting, because we had to

capture things really, really quickly. Kurt had no patience to do something over more than three or four times. Sometimes I was lucky if I got two takes out of him on vocals. The thing that people don't realise though, is that before we started recording *Nevermind*, they spent about five or six months in Seattle practicing every single day; like eight or sometimes ten hours a day, just playing the songs over and over and over again. So when they came into the studio they were tight. They may have sort of looked and acted like slackers but they wanted to make a really tight, focused sounding record. The only thing is, Kurt just didn't want to have to go back and do it. If they didn't get it in a couple of takes, we would have to move on to something else.'

A short thread of patience, as well as a whole-hearted commitment to every take, would be the key factors in pacing the album's recording.

'He got frustrated if he didn't get something quickly,' remembers Butch, 'and I think because of his punk background he felt like he was cheating if you did a part too many times, you know? When he would sing, he would sing so hard on the louder songs that he would blow his voice out after two or three takes, so I would usually get him to do a 'run-through' - I would tell him that I needed to get a mic check and of course hit record. I would already have the levels set, so I would just have him do a take all the way through and then I would usually get him to do maybe two more takes. On most of the songs on *Nevermind*, there would be three vocal takes and he sang really consistently, so I could go through those three and could usually find a double in there, and in some instances I had him go back and sing a double.

'Initially he didn't want to do that, and I told him one day, 'Well John Lennon doubled his voice all the time,' and Kurt thought about that for about two seconds and sort of went, 'Okay, I'll go in and double it,' because he was a massive Beatles fan.'

Almost fifty percent of those first sneaky 'run-throughs' were the takes that made the record. In order to keep proceedings moving along at a pace that Kurt felt comfortable with, performance was key for Nirvana. The introduction of a certain charismatic drummer made a huge impact on the necessary momentum, as well as adding an emotional lift that kept everybody buoyed.

'Dave Grohl, besides being an incredible drummer, brought a breath of fresh air; he was a goofball, constantly joking around,' says Butch of possibly the world's most liked drummer.

'He had this insane energy, he still does. I mean, he's a complete multi-tasking workaholic you know? I love him for that, because he's so much fun to be around. The greatest thing for me that happened when I went into work with Nirvana when we did *Nevermind,* was meeting him because he brought such a level of power and tightness to the band that hadn't existed before, and he made it very easy to record the drums as well as getting great performances. There wasn't one song on the record that took more than three or four takes to get. Some of them were like, first or second take. And Chris was great on bass. He also had a great very laid-back demeanour and was really easy to work with.'

It's testament to Nirvana's undeniable possession of that special indescribable something, that on a record that would go on to sell more than thirty million copies, just two of the album's twelve (thirteen if you were lucky enough to get a copy containing hidden track *Endless, Nameless*) songs would prove tricky to capture.

'One was *Lithium*,' Butch remembers. 'Initially we kept playing it and for some reason Dave kept speeding up a lot. He didn't do that very often, and both Kurt and I noticed it, and we were trying to keep it a little more mid-tempo so that it sounded heavier. After about three or four takes on whatever night of the week that was, Kurt got really frustrated and started smashing his guitar, and he went into that song *Endless/ Nameless*, which was at the end of the record. Of course, I had the tape rolling luckily, so I captured it all on tape, but the next day I asked Dave, 'Have you ever recorded with a click-track before?' He never had, and I could tell it kind of broke his heart, but I ran a click-track through to him and I figured out what the tempo was, or where I thought it would be good, and ran it to him in the headphones, and he nailed it on the first take, you know? I was like, 'Damn that guy's good'.'

At this point Butch laughs. It's clear he still has endearing memories of working on the record and the ray of sunshine that is Dave Grohl, whom he would not work with again for another 20 years.

The second track that threw down a challenge was *Something In The Way*. Kurt's need to virtually collapse in on himself emotionally, to find the song's heart, took the track right to the edge of being almost too delicate to capture.

Butch recalls, 'We tried to record with a full band and it didn't work. We tried to record it in the big room at Sound City, and I kept telling Dave, 'You've gotta play quieter, you gotta play quieter', but the room is so big and loud and it just didn't sound right for the song. Kurt tried it on his acoustic and he tried it on a clean electric, and he got really frustrated. After about four or five takes he just walked into the control room and said, 'It sounds like this', and started laying on his back playing the song, and I was like, 'Wait stop!''

'That's when I said, 'Everybody stay out of the control room'. I had to turn off the fans and the telephone and everything, he was barely singing and playing, laying on his back on the couch; I recorded him right there. It was pretty magical. I then had to make a…sort of a master take…and Chris and Dave had to come back and overdub that. So I created a click-track by tapping my finger, to match up with his guitar, so that they had something to sort of lock in. That was one of the most difficult songs - it's not easy to go back and overdub bass and drums to an acoustic guitar performance, but we managed to do it.'

But of course, also, there was the fragility and unpredictability of Kurt's mental state making the process of being in a studio trying to record within a certain timeframe, at times impossible.

'Kurt was very bipolar. He could be incredibly focused and in a great mood ready to play, and then a light switch would go off and he would just get up and go sit in a corner. You could see something sort of close off inside his head, and he wouldn't communicate. Sometimes he would get up and leave the studio, or I guess just sit in a corner. I'd known about that when he came to Smart and they did the Smart sessions, which were the demos for *Nevermind*, because I kept asking Chris, 'Is Kurt okay?' Chris would say, 'He just gets in these black moods, you just gotta let him come out of it. He'll come out on his own' and several hours or sometimes half a day or whatever, I could never predict that, he always did. All of a sudden he'd come back and pick up his guitar and say, 'I'm ready to play'. So I just had to know when to leave him alone, and when that happened I would go in and tweak the drums. It gave me time to actually get guitar sounds and work on the bass sound, and we'd change things up a little bit for each song. So, I used that moment to do something…to be ready so that when he picked up his guitar we were ready to go and he didn't have to wait around while I was still tinkering with the snare drum sound or whatever.'

I'd always wondered how Kurt in his darkness and Dave in his radiance functioned together as bandmates. I've met Dave personally, several times over the years, and he was a benchmark for us interviewers, as well a great role model for up-and-coming bands, diffusing permission for the self-inflated ego. His enthusiasm never waned. I ask Butch how this dynamic played out creatively.

'It was good that Dave joined the band. Besides being a great musician, he brought great ideas. He wrote parts that were hooky and drum fills that became motifs, and Kurt appreciated that. I think Kurt needed to have that vitality, you know? That sort of…spark or energy around him, it really helped lift the proceedings.'

It also helped that whilst Nirvana were recording *Nevermind* in LA, they were having the time of their lives. Butch recalls with a smile, 'They were hitting the streets, with some money in their pockets for the first time. They were staying at Oakwood Apartments …people sort of laugh and call them the Cokewood Apartments; that's where they would put all of the rock bands up that came to Hollywood - Kurt told me the apartment they were in was bigger and nicer than anything he'd ever lived in in his whole life, you know? They'd been living in squalor in Seattle. The place they were writing in before they came to record *Nevermind* didn't even have any heat, which is one of the reasons they would go to the rehearsal space for eight or ten hours a day because, there was a heater there. But they were having a great time, and it really wasn't until the weight of the success of Nirvana started to really eat at Kurt that he started to pull away from the band. It was after *In Utero* I think. I think Kurt got fed up with being one of the biggest rock stars in the world; he just didn't like that attention. And because he would have these incredibly dark mood swings, when you have all the success at your fingertips, it makes it worse somehow when you still feel like shit.'

Twenty years later, Butch would be deeply involved with Chris and Dave again for the 20th anniversary box set, and whilst doing the heavy load of press they did for that release, the three of them would admit that *Nevermind* radically changed all of their lives forever.

Post the explosion of Nirvana, there was a steady flow to Butch's door of labels, publishers and managers who came seeking his magical elixir to grunge fame and fortune. Not believing that he could offer what they were after, he continued to work as he always did, with bands that offered something a little intriguing, a little different. In 1992, he got busy with both Sonic Youth and L7, which only further reinforced his ability to take what was a little rough around the edges, put it into his rock tumbler, and come out with something smooth and shiny but no less rock.

This was not an easy feat for a band like L7 consisting of four women, famous for making music anything as heavy as their male counterparts, and for extracting a tampon live on stage and throwing into the crowd. L7 were no contrived feminist answer to male alternative rock. They were a fierce inspiration to a generation of girls uncertain of what it meant to be a woman. In the murky waters of post-feminism, musically, they were an influential prelude to the Riot Grrrl movement that was beginning to rise in the early nineties.

'The L7 gals were crazy,' exclaims Butch (or Mr Vig as the L7 ladies called him) animatedly, '...and fun and wild!

Bricks are Heavy was one of the most interesting albums I have ever done. I had a gas working with them, because they really were pretty full-on, and obviously it's different working with a band of four women than it is with four dudes. It's a different chemistry and it was exciting. They were having the time of their lives.'

For three or so weeks, L7 tracked at Sound City before returning to Smart. It was here that they finished the overdubs and the mix, and also where, despite being on a shoestring budget, they managed to set the town alight.

'They came in and kind of…took over the entire city. They were going out partying every night. We had rented a house a couple of blocks from the studio for them to live in, and that became a party palace. Every night there were just crazy parties going down. The same thing that sort of happened with the Pumpkins in Atlanta happened there. Like, all the bookies, drug dealers, crazy street party people…that band met everybody in Masa, every character there was! And they were all coming by the studio. It was a party. It was fun.'

Yet somehow the work was still getting done. 'I mean, I was always in the control room, they would wander in and out,' Butch said. 'We tracked all the drums and most of the bass at Sound City, and Suzie and Donita were over-dubbing guitars and we did all the vocals and mix…and they were a joy to work with because they had a crazy energy and I think they wrote some amazing songs on that album. And they rocked! I saw a bunch of their shows, I was pretty close to them back in the day, and you know…they did not wimp out.

They were as heavy as any band with men I worked with, and I found that exciting and refreshing.'

After L7, Butch began working with Sonic Youth, who were already six studio albums deep into their career and possessed an air of musical intelligence that Butch admits to having been a little intimidated by.

'I was a fan of their music you know, I knew their albums and I'd seen them live and thought they were incredible, and I guess I thought of them as being very cerebral and arty and sort of…stand-offish in a way. When I flew to New York to first meet them, I went to Kim and Thurston's apartment on the Lower East Side. I knocked on the door and walked in and Thurston said, 'Butch Vig, I want our album to sound like this', and he put on this band called Mecht Mensch; and it was the very first punk rock recording I ever did! It was crazy lo-fi…I mean, I think they only ever pressed like 500 copies, how the hell did Thurston get a hold of that? I just burst out laughing and he burst out laughing and he totally, completely disarmed me.

'It turned out that he had almost everything I'd ever done with all these obscure punk bands. He's a real archivist and a punk rock historian. I found them to be very funny and smart and witty and cool to hang with.'

Working with Sonic Youth was an educational experience for pop-hook-master Butch, who knew that there was no shot of producing any three-minute pop songs with this experimental pair. Not on their album *Dirty* anyway. It became Butch's role to go in and hear their music with the purpose of helping them achieve their vision, yet try to make things focused and…possibly…be able to broaden their audience. Quite the challenge for a band who have always been held close to the breast of fringe, punk, indie kids who've wanted to elevate themselves on the music-knowledge-hierarchy by knowing who Sonic Youth were. Needless to say, Butch did a bang-up job with *Dirty,* with many a critic heralding it, to that point, as their finest album. For Butch, well he squeezed in a little career highlight here too…

'One of my favourite songs that I've ever produced was on that album…and I remember clearly the night we did it and when we recorded it. *Theresa's Soundworld* had been a tough song to get, for whatever reason. Some of the performances, when they record, become completely different, you know? The arrangement can vary because they go off on tangents, and that's what makes them special. That's what makes them who they are. But for whatever reason, we'd been struggling with that song and I remember late one night we decided to try it again. I lowered the lights down, put the playback up on the big speakers and the hair on the back of my neck went up and the engineer and I were like, 'This is it!' I could just tell this was it. I was watching them and then I shut my eyes and the most…sort of beautiful symphonic sound came out…and I swear I held my breath for five minutes or however long that song is, you know? It just completely floored me and I remember to this day how amazing it sounded and I still absolutely love that song.'

After the joy of working together on *Dirty,* Butch and Sonic Youth would team up again two years later on the much looser, more warts-and-all album *Experimental Jet Set, Trash and No Star.*

'They said, 'We're going to do everything in one or two takes," Butch recalls. "If there's a buzz or a click or a hum or a mistake, we're gonna leave it…and that's what we wanna do'. I said, 'Okay'. And that was the mission statement right there. We recorded that at Sear Sound, which is a tighter, sort of more intimate control room and studio, so the sound was a bit more dry and in-your-face. I remember that record as just…laughing a lot because the band were in really good form. There was a looseness to it, it was less serious than making *Dirty* and it really was a lot of first takes, second takes; if someone made a mistake, unless it was something that they really hated, we would just leave it. It was a really, really fun record. I found out at the end of the record that Kim was pregnant too at the time. I didn't know that. She didn't tell me until we'd finished the recording.'

Coco Hayley Gordon Moore was born on the 1st July 1994, two months after the release of the album she contributed too in utero.

Around the same time that Butch found himself enjoying the company of Thurston Moore and Kim Gordon, his own band Garbage would come to life. Birthed from both the spill over of ideas that Butch was accumulating along the long production highway he'd travelled and a tickle of boredom that came from having produced what felt like 'a thousand punk rock records with guitar, bass and drums'.

Of Garbage's sound, Butch admits to it being a million-piece pastiche of musical influences, from wide and far, from the obvious to the highly unlikely. 'I started hearing things on the radio like Public Enemy and to me, that was like the scariest rock and roll music I'd heard at the time, and I couldn't figure out how they were doing that. Then when I started hearing about all these samplers that were coming out, I went out and bought a couple. I bought an Akai S1000 and a Kurtsweil k2500 and started figuring out how to use them. And the great thing is, you can blow music in and start creating loops and manipulate it and process it; and that became the main instrument when we started writing Garbage songs. Everything on the first album, on our debut album, pretty much went through one of those samplers. That to me became freeing in a way, because I felt like I was almost back in college taking electronic music. You can start changing the rules of what you think a song should sound like and we - after Shirley joined us - wanted to write hooky songs, but we wanted to embrace pop music and punk rock and fuzzy guitars and film moments and electronica and hip hop beats and sometimes have all those in the same song.

Essentially, we wanted to make songs that were rock songs, but give them a completely different sonic feel, and to this day, that's still one of our inspirations in Garbage.'

By this point, Butch and I had been chatting for just over an hour and one of the bar staff come over to check in. Butch says he's fine in terms of beverages and as the young man turns to me I just want to cry out to him, 'This is Butch Vig! He produced Nirvana! He knows Billy Corgan and Dave Grohl and Sonic Youth and Against Me! and Greenday and Muse…and he's in Garbage!' Instead I take a little breath and say,

'Thank you, I'm fine too.'

I look at my long list of bands still to cover in so little time: AFI, Green Day, Jimmy Eat World… we decided to go with Against Me!

Butch had formed an immensely close relationship with founder, guitarist, songwriter and lead singer Tom Gable, during their time working with the band on *New Wave* in 2007 and 2009's *White Crosses*. In 2012, after a lifetime living under the torment of gender dysphoria, they transitioned into Laura Jane Grace. She continues with Against Me! and has been quoted as saying, 'However fierce our band was in the past, imagine me, six-foot-two, in heels, fucking screaming into someone's face.'

It was during the recording of *New Wave* with Butch that Laura decided to lyrically out herself on the song *The Ocean*: 'If I could have chosen, I would have been born a woman / My mother once told me she would have named me Laura / I would grow up to be strong and beautiful like her / One day I'd find an honest man to make my husband.'

No-one at the time picked up on the literal meaning of the lyric. In retrospect it's an intriguing window into how desperately Laura was crying out to be seen, but how terrifying that step must have been to take. Another five years would pass before she publicly announced her transition.

'I remember when we recorded that song,' reflects Butch, 'I asked specifically '…what is *The Ocean* about?' And the answer was, 'I was just sittin' by the ocean smokin' a joint one day and those lyrics came out.' Obviously playing a lot closer to the chest. When Tom called me and said he was going to become Laura Jane Grace it surprised me but it didn't in a way… I knew that she always beat to a different drum and always followed a singular path and was going to do whatever she needed to, to be true to herself. I remember also thinking, 'God, you can't live in Florida. You gotta move somewhere where people are more tolerant.' But Against Me! fans get it. Because their music and their lyrics have always been kind of…open book. So, I think of all of the fans of hardcore bands, they're probably more of the accepting tolerant ones out there because part of what has always been written by Against Me! are songs about injustices and people who need help or are searching for a focus. I'm sure there have been very tough things for her in that transition but I think that having that kind of music…having music, to be able to use that as part of your background, and as part of a form of letting yourself out in the world, is important and I know that's something that Against Me! fans have embraced.'

With a sudden decree of emotion, Butch says, 'I absolutely adore Against Me! Absolutely adore 'em.' I fell in love with them after they got signed to Warner Brothers. Their A&R guy sent me some of their earlier records and said, 'You have to go see 'em. They're amazing. You're gonna fall in love with them.' He kept talking them up to me and I listened to *Searching For A Former Clarity* and I liked it. I fell in love with them as people then, I saw them live and thought, 'Oh my god, they should be as big as The Clash,' and I still to this day think they should be as big as The Clash. I absolutely loved working on *New Wave* with them. Laura wrote incredible songs and it was my job to just help them focus.'

Butch's intention in that focus, was to ensure that Against Me! maintained on record, the energy of their live shows; renowned for intense participation and support from their crowds, fed by the full-force atmosphere of the band. His vision was to make the sonics more widescreen without diluting the passion. The key for Butch was in getting involved with the band very early on in the album's process, to assist, as much as they needed, from an arrangement perspective onwards.

'At one point I suggested, 'Have you ever written a song that's sort of a cross between a David Bowie song and *Walk on the Wild Side'* by Lou Reed? And they took what I said and wrote *Thrash Unreal*, which doesn't sound anything like David Bowie or Lou Reed but kind of got what I was saying. So, sometimes I could just say something to the band and they would translate that into something that would take the song up to a huge level. Looking back at all the bands I've produced, I kind of feel like I have a relationship with that band and with Laura now, that is quite exceptional because it really is a close nurturing relationship back and forth. It's one of the true instances where I think I could say something and they would take it to heart and really go elevate their game.

Just before it was time to record, I said, 'You better come out to LA and we'll do some pre-production' and they were like, 'What's that?' Well they rehearsed...a lot! The first day they came into the studio, I made them play over and over. I would break down what they were doing - kick drum, snare drum, bass patterns, so everybody was aware (of) what they were all playing so that I was still capturing what they were doing, but they became very aware of exactly what they were playing. We just kept playing it over and over so they could play it tighter and more focused until they played it so much, that when we went in to record there was not a lot of thought process, it was more about execution and made the recording for the most part pretty painless.'

New Wave was a cracking success for Against Me!, seeing them chart for the first time, nearly breaking into the top 10. With a culmination of that and their established relationship with Butch, it was to him they returned for the next album, *White Crosses*. As if you wouldn't. The band wasn't coming in with the same configuration however, with former drummer Warren Oakes, replaced by George Rebelo from Hot Water Music. It was a shift that would alter the band's state of play significantly.

'When George came in it brought a completely different feel. Warren had almost a loose kind of shuffley feel. And honestly, it took a lot of work to get Warren's drums really tight and focused and George almost looked at it more from a studio perspective. He was more accomplished in what he could do; and he was very easy to work with so, in some ways it was easier to get the performances, especially the drum performances. But once again, when the band brought in the songs, god, I just fell in love with some of the tracks on the record, like *Teenage Anarchist*. My daughter still plays that in the car, and I have clips of her singing the chorus of that and she's only seven!' Butch suddenly breaks out into song! 'I was a teenage anarchist looking for a revolution..."

'Man, when they brought those songs in, again I'd just felt that they had really written, an amazing batch of songs and the song *White Crosses* is so epic sounding which is about Laura had been up all night drinking and I think took some speed or something and was just wondering around, coming home at sunrise, walking in Saint Augustine along the beach, and there's all these tourists getting up and sort of seeing you know, how sort of stark and weird the city is with different eyes. It's a slice of life. All the lyrics are literally about a six-block walk home and finally, right before you come home, coming around the corner and seeing all these protesters with all these white crosses on the church lawn - it was an anti-abortion rally; and just basically almost a complete meltdown at the time. Laura almost had a complete meltdown.'

The ability of Laura to translate all of this depth and perception into song was one of the master strokes that ran its brush several times through the track *White Crosses*. 'It's a real life story too, about a friend who...was killed by her boyfriend drug dealer, and when Laura went to the funeral, the mum brought up that she had had their name tattooed on her arm before she died,' explains Butch. 'It was very complex and the mother said some things at the time...again this was how close our relationship was, and Laura said (to me), 'I don't know what to do. I think she sort of feels like maybe one of the songs I wrote on *New Wave* was about her' - about the daughter who was killed. The mother thought that, and was very upset, and Laura said, 'No I didn't write that about her, *Thrash Unreal* was not written about her.'

Turns out, *White Crosses* did, in a way, stem from the response to the upset and the shame of that encounter with the grieving mum. 'It's just an incredibly powerful song. I'm lucky I have a relationship with the band, with Laura, that I'll get a call and really dissect from a psychological point where that song is coming from. That doesn't always happen with artists, where you get very closely involved in where they're coming from, especially from their heart.'

From this darkness and suffering of Laura's experience, Butch and I decide to end with Dave Grohl, and talk about their experience of recording together again after 20 years, for the album *Wasting Light*. Whilst they'd remained friends, toured together across the festival circuits in both of their respective bands, and run into each other often in LA, the success of *Nevermind* had always remained a bit of a back-monkey feeling the pressure of expectation. But after reconnecting in studio for the Nirvana greatest hits, Dave made the call and asked Butch to work on the next record for the Foo Fighters.

'He dropped two bombs on me the first day I went out to meet him,' Butch says after he'd agreed to take on the task. 'I went out to his house and he said, 'Okay...first of all, I wanna record on analogue tape.' Aand I was like, 'Ooooookayyy.' And I'm thinking, 'It's fine to record to analogue tape. I've done that.' I still do it now in the present time, but usually I take it and then immediately put it into ProTools so you can manipulate it and edit it and make playlists and make your life easier in general. But then he said, 'No ProTools. I wanna keep it on tape - the entire project. I wanna mix it from tape, I wanna master it from tape…' I was like, 'Holy shit, he's gonna make me go back and relearn everything I learnt twenty years ago.' I still thought 'okay, I can do that,' whilst in the back of my head I'm going, 'Oh shit, oh shit, oh shit.' And then he says, 'Okay, the second thing is I wanna record it in my garage. I don't wanna do it in my studio.' Now you have to realise he has a million dollar amazing studio. An incredible studio! And he said, 'We're not going to record it there. We're going to record it in my garage.' We went downstairs, he rolled up his garage and literally, it's like a 20x18 rectangular room with dry wall on the sides and a refrigerator and some garbage cans in the corner and he had a drum kit set up…and he started playing it…and it sounded *good*. It sounded really tight and trashy and punchy. And I was just listening to it going, 'the drums are going to sound cool in here man.' So I said, 'Okay, we'll do it gorilla style."

With the time and expense involved in using tape, everything about the record became about performance, the band were completely up for the challenge. If anything, it proved a motivating chance for them to really shine, without the safety net of Pro Tools. Butch and engineer James Brown's roles became all about focusing everyone to get things spot on, right from the moment the record button was hit.

'We worked on the demos a lot. I would go out with Dave, we'd work on songs, he'd work on the band, we'd do live demos, then we would go into rehearsal before we'd record it and we would really go through the songs so that once again, when we went into record, we pretty much knew exactly what everybody was going to play and then it was just a matter of… go for it.

There were only two really low moments for me…doing it in Dave's garage, we set up a little control room upstairs above the garage, like this little loft study, and it was not acoustically designed for a studio. So, it was kind of hard to get your head around what was coming out of the speakers. If you sat up close to the speakers there was no bottom end and if you moved back at all it was super bassy. The room was not tuned. So, it took a while to figure out what the balance of tone was coming in and it was probably harder for James because he really had to be able to move around a lot and trust what he was getting out of the speakers. On the first day we went down and they did a take, and I think we went back and did a second take…and Taylor played a couple of fills differently and I liked the drum fills in a couple of spots so I went, 'I'm gonna go edit those in.' I went back downstairs, old-school style, and I sliced the tape with a razor blade and I cut…and I was sweating - I hadn't cut tape in 20 years you know, and I thought, 'If I screw this up, I've just completely fucked up the master tape'. But then I was like, 'Pfft, I've done this a thousand times.' *Then* I look down and I notice the tape was shedding all the oxide. The backing was coming off and I freaked out and called James Brown, the engineer, down and we were like, 'Oh my god!' We called the tape company and said, 'Can we get another batch sent up, we're not sure about this?' And they said, 'Well, sometimes the batches are not as consistent so maybe you wanna go to another batch.' We were like, 'Ah yeah, I think we better get another batch in right away.' So, I went upstairs and I said, 'Dave, the tape is coming off…the oxide is coming off. I think it would be smart to back this up to Pro Tools so we have a backup.' He said, 'If you bring in a computer, I'm going to fire-bomb it and I'm going to throw it out the window. If the tape disintegrates, we'll record the song again,' and I looked at him and thought, 'Damn, he's got balls if he really gonna keep it analogue, even if the tape is fucked up and doesn't work. If he's willing to go back and do it again then I gotta give that man a lot of cred.' So that was our MO. No computers the whole way through the record.'

Everything was mixed then to half-inch tape and mastered at the lodge from there. Once the process was completely done and dusted and all the mastering approved, Dave took all of the two-inch 24-track and had it all cut into little slivers and put in the first pressing of the CD. Hundreds of thousands of strips of tape, leaving behind no master, those original recordings to analogue are gone, except for the little slivers that fell into the laps of those who bought the very first pressing.

With Butch all talked out, and it being time for me to head back to my own beckoning life in Northern NSW, we shook hands and parted ways. As I wandered out through the excessively opulent foyer, I couldn't help but chuckle at how easily this man could move through the world unnoticed. A man who had not only witnessed with his own eyes the making of grunge's biggest albums, but had a firm hand in the direction in which they would unfold. It's a testament to the immensity of Butch Vig's career when you can chat for an hour and a half and not even get around to talking about Muse or Green Day. These were chats for another day.

19

Home

I had another plane to catch - this time home, to begin penning the tale that little did I know as I floated contentedly from that hotel foyer, would eventually bring me to this unexpected locale; a soiled sanctuary where I could find some solace amongst my life's many pieces. Little did I know that I would reach a place again and again of resolution between then and now, that this book would *not* be released; life too intense to labour this literary effigy to these unsung musical legends to its birth. Yet birth it has, thanks to the fiery process of internal persistence that brought me here, to this dodgy motel, behind this barricaded door laying out these final flourishes of an epic odyssey. A different person - both in appearance and in nature - to the one that began that equally loose yet professional journey all those years ago, having been schooled by life as well as by every producer I have ever sat with, all of whom shared their gems of wisdom so candidly, with unparalleled interview-generosity.

Of the smorgasbord of lessons learned, one could not be more clear in this moment - never underestimate the power of collaboration, of a strong connection; the flourish, the tiny nuance that someone may bring to your creative process and to its final result. For that stroke of genius - be it deliberate or accidental - could be the crowning moment of difference that hooks the hearts of millions.

Thank You

To Jazzy and Tiger, for whom I would trade every adventure in these pages, to have all the time over again to spend with you. To Obi for bringing the light, and Shane for constantly waving away the darkness and holding down the fort. To Jordie Kilby, my producer and friend, whose obsession with the ins and outs of music, birthed this crazy odyssey. To Linda Bracken, for supporting me to continue The Producer Series in a way that fulfilled so many childhood dreams, and some. To Kelly Sullivan, for being brave enough to be in your talent, so this book could have not just cover art but art for a cover. To Karen Penning from Harper Collins for bringing to life, all those years ago, the idea of turning the radio series into this here publication - the most enormous professional task I've ever undertaken. Your enthusiasm set something in motion that could not be stopped, even under life's greatest challenges. To Ebony McKenna, for the invaluable eyes and ears on these final stages, without which I would not have crossed the finishing line. To Jenny Valentish, for being the first brave soul to bring order and refinement to my tens and thousands of words. Tal Wallace for assisting me on the gruelling task of transcribing - hundreds of hours of transcribing. To Adelle Jarvis, for too much to put here but in particular, a quality of friendship that inspires a human to be brave. To Kate McMahon for being my wingwoman, no matter how inappropriate and wild the adventure.

AND to those whose words, generosities and stories make this book a book worth reading. Whose personalities, gifts and idiosyncrasies have brought wonder, emotion and a feeling of connection to the lives of millions. The Producers and the Artists whose relationships - smooth or turbulent - have enabled great songs to soundtrack everyday people's lives in ways that will never be fully known. To every Producer I spoke with, you gifted me the most in-depth, down-to-earth and intricate interviews of the thousands I've conducted in my career. Thank you.

www.ingramcontent.com/pod-product-compliance
Lightning Source LLC
Chambersburg PA
CBHW021139080526
44588CB00008B/133